From the Senedd to the Roofs

Collected Columns
(2023-2024)

Ben Wildsmith

Foreword by Martin Shipton

Published by
Llyfrau Cambria Books, Wales, United Kingdom.
*Cambria Books and Cambria Stories are imprints of
Cambria Publishing Ltd.*
Discover our other books at: www.cambriabooks.co.uk

Ben Wildsmith is a *Nation.Cymru* columnist, writing about politics and rugby twice a week. His book, *Flags & Bones* (Cambria Books, 2023) pulls together his irreverent journalism. A Hay Festival Writer at Work, he has also published short fiction and poetry. He lives in Rhondda Fach with his wife, Susie, and a mounting sense of dread.

Cover art and design by Siôn Tomos Owen

CONTENTS

Foreword

Categorising Ben Wildsmith's imaginative columns for *Nation.Cymru* isn't an easy task because they don't fit into any clearly defined category.

Most of them are political in the broadest sense, of course, but no one could accuse Ben of conforming to normal discursive expectations.

Often when you read an opinion piece or a newspaper leader article written by someone you tend to agree with, you follow the writer's train of thought and know where he or she will lead you. This can lead to boredom.

Ben is different. You could bet more than you can afford and be sure that any one of his columns will take you on an excursion whose byways you couldn't have predicted in advance. That, of course, is what makes them compelling.

The rule applies even if his starting point is straightforwardly polemical. As a man of the left, it's no surprise that Ben opposes the two-child benefit cap initially imposed by the Tories, and now continued by Labour. But while a more conventional columnist would either build a convincing case from statistics or write an emotive piece that tugs at the heartstrings, Ben's expertise as a creative writer soon has him operating like a Metaphysical Poet, 'combining heterogeneous ideas together in a violent way', as Samuel Johnson unflatteringly put it. (I've never gone along with Johnson and prefer TS Eliot's view that the heterogeneous ideas are 'compelled into unity by the operation of the poet's mind'.)

So far as Ben's columns are concerned, the unexpected comparison invariably involves the illustration of a moral point. Thus, before we are told the theme of the column is the vote that kept the two-child benefit cap, we are introduced to an act of animal cruelty, coupled by some self-deprecation: 'I only watched a few seconds of the video showing Olympian dressage star Charlotte Dujardin whipping a horse 24 times. I'm weak, I suppose, such things upset me for so long after viewing them that I just can't cope with it. She's ruined, of course. Bracketed forever with that woman who threw a cat in a bin, Dujardin is on the national shit-list: someone over whom we can all feel morally superior.' For Ben, the Labour MPs who voted in favour of the benefit cap are on that shit-list too. Many of us will agree.

Originality makes columns come alive. Otherwise, they're too short to make an impact. Ben's are always long enough and lively enough to grab our attention.

Martin Shipton

Introduction

After the kaleidoscopic dysfunction of Boris and Liz's not so excellent adventures in Number 10, it seemed we were approaching calmer waters. Rishi Sunak's initial presentation suggested a serious, conscientious approach to the nation's affairs. Perhaps we wouldn't be learning of cleaners mopping up vomit at the epicentre of power, or of plans being drawn up to invade the Netherlands.

I wondered if I should concentrate more on personal writing in my columns. Gentle tales of my mishaps as a middle-aged child in 21st-century Wales might endear me to the nation. Why-oh-why-oh-why, dear reader, does modern life insist on differing from what has gone before? Allow your avuncular columnist to take you by the hand and soothe your discomfort with self-deprecating reports of his inability to do anything properly.

But no. Just two hours after becoming Prime Minister, Sunak appointed Suella Braverman as Home Secretary, and it was clear that the UK's death spiral was not only continuing but accelerating. It's a bit rich to be exaggerating the travails of day-to-day life for comic effect whilst the government is threatening to defy international law in front of podiums emblazoned with 'Stop the Boats'. So, *A Wry Look at Valleys Life with Ben Wildsmith* never materialised.

More worryingly, it soon became untenable to point an accusatory finger at Westminster from the supposedly less chaotic political environment at home. Vaughan Gething's leadership campaign resulted in journalistic scrutiny of the Labour Party in Wales that was unprecedented. Much of the investigative journalism about this story appeared in *Nation.Cymru*, with Martin Shipton and Emily Price ensuring it became international news.

Shifting focus from Westminster to the Senedd was a queasy business, I found. Tory-bashing is my stock in trade. They may provide the country with scant legislative nourishment, but their endless rollcall of grotesques, spivs, racists, homophobes, misogynists, crooks, and Nadine Dorries ensure that satirising them is easy work.

Labour is a very different beast. Nowadays, its leading figures are largely drawn from the professions and public sector management. Its pitch to voters is that, in contrast to the Tories, it is serious, honest, and professional.

Tory politics is a branch of the entertainment industry. I was often perplexed at how cheerfully they would react to condemnation, with Andrew RT Davies going so far as retweeting some of my more scurrilous accusations.

Labour, on the other hand, cannot afford to allow mockery. Having abandoned socialism in favour of 'third way' market solutions, its viability rests on the electorate trusting the party to be honest. It cannot, therefore, countenance suggestions to the contrary.

As the party in the Senedd became overwhelmed by the questions surrounding Mr Gething, elements within it quickly demonstrated the lengths to which they would go in self-preservation. Not only were suggestions of impropriety against Gething unfounded, they claimed, but the journalists posing them had a racist agenda.

Keir Starmer's 'changed' party has removed so much of its ideological foundations as to be unrecognisable. In place of public ownership and redistribution of wealth, it promises to administer the economic status quo more fairly and honestly than its opponents. For that appeal to work, the party must be beyond reproach in its dealings, both personally and collectively. Most particularly, it must be *seen* to be beyond reproach or risk losing the trust required to operate without a recognisable ideological position.

So, anybody questioning the party's moral standing is

guaranteed fierce blow back. Just as journalists in Wales were smeared as racists for pursuing Vaughan Gething's campaign contributions, Labour MPs in Westminster were immediately suspended for opposing, on principle, the retention of the two-child cap on benefits. The appearance of moral superiority over the Conservative Party is like the glass and a half of milk in Cadburys chocolate: they never tell you how big the glass is.

I've lost friends writing these columns. During the election, I was accused of helping to facilitate a Tory victory. After the election, I'm routinely told that I haven't given the new government enough time to establish itself before criticising its decisions. If I'm taking aim at big, daft targets like Andrew RT Davies, it's slaps on the back all round. If it's the renewed demonisation of the disabled by Labour, then I'm peeing on Nye's grave.

There's a degree of wishful thinking about this which is understandable. Good people *want* substantive change to the cruel misgovernance of the UK which has impoverished our communities in Wales for so long. Keir Starmer said 'change' a lot during the election campaign, and he's all we've got. Perhaps there is a long-term plan that he is yet to reveal. Hush now, or you'll awaken the Tories again.

Here in front of me, though, are pensioners losing assistance for fuel, the disabled losing mobility benefits, DWP 'work coaches' being sent into psychiatric wards, and British weapons falling in Gaza.

With Labour in the Senedd offering little if any divergence from the Westminster line, Wales seems captured as never before. The historically radical demands of the Welsh Labour movement are reduced to the cooing of conformist sycophants. Down the pike heads the antidemocratic outrage of closed lists, entrenching groupthink as an end in itself.

So, I'm not being funny or nothing, but go whistle if you expect me to believe this is as good as it can be. I spend my days at work supporting people whose lives have been blighted by abuse and trauma. *Their* days are already atrophied, fearful sketches of how they would have been in their fullness.

Each performative, get-tough budget cut that I'm required to enforce upon them brings more anxiety, more loneliness, more proof that they aren't valued.

There's some laughs here, I hope. If it gets too depressing, skip to the rugby reports. Oh, hang on…

Ben Wildsmith, October 2024

The Gambler
17 Feb 2024

Calmly and easily, the nurses busy themselves around this ward, administering a tablet here, a smile there, a squeeze of a hand. It's bright in here, and quieter than the ones people graduate through to reach it. It's the pinnacle of most people's lifelong journey through the NHS, from squealing into life in Obstetrics to here. It's taken Louise 46 years to arrive, after all those visits to A&E, operating theatres, and psychiatric wards, she's completed the game.

Around her bed, the support workers who tried to cushion her bumpy ride are bereft. Inevitability is no balm to the wrench of losing someone you care for.

They've been busy today, both of Louise's brothers are in prison so urgent calls had to be put in to the chaplains who can advocate for compassionate release when a relative is dying. They arrived earlier, handcuffed to officers, and unwound with grief. As Louise lay motionless the elder brother just wept, the younger plead,

'Not now, Lou, not now, please...'

The streets are hard on a person. For a night, a week, a month, six months that kind of homelessness is such an offence to the soul that it can provide a spur for change, the sort of 'short, sharp, shock' that idiot politicians think will work for anything they disapprove of. The real trouble sets in when the shock wears off, when there's no point in becoming sober anymore, when you don't notice if your clothes aren't dry, and your cough replaces your smile. Once that perversion of normality settles on a person it never really leaves.

There are moments though. Perhaps a support worker had a free afternoon and could take her to Barry Island for a couple of hours. She'd rave and laugh all the way then sit on the wall and smile at the sea, silent until it was time to go home. Because there was a home in her last few years, a little flat that she kept immaculate – 'Get your feet off my rug!'

In her pomp she was magnificent, singing in the city centre for strangers, enough for a can. Everyone knew her: police, magistrates, judges, doctors, probation officers, prison officers.

'What are we going to do with you, Lou?'

'Got a pound, Your Honour?'

'Louise!'

'God loves a trier!'

She needed to be visited daily by her support workers, first thing in the morning, don't be late. We brought her food, rationed out her cash, took her to the hospital if we could. The police knew to call us if she got out of hand in town.

'Can you pick Louise up, please?'

Cursing the world and its mother she'd be coaxed into the car and brought back home. We'd put a blanket over her if she fell asleep on the sofa and refused to move.

There were only flashes of what had sent her life that way. She didn't do self-pity. Little Louise remembered hiding her dad's lager, not letting him have any until he'd eaten the toast she'd made for his breakfast. Her mam had been the same too, she knew what was coming.

Mostly, though, the stories were uproarious.

'I was in prison, right, and I didn't have any burn. So, I find the nearest muppet, not a tooth in her head, and sell her my false teeth! She comes back half an hour later and tells me they don't fit! Well, you can't have your money back, I tell her. I can't have them now, can I? It would be *unhygienic!*'

Once, when we took her to Penarth, she collected a handful of smooth stones off the beach. When I took round her shopping the next morning, they were on her mantelpiece, one for each of us with our names carefully written on them, and the date.

She once told me she'd never had a steak, or champagne. We got her a steak.

As she slips away, tiny and silent, we sing to her: Kenny

bloody Rogers like she always sang to us.

You've gotta know when to hold 'em,
Know when to fold 'em,
Know when to walk away and know when to run.
You never count your money,
When you're sitting at the table,
There'll be time enough for counting when the dealing's done.

2023

Now's the Time, Mr Drakeford

21 August 2023

It's natural to compare the Welsh experience of devolution to that in Scotland. As Celtic nations that dress reliably further to the left than England, we have much in common. Where we differ, however, is that Scotland has, in recent years, managed to project an existential threat to the union. For a while there it seemed almost assured that flashing a blue passport at Carlisle would be a chastening experience for us here. How that has unravelled in Edinburgh is beyond my remit, but equipped with a tinfoil hat, I could advance a theory or two.

Instead, let's look at the wider picture. With Scotland temporarily in recess, the devolutionary problem for Westminster is Sadiq Khan in London. Bit by bit, and seemingly in defiance of his party leader, Khan is positioning London at the vanguard of progressive governance. It has been telling that his defence for ULEZ charges has been unapologetic. Where a cautious politician would have confected an economic case, Khan has stood on principle and written a book on the importance of air quality.

Here's today's *Mail on Sunday* channelling Goebbels to show how well that has gone down with vested interests.

'Sadiq Khan plunged into race row after his official website publishes picture of white family and says they don't represent real Londoners.'

I'm going to assume that you are as horrified by that as I am. They are saying the quiet bit out loud nowadays and that means they are rattled.

The most meaningful point of difference for Wales in recent years was the handling of the pandemic. During that period Mark Drakeford carved out a UK-wide profile and seemed a world away from the panicked confusion in Downing Street. Whether what he decided was right or wrong, he took it seriously.

Not so his constitutional responsibilities now. The First Minister has shown enough of his hand that we know where he stands. Over the years, he's advanced federalist ambitions and gone as far as to hint at the unthinkable: that the Welsh Labour party should be self-governing.

In the autumn of his political life, he should be standing up for these sentiments fearlessly. Whether we push further for independence or not, that's an argument we should be having from a position where our self-determination is unquestioned.

Nobody in possession of self-respect, regardless of loyalty to the UK, should accept that matters like transport should be remotely decided. We live here; therefore, we know what type of train line we need, right?

Westminster politics are an international disgrace; a farce that elicits giggles from waiters when we go on holiday. I'm *Welsh*, we plead. Don't lump me in with them.

So, Mr Drakeford, you've told us that devolution is the way for years. Let's hear you telling them the same thing. If Wales is viable in the union, we can demand things, can't we? If we're being disadvantaged, we should be a problem, if we're leading the way we should be terrifying the *Mail* like Sadiq Khan's London.

Khan has the advantage of being right there in the face of Westminster. Those MPs must navigate London and the democratic decisions its citizens have made. Lacking that visibility, Wales needs to be louder and to make a point of it. If Westminster charlatans are lying about our NHS to excuse their betrayal of their own, we should be heard. If we are paying for somebody else's train ride, we should be heard. If our farmers are disadvantaged by Brexit, we should be heard.

If devolution works, Mr Drakeford, and you've been insistent that it does, why can't I hear you?

Filling in the Blanks

28 August 2023

In August of 1983, I reached one of those forks in the road when you experience something so enjoyable that it hooks you for life.

I was on a weekend break with my family in Penmaenpool and the journey there had been eventful. As we sat at the lights near Y Trallwng, a black BMW came hurtling down the dual carriageway behind us without a hope of stopping in time. The crunching sound behind me was so unusual that it registered more prominently than the feeling of my face banging into Mum's headrest and her scream.

The rear of the car was totalled but it still moved so we carried on to the Mawddach estuary; all of us in shock and processing what had happened.

I was a big boy now, at 10, and had been thrilled to be getting my own room for the weekend. After a quiet dinner I assured my parents I was OK and went to enjoy it. The next few hours were awful. I'd drop off to sleep and start dreaming about my surroundings. Cormorants and oystercatchers flew around the room until the roar of a German engine scared them off and that crunch from behind woke me up, crying and panting. There was no way I was going into my parents' room, though, not at my age, so after several attempts at sleeping I put the telly on.

In the middle of the night, live from America, Gorseinon's Colin Jones was fighting Milton 'Ice Man' McCrory from Detroit for the WBC Welterweight championship. Over 12 rounds in Las Vegas, he banged and sweated towards a split decision loss that could have easily gone his way. I was lost in it, bobbing and weaving as I sat upright in bed willing Colin on. By the time I went back to sleep, I was disappointed instead of traumatised and boxing had got me. When Jones challenged for the title again, against Donald Curry, I was nervous weeks in advance, as I was for Pat Cowdell, Barry McGuigan, Frank

Bruno, Herol Graham…

So, I'll be forking out my pay-per-view money to watch Daniel Dubois take on Oleksandr Usyk tonight despite his vanishingly slim chances of victory. I've watched the press conferences, the weigh-in, dozens of interviews and a couple of documentaries. All this peripheral stuff serves as the sizzle on the steak, whetting appetites to see two extraordinary athletes risk their lives for glory.

Another boxing event this week, however, has eclipsed the heavyweight championship on social media. In October, Logan Paul, the YouTube star behind the Prime energy drink will be boxing Dillon Danis, an American MMA fighter. Neither has a boxing background and no titles are on the line, but it is predicted to be one of the most watched contests of the year. Danis, knowing that the event could propel him to superstardom, has been putting in the hours on Twitter to hype the fight, for which a press conference was held on Tuesday. Specifically, he's been posting dozens of photos of Paul's fiancée in affectionate poses with other men. Slut-shaming, in other words.

At the press conference, Tyson Fury's father, John, had a role to play. His younger son, Tommy off *Love Island*, is fighting another YouTuber, KSI on the same bill. Fury Sr. concocted a flimsy row so that he could throw furniture about and challenge anybody in the room to a fight. The assembled social media stars on stage shrunk into the shadows as this 60-year-old rampaged through his act.

For an event like this, you see, there is a missing ingredient: authenticity. John Fury's performance was dependent on background knowledge from the audience. He has a reputation as a bare-knuckle fighter in his youth and spent four years in prison for gouging out a man's eye in 2011. A boxing match between two pretty-boy influencers lacks *jeopardy*, so John, do your thing. The cheque is in the post.

All public events need hype, and politics has always involved an element of it.

The 1978 'Labour isn't Working' Conservative poster is

touted as the moment that PR became dominant in British politics. Created by Saatchi & Saatchi, it marries a powerful visual image with a simple slogan to pin blame on the incumbent government for growing unemployment. Yes, there had been an international financial crisis caused by oil prices, but for the electorate, this image caught the moment, and we all know what came next.

If Osama Bin Laden's ambition had been to kill as many Americans as possible, he could have killed a greater number, and more easily, than he did on 9/11. His objective was the image freezing into the collective consciousness, as we all saw the human experience bent to his will before our eyes. It was an advertisement for Armageddon.

But at least it was an advertisement for *something*. The use of outrageous imagery to captivate the public has traditionally involved simplifying a complicated matter into something we can understand or even enjoy. So, for instance, the careers of two boxers might involve losses, controversial decisions, gruelling years as amateurs and injuries. On the poster for their fight, though, you'll see two airbrushed titans glaring below a slogan like 'Judgement Day' or, if that one makes money, 'Judgement Day 2'. All the struggles the fighters have been through to get there are implicit in the image, there for you to decode.

But decoding stuff is boring. As it's become apparent that the image is king, why bother with all the problematic gubbins it's supposed to represent? As long as the press conference does the numbers, it doesn't matter if the fight is between Noel Edmunds and Prue Leith.

But how many empty charades can our culture accommodate before substance is eliminated entirely? The Republican primary debate went on this week minus Donald Trump, who is virtually guaranteed to win the nomination. Whilst the other candidates debated whatever it is they think his voters care about, the lad himself was proving that they don't care about anything at all. Staring defiantly into a Georgia Department of Justice camera, Trump burned everything you

11

need to know about next year's election on to the whole world. Vote for Jesse James.

Here in Wales, Andrew 'Real Ting' Davies has tweeted that Labour wants to give £1600 a month to asylum seekers every day for weeks on end. It's not true, he knows it's not true, even his supporters up the golf club know it isn't true. None of that matters. It brings eyeballs, get over it.

The sizzle from a steak should signify the existence of an actual steak, not steak-flavoured candyfloss that disintegrates upon contact with the air. If Marcel Proust had posted 'Hmmmm…' on Instagram alongside a picture of a cake, it would not have been enough to win his reputation.

When Colin Jones went life or death against McCrory all those years ago, it took away a little boy's nightmares. The genuine drama of the fight gave my brain the space it needed to file away the day's trauma properly and see me right. It inspired a lifelong passion for the sport and gave me something to talk about with people who love the same thing. It was real: for him and for everyone watching.

The crash would have made a great YouTube short, I suppose.

A Vacuum Abhors Nature

03 September 2023

When, in 2019, Michael Gove said, 'We know we must do all we can to protect our precious natural environment,' we were yet to discover that his own natural environment was the dancefloor of an Ibiza night club.[1]

I have some sympathy here. As a child of the suburbs, I grew up in magnetic thrall to the city; that was where it all happened and where I wanted to be. Consequently, my understanding of the natural world is shamefully sketchy. I like how it looks but am less keen on its tendency to sting my neck or stick to my unsuitable shoes. I prefer to experience the countryside – as I do anything that poses the remotest peril to my soft-sinewed, precious wellbeing – in books or from the decking of a nicely appointed gastropub.

'Is that a red kite?'

'No.'

'Oh… More tartiflette?'

I am aware, however, that this is a wretched state of affairs. I have a friend who races home of a Friday to assemble his kit for a weekend's bivouacking. He's never happier than tethered to a snowy mountainside with his Calor gas stove, Ordinance Survey map, and Swiss mountain knife. Where my Facebook feed is full of pictures of Mrs W.'s cooking and doggo memes, his features him staring flintily across ravines with an expression that suggests hard-won comprehension of man's humility before the elements. I haven't told him that I put the central heating on at one minute past midnight on September 1st, he's not my dad.

Nature is bracingly three-dimensional. To reckon with it

---

[1] Distressing photos of Mr Gove throwing shapes on the dancefloor had appeared in the press without trigger warnings.

meaningfully requires an acceptance of dangers that can't be bargained away. It's no good complaining to a riptide that it is interfering with your freedom of speech as, indifferently, it drags you to an eternal, watery silence.

The current Westminster government floats miles above the mundane realities of organic life. Like monks devoted to an arcane and peculiarly absurd religion, ministers address us solely in terms of abstract concepts. Each day, freedom of speech jostles with 'sovereignty', 'British values', and 'common sense' to be wrapped up in a union flag and unfurled in the face of catastrophes that would be better addressed by someone who knows how to use an adjustable spanner.

This week, it led them into conflict with RSPB England.[2]

> LIARS! @RishiSunak @michaelgove @theresecoffey you said you wouldn't weaken environmental protections.
> And yet that's just what you are doing.
> You lie, and you lie, and you lie again.
> And we've had enough. 🎩 pic.twitter.com/ZHlRmd5po3
> – @RSPBEngland (August 30, 2023)

The society styles itself as 'nature's voice' which, it turns out, sounds less like an Enya track than its commemorative tea towels might lead you to assume.

The response to this glorious example of seditious ornithology was swift and hilarious.

Mark Jenkinson, MP for Workington and proponent of new coal mines, wanted the radicalised twitchers closed down.[3]

Inevitably, he was joined by our own Andrew 'Red-throated Tit' Davies who upped the ante by suggesting[4] that charities shouldn't be allowed an opinion on anything at all.

---

[2] This tweet has since been deleted.

[3] https://twitter.com/RSPBEngland/status/1696845799383003180/photo/1

[4] https://nation.cymru/news/andrew-rt-davies-calls-for-rspb-to-be-stripped-of-charitable-status/

So, the RSPB has been cast on to a crowded naughty step alongside delinquents like the Supreme Court, junior doctors, the civil service, the Welsh and Scottish governments, the BBC, the National Trust, and the RNLI.

Meanwhile, on the forest floors, our nation's mushrooms were preparing to poke through the autumn soil with their traditionally ambivalent attitude towards human wellbeing. This year, however, the high-stakes game of spot-the-lethal-breakfast-ingredient has been lent piquancy by our apparent desperation to accelerate human extinction. You can purchase mushroom identification books that help you discern which 'shrooms are fun guys (Editor: last warning, Ben), and which will elevate an omelette to the climactic experience of your adventure here on earth.

It's not unreasonable to assume these books to be written by the sort of cove who can peer meaningfully at a troubled sky and announce the precise minute that rain will commence. During my brief period poncing about the Powys hills like a lace handkerchief in the wind, I lived next door to a *man of his own square mile* who could do this. He was always right, and that's the sort of fellow you want advising you on mushrooms.

This season, however, Amazon is offering unreliable foraging guides that have been written by Artificial Intelligence.[5] In lower moments, I've toyed with the notion that the potential consequences of this would provide a seemly conclusion to this period of the planet's history. If functionally useless carbon units like me are persuaded to poison ourselves by machines we imagine to be our superiors, then we had it coming.

But I mustn't think like that, must I? As a damp summer recedes before September's golden decay, with idiocy clanging around the nation like a knell, eventually the old will yield to the new.

---

[5] http://www.theguardian.com/technology/2023/sep/01/mushroom-pickers-urged-to-avoid-foraging-books-on-amazon-that-appear-to-be-written-by-ai.

A Whole Other Country

10 September 2023

Speaking from HMP Cardiff, Sir Keir Starmer cuts a forlorn figure in his prison-issue blues.

'Nobody told me about the new speed limit,' he protested. 'I never drive above 25mph because of my tendency to drift into the right-hand lane, so I assumed I was safe.'

Sinking tearfully to his knees, Sir Keir looks confused. 'Patriotism… toolmaker… fiscal responsibility…' he babbles.

Sensing his cellmate's distress, the story is taken up by Ron 'Viral' Thomas, currently serving 15 years for crossing the Cardiff/Caerphilly border during lockdown.

'It's shocking. They won't let him have a Union Jack in his cell and are charging him a tourist tax for every night he is here.'

It can sometimes seem as if Mark Drakeford is the only person in the UK who views devolution positively on its own terms. For supporters of independence, it is window dressing that obscures Wales' subservience in the union. Unionists, meanwhile, fear that it's a gateway drug that leads to separatism.

'I stopped paying prescription charges and thought I could handle it. The next thing I knew, I'd converted the Welsh Office into a youth club and seceded from NATO.'

The matter is complicated by the awkward reality that we're a *de facto* one-party-state. With Labour seeming certain to win power in Westminster, the Welsh Government will lose its comfortable position in opposition to remote Tory rule and must reckon with a UK Labour government with centralising instincts and a mandate from erstwhile Tory voters.

So, the time is ripe for Welsh Labour – a non-existent entity – to carve out an identity separate from Head Office in London. Drakeford has long hinted that this was an ambition and this week we saw a step in that direction.[1]

> "I've not had that conversation with him, nor should I need to." First Minister of Wales Mark Drakeford tells @PGMcNamara that he did not consult Labour Party Leader Sir Keir Starmer MP about lowering the speed limit on most Welsh residential roads to 20mph.[1]
>
> – @Channel4News (Sept 8, 2023)

Sir Keir can, it seems, read *Nation.Cymru* if he wants to find out about devolved matters in Wales. Mark Drakeford is too busy for his bullshit and is living his best life.

This, for me, is peak Drakeford: galvanising Wales with a long overdue assertion of self-determination but choosing to do so in support of a measure that has enraged half the nation. He could have gone rogue over the NHS, or the Crown Estate, or drugs policies. But no, the flag has finally been planted on behalf of your right to attend a speed-awareness course.

We can, however, unite over Channel 4's Paul McNamara reacting with mirthful disbelief to the notion that the First Minister might decide anything at all without clearance from Starmer. For all Drakeford's insistence on the primacy of his mandate, it's clear that even Channel 4 News, traditionally the progressive end of TV journalism, sees Welsh democracy as inauthentic; a 'My First Sovereign Decision' playset granted by the grown-ups in Westminster.

Looking at the chaos of Westminster politics over the last few years, it has been comforting to emphasise our distinctiveness and fall back on traditional contempt for clueless toffs and those in England who, seemingly against their interests, vote for them. Labour in Wales benefits electorally from the very existence of people like Boris Johnson and Jacob Rees-Mogg: cartoonish villains who look and sound as if they would force our kids down the pits if given the chance.

With Starmer in charge, that dynamic will change. As the

---

[1] https://x.com/Channel4News/status/1700107244526797261

17

Welsh Government seeks to position the nation at the forefront of progressive governance[2], particularly on environmental matters, UK Labour is busily reneging on promises to do the same. It is difficult to see a way through this that doesn't involve conflict within a party that also has to coexist with powerful devolved entities in London and the English North.

Wales is perennially at the sharp end of the UK's woes. Disadvantaged in terms of investment, transport links, and influence, our case has always needed to be argued. If our advocates are wearing the same kit as the Westminster decision-makers, they will need to hold it to account and be seen to do so. Mr Drakeford made a welcome gesture this week, but it needs to be a taste of what's to come rather than an exception.

---

[2] OK, scratch that.

Passion, Pressure and Mantovani

11 September 2023

We had Radio Wales on as we came home from watching the game and when the coverage ended, they played what sounded like Mantovani. Presumably, the NHS had been in touch to demand the nation be soothed back to cardiac safety.

It's never straightforward, is it? There was a moment, on 60 minutes, when I did it to myself again. I looked at the score, then at the clock with the little yellow card symbol above Fiji, and relaxed. I sat back in my chair, took a leisurely swig of Diet Coke and said, out loud mind,

'That's us into the quarter finals.'

Fifty years I've had to learn better than that but, once again, hubris got the better of me and I set myself up for 20 minutes of pure blydi torture.

Earlier in the week I'd been making the proper psychological preparations. *Of course,* we were going to lose the opener. Wales always start slowly, and Fiji are the form team. Even the bookies had Fiji winning, so the wise course of action was to write this one off and hope that Wales was gelling by the time Australia came around. I was even slightly upset when Warren Gatland announced that the squad had no injuries. For purposes of rationalisation and self-care, we are usually provided with a raft of key injuries upon which to ascribe defeats. If it all went 2007, what was I to blame this time? The Tories, probably.

There was a subdued atmosphere in Pontypridd's District Club as the big screen blared the huge Bordeaux stadium into the darkened bar. Before the game we had the inevitable montage of 1970s moments, complete with tearful doggerel and weapons-grade cliché. The camera panned around the crowd and settled on a couple of blokes wearing daffodil head dresses. My pal, Phil, winced visibly.

19

'Grown men, they are.'

And we were underway.

Wales looked well-drilled and exceptionally fit. In the early exchanges, the defensive line was organised, and players knew where they were supposed to be.

When Adams went over it seemed totemic. If he starts scoring tries, he tends to carry on scoring them and his raw aggression near the line, looking for all the world like a staffy entering a butcher's shop, is a rousing sight: the sort of spectacle that inspires a team to greatness.

The sheer physicality of Fiji, though, is something for which there's no sure answer. When Waisea Nayacalevu bounced Dan Biggar off one shoulder and Aaron Wainwright the other on his way to Fiji's reply, it was clear that nothing should be taken for granted. Well, it was clear to everyone who isn't as twp as me that nothing should be taken for granted.

In the second half, Rees-Zammit's try showcased not only his whippet speed but also the Penarth assurance he carries through life. Having left the Fijian defence for dead, he produced a 'what did you expect' smile for the cameras. Wales will be a serious threat from either flank in this tournament.

Elliot Dee's try should have been it. Fiji had begun to tire, and it seemed that sensible game management would be enough to see Wales home. This Fiji side, though, is irrepressible. Their intensity was evident before the game and the onslaught they produced in the last quarter would have tested any side.

This version of Wales, however, is a tough nut to crack. Typified by Dan Biggar, the players ae fierce in defence and ready to take a chance when it arises. They must have been black and blue at the end of this. Play them some Mantovani, Warren.

Send in the Clowns

17 September 2023

I'm supposed to be light relief here. Whilst everyone goes nuts about the 20mph speed limit, or what we call our national parks, my enviable role is to make a paper plane with 'wankers' written on the wings and lob it into the political space. It's an easy job. Over the 18 months I've been doing this, we've had the death throes of Boris Johnson's playpen tantrum, Liz Truss's reckoning with reality, and Rishi Sunak's realisation that being the bestest behaved boy ever doesn't guarantee a transition from Head Prefect to world statesman. If that wasn't enough, nearer to home Andrew 'Reet peTite' Davies has reliably acted as a comic foil to Mark Drakeford's crushing worthiness. The only anxiety I've had is whether satirising all this detracts from its inherent comedy.

Humour is best positioned as a valve to release the pressure of relentless seriousness. When 'We're Going to Hang out the Washing on the Siegfried Line' was sung by marching soldiers in 1939, it was in the expectation that the politicians responsible for their prospects were engaged with the matter as if their own lives depended upon it. Without that belief, no light-heartedness would have been possible.

In more recent times, *Spitting Image* thrived because the absurd seriousness of its targets demanded satirical puncture. A man like Douglas Hurd, for instance, was so concerned with acting as a vessel of traditional rectitude that the only sane response to him was to render his neglected hairstyle as an ice-cream cone. Likewise, Margaret Thatcher's maniacal certainty, and seeming disregard for criticism, gave birth to a host of comic imitators who only needed to exaggerate her by a few degrees to satisfy their audience's need for well-crafted mockery in the face of her relentlessness.

Historically, politicians were earnest oddballs whose obsessional nature was simultaneously a professional strength and a source of mirth for anyone with a balanced life. Think of the hours that Gordon Brown must have spent reading up on economic theory when you were down the pub or playing Angry Birds. Traditionally, we have allowed dweebs to indulge their obsessions on our behalf as long as we get to take the piss when they get it wrong. That was the trade-off.

The current traffic from Westminster to jobs presenting shows on the grubbier fringes of satellite TV reveals a fundamental change in the sort of personality who thrives in contemporary politics. Theresa May is an almost forgotten figure now, but it is only a couple of years since we observed her excruciating attempts to express well-meaning awkwardness on a stage that has no room for self-doubt. Since then, her kind has been wiped out in favour of post-Johnsonian politicians who can avoid criticism by outpacing it with self-parody.

When Suella Braverman tweets her latest fascist-adjacent take on immigration, it's with the knowledge that instead of leaving her vulnerable to accusations of inhumanity, any resistance will only serve to strengthen her brand. After all, if the Home Sec. gig gets pulled, she can perform the same act on GB News for more money.

Politics has always been 'showbiz for ugly people', but its current incarnation seems to operate in a space that forgives triviality as if it were a given prerequisite of national life. The 20mph furore currently raging here and in the English press is less to do with the policy itself than the novelty of democracy throwing up a real-world outcome. You actually do have to drive slower because of this democratically mandated change to motoring regulations, and that is a shocking revelation in a political hall of mirrors where narrative has replaced outcomes. You'll notice, for instance, that no immigrants have been removed to Rwanda. Neither has the UK left the ECHR. Boris Johnson certainly didn't build a bridge between Scotland and Northern Ireland, or one built out of plants across the Thames. These are all storylines in a soap opera, whereas your upcoming speeding fines are very much non-fiction.

According to an international poll[1] published this week, 42% of people aged 18-35 believe that military rule is preferable to democracy. I stand with my bucket of glitter each week, ready to throw it over politicians who have equipped themselves with a collapsible car. With potentially 12 months to go before an election, and the prospect of American democracy collapsing into mob violence in the interim, I wonder how strained the laughter will become.

[1] www.theguardian.com/world/2023/sep/11/younger-people-more-relaxed-alternatives-democracy-survey

The key to tournament rugby…
is winning when you're awful
17 September 2023

The Portuguese invented fish & chips, you know, so it never does to underestimate them when it comes to participation in what we imagine to be our cultural touchstones. For a while there in the second half it looked very much as if we'd shown up on Caroline Street half an hour late and ended up with the last saveloy in the cabinet. The look on Taulupe Faletau's face after he'd secured our inevitably crucial bonus point was less of triumph than peeved disbelief that, at his age, he'd had to dig us out of a hole once again.

It's alrigh' though, innit? The key to tournament rugby is winning when you're awful, and hopeless as we were today, the bonus point was all that was ever in peril.

For rugby more widely, this RWC seems finally to be delivering on its objectives. Ever since Dame Kiri burned 'World In Union' on to our collective consciousness in all its banal emptiness, the organisers have required us to buy into the idea that Rugby Union is a global game. Never mind that you could assemble 15 randoms from Ynyshir Road who'd give most participatory nations a run for their money, this was 'elite sport' in competition with soccer and the Olympics.

Until now, this has felt less of an aspirational goal than a marketing irritation. Be honest, if your other half had absolutely insisted on a trip to the garden centre this afternoon, you'd have gone.

'Ah, it's only Portugal,' you'd have thought. 'All I'm risking is whether we stuff them by 40 or 60. 'There's also the risk that my wholly uninformed opinion on the makeup of the front row might be exposed, but he/she/they will go proper nuts if I don't pay rapt attention to the design options for our proposed gazebo, and it's obvious Australia is the next proper game...'

Wrong!

From Montevideo to Lisbon, it seems that there are people who have a spookily accurate grasp of what constitutes a legal entry into the breakdown. Who knew?

As things stand, the more serious nations tend only to be represented in rugby by the more bohemian elements of their populace. Imagine what would happen if mainstream sportsmen from the USA or Germany decide to take up the game. I think it's fair to speculate that such a development would put a dampener on the *joie de vivre* historically associated with the game.

'Chad Sportenstock disgraced his nation today after celebrating the USA's win against Waleshire by driving a golf cart down the M4 at midnight. His teammates are currently holding a prayer vigil for the fallen idol, who has lost his sponsorship deal from Clark's Pies.'

It looks, though, like RWC, originally the brainchild of Wales flanker John Taylor, has been right all along. This illogical, infuriating game appeals to people in a different way to soccer. It beguiles, confounds, and thrills anybody who has the willingness to learn its ever-changing rules. Well done, Portugal. Mine's a large haddock.

Friends and neighbours, we cannot go on like this

24 September 2023

There are ten types of people in this world: those who understand binary, and those who don't.

In the thuddingly tedious, infantile hellscape of UK politics, you can distract yourself from deepening shame by playing a simple parlour game. It goes like this. Find out what someone believes about a random news story, then use this information to predict their views on every unrelated topic.

This week, for instance, we are all required to have opinions on two matters: the sexual opportunism of an overheated vaudeville act with philosophical pretensions, and how quickly you should be able to drive through Ferndale on your way to pick up your wife from the bus stop outside Tylorstown Welfare Hall.

In saner times it was permitted to hold opinions on these matters which were independent from each other. I can't remember the debate over compulsory seat belts being coloured in any way by people's stance on Frank Bough's efforts to reposition knitwear as the libertine's garment of choice.

If, however, somebody offers their opinion that YouTube's decision to demonetise Russell Brand's videos is a sinister curtailment of free speech, you can safely run to the bookies and bet the farm on them being opposed to the 20mph speed limits here in Wales. If your co-worker admires Meghan Markle's approach to marriage, you can safely assume that they are accepting of climate science. And, just to maximise the Twitter abuse I receive this week, if your butty reckons, like me, that our rugby team should replace the three feathers on their jerseys with a dragon, then don't get them a Jeremy Clarkson boxset this Christmas. Not if you're expecting an affectionate time on Boxing Day.

26

Logically, these matters have nothing at all to do with each other but let's face it, logic went out of the window some time back. When the heavy axe of the Brexit referendum splintered everything asunder in 2016, every conceivable facet of human existence fell on one side or the other and began drifting in opposite directions. Since then, the polarisation of political opinion has become so absolute and all-encompassing that we don't really need to develop positions of our own. To save time informing ourselves about the confected bilge that is pumped our way in the name of current affairs, we need only to see what the other side thinks before taking the opposite stance.

Oh, apparently Russell Brand is being cancelled because of thus far unproven accusations about his private life. What does Toby Young think about it, and just to make sure, Darren Grimes? They're urging caution. In that case, he must be a wrong'un and deserves everything he gets…

Or, if you clung on to a different piece of driftwood in the post-referendum Titanic re-enactment.

What's that, particulates in the air from older vehicles cause demonstrative harm to the developing lungs of children? Surely then, we should encourage a reduction in the manifestation of this public health menace… but hold on! Sadiq Khan believes in this science so, by definition, it must be wrong…

Friends and neighbours, we cannot go on like this. Firstly, next to nothing is getting done by our politicians. LBC's James O'Brien, whose intelligence is eclipsed only by his delight in his intelligence, likes to characterise the tribal nature of current politics as 'footballification'. That suggests, though, that an actual game is being played. What's actually going on is a UK full of spectators wearing shirts whilst the players perform pitchside interviews without bothering to kick a ball. Andrew RT Davies I'm looking at you.

There is a general tragedy inherent to this, as we all watch our standards of living decline by the month without any apparent democratic redress. More particularly, though, the people whose lives are genuinely affected by the daily 'issues' these shysters exploit find their personal heartbreak cheapened and commodified by a system that is supposed to protect them. Rape complainants; children with poorly lungs; refugees; motorists on their way to shitty, underpaid jobs; junior doctors; trans people; female athletes; all of us in the end are being fed into a meat grinder by people whose only ambition is personal attention.

As Rupert Murdoch retires, we need to recalibrate our political machine to nullify the malignant division that he has sown in our communities. The seductive, binary satisfaction that ruined our consensus in 2016 needs to be replaced by voting systems that force our politicians to seek agreement and eject those who refuse to try.

There are only two types of people in this world: those who care, and those who don't.

Wales Ditch the Agony for the Ecstasy

25 September 2023

If there's a doctor reading this, I'd like to know if the calm All Black fan-style experience I've just had as Wales romped to victory tonight against Australia means that I get some life-expectancy back for all the times I've experienced carcinogenic levels of stress watching them over the last 50 years? Jiffy's 'never in doubt' quip when we nicked a last-second victory over France 20-odd years ago summed up nearly every high-stakes win we've had since: reliant on luck, in jeopardy throughout, and enjoyed as if we've been released from the jaws of a lion that can't stomach the aftertaste of Brains SA.

Who knew that watching Wales in a make-or-break RWC tie with a southern hemisphere nation could be a serene experience?

'I've cancelled your spa weekend, sweetie, Wales are playing Australia it'll chill you right out.'

This one was personal for me as I've recently been visited by the Australian branch of my family. Naturally, I made a vehement effort to usher them towards the light with a tour of the Principality and an ideological re-education of which Chairman Mao would have approved. So, an Australian victory would have hit me particularly hard this time. C'mon boys, you can capture my nephew for life if you pull this off!

Like you, though, I expected to be put through the wringer once again. We'd start brightly, establish a lead, and then lose it in the dying seconds of the first half. After the break, we'd drop the restart and concede three tries in 15 minutes before rallying in the last 20 but falling one point short of a losing bonus point and coming home to 483 articles about how the chickens had come home to roost as regards the WRU's mismanagement of the professional game.

I wasn't the only Welshman with a personal stake in this game, though. Gareth Davies' humiliation at the hands of Margot Robbie in *Barbie* has clearly cut deeply. Any notion that his job was 'beach' faded from global consciousness when he crashed over the Australian line with only seconds on the clock. Could he become a surgeon purely because he imagines it? Nobody would bet against that outcome now.

I'm always a bit over-rapt, myself. I don't possess the *sang-froid* to watch Wales play as a dispassionate reporter. Or, to be honest, as a normal human being, every collision, front-row encounter, and Wayne Barnes thought process registers with me like a threat to my personal wellbeing.

My goodwill towards old Wayne has flourished this evening, though. I was impressed at how his understanding of the game seemed to improve once our utter supremacy rendered the rules a mere sideshow to Josh Adams' emergence as the Bully XL of Australian nightmares.

And this is where tonight's performance really hit the spot for me. Whether in defence or attack, the Welsh pack seemed to advance and that bought us the right to go wide if something looked on. We've always had good wingers, but the Gerald/JJ double-trauma fear hasn't inhabited our opponents for a while. Give either the ball, and something destructive will ensue.

So, how are you going to approach the quarter-final of a world cup when we are expected to win it? It's a new one on me, and my nephew.

State-Funded Satirist Pens Balanced Article

1 October 2023

Absolute scenes in the Senedd this week as First Minister Mark Drakeford further tightened his grip on freedom of speech in the nation. Wearing his customary peaked cap, epaulettes, and mirrored sunglasses, the Premier swept into the chamber accompanied by an escort of female bodyguards, who are recruited from his tribal stronghold in Carmarthenshire.

There had, he raged, been threats against his personal safety. As a punitive measure, his government would be reducing the national speed limit to 10mph over the Christmas period.

'Your Judeo-Christian festivals mean nothing in the New Wales,' Drakeford glowered. 'Loyal citizens may celebrate a responsible Ecomas in the safety of their own homes. Dissidents will be struggled with by the masses and held to account by licensed journalists.' A spontaneous round of applause broke out in the press gallery, where correspondents had been issued with new iPads by the regime.

There you go: three solid paragraphs of anti-Welsh Government satire, as demanded week-on-week by puce-faced Twitter commentators with profile pictures that feature them holding large game fish aloft. *Nation.Cymru* has listened to you, and we hope you enjoy this new direction. Stop the boats![1]

Mindful of your insistence on 'balance', however, you'll forgive me if I briefly cast an eye over this week's contributions from Andrew 'Reliable Target' Davies.

It seems that Windcheater Winston feels that his treatment at the hands of this outlet has been too robust. In response to

---

[1] At this point in the political cycle, I was routinely accused of being in the pocket of the Welsh Government.

31

Mark Drakeford's disclosure that thousands of threats[2] had been made against himself and Deputy Minister for Climate Change, Lee Waters, Davies complained that *Nation.Cymru*, a 'purported news site', had 'painted a target' on the backs of him and his family.[3]

Suggesting that *Nation.Cymru* be defunded, Davies sought to draw an equivalence between our coverage of him and threats on social media to coordinate physical attacks on the First Minister.

Who knew that the horny-handed son of the soil was such a fragile soul? I'd been given to understand that this plain-talking defender of free speech welcomed a bracingly agricultural approach to political discourse. The idea of his whimpering into the silage due to journalistic doggedness seems off-brand.

Davies' own approach to the national debate is notable for two reasons: a propensity to misrepresent facts in the service of narrative — see the 'blanket' 20mph limit or Labour's supposed desire to hand £1600 a month to asylum seekers — and a willingness to repeat such claims relentlessly, and long after they have been discredited.[4]

Davies is an internet troll. His Twitter account exists not to inform nor persuade the electorate, but to inflame it. A sympathetic explanation for this behaviour is that Davies hopes that entrenching division will shore up the existing Conservative vote in the upcoming Westminster election. A glance at the polls[5] however, suggests that this strategy isn't bearing fruit.

Another, less palatable, explanation for Davies' online behaviour is that it is unrelated to electoral behaviour in Wales and not aimed at us at all. The Tories in *England* are facing the

---

[2] https://nation.cymru/news/vile-threats-to-first-minister-investigated-by-south-wales-police/]
[3] https://x.com/NationCymru/status/1706703898348495059?s=20
[4] I'm editing this book in October 2024 and he tweeted the same nonsense yesterday.
[5] https://redfieldandwiltonstrategies.com/latest-welsh-westminster-senedd-voting-intention-16-17-september-2023/

loss of previously safe seats, and their biggest fear is that elderly, traditionally Conservative voters will stay at home on election day. It is to these voters that the culture war is pitched. The fringe fearmongering that used to be the preserve of UKIP *et al* has now been deployed by a government that sees an existential threat to the Conservative brand. Knowing that we are an electoral lost cause, the party has utilised Davies to peddle misinformation about life here in Wales and spook English voters about the prospect of Labour governance.

He is, however, a minor player in the wider game. The disintegration of UK politics is happening at a dizzying speed. In the last week alone, we have seen Suella Braverman unleash an attack on multiculturalism that drew condemnation from the United Nations, while over on GB News, where Davies appears alongside Lee Anderson, Jacob Rees-Mogg, and Nigel Farage, a female journalist found herself attacked in sexual terms by Lawrence Fox. This is desperate, grim stuff and, after the election, we can expect to watch the protagonists play musical chairs, as they seek to cling on to whatever political or media positions remain open to them. We'll see what all Davies' tweets are worth to him then, I suppose.

The direct losers from Davies' clownish political persona, and disinterest in the nuts and bolts of Welsh policymaking are serious Conservative politicians and voters who would like to see a centre-right government in the Senedd. Wales is, and always has been, to the left of centre in relation to England. It follows, therefore, that electoral success for the Conservatives is unlikely to come from the extreme right wing of the party. In pursuing the approval of that faction in England, Davies has left mainstream conservatism without a voice on his own watch.

There is *plenty* to take issue over with our Labour government. From NHS outcomes to Cardiff Airport, and a perceived over-cautiousness in approach, an engaged opposition could hold it to account in a way that made it a potent force. Instead, the Welsh electorate has been used as scenery in the disaster movie of Westminster politics by a politician who seems ambivalent at best as to whether the democracy that has sustained him thus far should exist at all.

If Davies has a target on his back, it is not because the press has painted it on him. Rather, he has chosen to place himself beyond the pale of reasoned debate in Wales, and the incoming arrows he should worry about are from sensible Conservatives who have had enough of being humiliated by his leadership.

Georgia are the new Wales

8 October 2023

We need Georgia in the Seven Nations ASAP, don't we?

The Rugby World Cup, traditionally, has been where rugby shows its professional face to a global audience. The game is branded, blow-dried and *World-In-Unioned* to resemble a product that sits alongside other sporting occasions as a fitting vehicle for corporate advertising and slow-motion montages that have been filmed in advance.

ITV today tried to lure us into its American football coverage.

'Is it too simplistic to suggest that fans of rugby would enjoy its American variant?' the presenter asked.

Well, yes butt, clearly.

It always feels a bit wrong to me. Weird, unfamiliar presenters speaking with that over-earnest urgency that accompanies Premier League football, adverts all the time, and, often, a cautious brand of rugby that jars in a game that's all about adventure.

Wales fancied a bit of that today. Now that we're a well-drilled machine of the global game, routinely racking up victories wherever we go, it was time to execute the plan against a second-tier nation before assuming our inevitable berth in the quarter finals.

'Just drill the ball relentlessly into the 22 and wait for Johnny Foreigner to make a mistake,' has a rather English tone to it but banal efficiency is the name of the game once a side operates in the rarified atmosphere that Wales finds itself in. Another day, another routine win in service of the ultimate goal.

Can't lie, I'd got the kick-off time wrong. At ten to two, I was still in my pyjamas, planning a trip out to watch the game somewhere picturesque. How quickly success breeds complacency! One minute you're weeping into your Butty Bach as Georgia consign us to the scrapheap and less than a year later, you're so relaxed you've forgotten what time the game's on.

Fortunately, the pub is within wheezing distance, so I made it in time and found everyone else in cheerful laxity too. With no peril to enthral us, conversation was varied. Who, for instance, is employed by TV companies to scan the crowd for attractive women to train the camera on during breaks in play? More pertinently, how has this practice survived into the twenty-first century?

Georgia looked lively towards the end of the first half, but Wales continued to impress with their intensity exemplified by Tommy Reffell, who gave a timely reminder that Jac Morgan has to be world class to keep him out of the side.

Outside at half-time, the Rhondda smiled in the embrace of an Indian summer. So, when Rees-Zammit took advantage of an interception to glide home for one of three tries, there was little wrong in the world. His easy grace seemed of a piece with the day and less obsessive pub-goers turned their conversations away from the game.

'You know what his missus is like…'

Georgia wasn't having it, though. The commitment they showed in the second half was unending. Employing wild physicality and nineteenth-century facial hair stylings to terrifying effect, they took apart the Welsh defence as no other side has been able to during this campaign.

The mid period of the second half suggested that they might just pull off the impossible as the Welsh scrum creaked, and Georgia built momentum.

With jeopardy restored, the pub once again became a rugby crowd, gasping and shouting with every collision. We even experienced the nostalgic treat of a 30-man brawl that resulted in a yellow card each for the sides.

When Wales eventually stretched away, I reflected that the Georgian experience mirrored many that we've all had supporting Wales. They were a step below us in class but skilled, fierce, and inventive. As we advance to the quarters let's hope that it's not long before this fine rugby nation joins the top tier of European rugby.

Put the Lelos into the dark, wintertime tumult of the Seven Nations and they'll surely deliver.

Who fancies RyanAir flights for a weekend in Tblisi?

When the dog whistle is replaced by a bull horn

8 October 2023

One of the defining features of truly dreadful people is that that they are blissfully unaware of their repugnance. If you do or say something socially unacceptable, your senses alert you to adverse responses, however polite or subtle they may be.

Embarrassment is a unique emotion in that it doesn't fade over time. Decades on from saying something that threatened your acceptability to a social group, the mere memory of the event will induce the authentic, gut-wrenching horror that you experienced at the time.

This is humanity at its base level. Underneath our intellect, and regardless of the individuality we've imagined we possess since the Enlightenment, lies the pack mentality that kept us alive when resources were scarce, and predators proliferated.

Back in the day, it was no good claiming to be a 'disruptor' if you'd snuck off from bear-guarding duties to record an edgy podcast about trading crypto arrowheads. You were out of the tribe and at the mercy of nature.

Fear of ostracism is the most powerful deterrent we have to keep us honest. Laws and penalties vary from place to place and over time. The turning away of a society from an individual, though, is the bedrock of our application of justice.

Whether you've been sent out of class for blowing raspberries, or to the Hague for committing war crimes, the process is the same and the implication identical: do this and you threaten the common good.

Imagine, then, what it must be like not to feel embarrassment. If things are going well, it would be liberating to be unconstrained by a continual emotional response to your social performance.

'I don't care what other people think,' we often lie as we transgress just a teensy-weensy bit so that we can poke our heads above the crowd and experience the sunlight of personal recognition.

We do, though.

Remember the last whispered joke you shared with your best friend; one that had you both breathless at its thrilling wrongness. Now picture yourself at an elderly relative's birthday party telling the same joke in earshot of Aunt Gwen, who still sends you an Airfix kit every Christmas.

You care what people think alright.

Which is why you're not going to make it as a politician.

When Suella Braverman made her sniggering speech this week, in which the traditional dog whistle was replaced by a bull horn, it was with disregard for the mores of most of the population.

To the baying delight of her audience in the hall, she dismissed those who disagreed as a 'privileged elite'. Listening to the speech in my car outside Lidl, I learned that compassion for refugees was a 'luxury belief' which would be tolerated no longer.

Later in the week, I heard a journalist from Led By Donkeys recount telling Ms Braverman that Rwanda, her proposed destination for refugees, had shot dead 12 asylum seekers in 2018. Initially unaware of the incident, she quickly rationalised it in non-luxury terms.

'That was five years ago. It's 2023 now.'

The Conservatives remain over 20 points behind Labour in the polls.

To thrive in modern politics, a candidate has to navigate not only the scrutiny of the press and the ballot box, but the 'hurricane', as Braverman might style it, of internet abuse that blows in the face of anybody who mounts a soap box.

The quantitative deficit between people who were willing to post a letter and those who will lob an abusive comment on social media is so great that it is throwing up mutant politicians.

Whilst a thick skin was always required in that game, the century variant rewards those with no finer feelings to protect.

However the next election goes, you will be hearing from Braverman until either she or you is reading the great opinion column in the sky.

If not in power, she'll be in opposition, and if that goes south, she'll be in the media agitating for her own reemergence.

The mountains of disgust she will produce are a monetizable product for which you, one way or another, will be paying the bill.

It's embarrassing, isn't it?

A Different Energy: The Gentle Good

Clwb Y Bont, Pontypridd

14 October 2023

I've heard too much news this week. Telly, YouTube, radio, Twitter, Facebook are swirling round me in a bloody froth of cruelty and despair. The jabber of partisan opinions that accompanies everything nowadays sounds hollower yet when applied to the horrendous events in the Middle East.

Don't you get it? This is actually happening, as you speak, unfolding in the lives of living, crying humans. Nobody cares what you think. Be quiet.

So, we go out, my wife and me. Since Covid, we're out of the habit, well I am. I'm becoming a miserable old sod.

It's alright, though. We catch the bus so I can have a couple and socialise more like a person who volunteers for it. Things could do with a little blurring, I reckon.

Clwb Y Bont in Pontypridd is an effortlessly welcoming venue. Its relaxed authenticity is reflected in the easy manner people take on in the place. Nobody is on anybody's case. Your anxiety starts to think it can have a night off.

Y Dail's urgent guitar pop is what Friday nights are for. Quirky chords, melodic bass, chiming keys and four on the floor are a platform for Ponty's Huw Griffiths to seize his moment and knock you into yours. It's delivered with the conviction of musicians who knew you'd love it but are keen to make sure.

The Gentle Good[1], Gareth Bonello, is a different energy altogether. Conceding to showbusiness by taking off his jumper before mounting the stage, he is a performer whose calm assuredness owns a room. Seated like a classical player, he

---

[1] The Gentle Good's albums can be purchased from thegentlegood.com.

sweeps arpeggios across his steel-strung guitar that flutter into place behind the woodwind sweetness of his voice. It's transfixing; music to fill a silence.

Behind him there is a banner: 'The Welsh Language Is For Everyone!'

The songs speak of landscapes and what it is to inhabit them. Bonello coaxes the rivers and peaks of Cwm Elan into the room with the nurturing empathy of their mother tongue. The music plants no flags. Rather, it takes you by the hand and shows you the riches beneath the soil.

Between songs, he patiently translates everything for those with no Welsh and the kindness of it prickles my shame a little. I should learn, I know I should, I'd like myself more if I did.

Once a song starts, I have to concentrate on the fine guitar work to compensate for the words. I'm missing out on something I could have if I'd only *learn*. I might. I will.

I'm terrified of being someone who never learns. In my fevered newsfest this week, did I really read about a *university professor* angrily blaming traffic signs for his inability to read them? Duw, Duw...

Waiting for the last bus back up the valley, conversations are ringing around the concrete in the key of RCT.

'I'm telling you, that dust comes from the *Sahara*!'

I check my phone for the latest news from Gaza. *Make it stop...*

When the bus arrives, we gather round it and nod at each other. There's pensioners, teenagers, and us in the middle. The doors open and nobody moves. We all want each other to get on first, waving our arms to insist. Finally, grace gives way to respect and the eldest lead on with the youngsters cheerfully taking up the rear.

The gentle good, indeed.

Ghosted

15 October 2023

The best piece of advice I ever received was never to bother someone whom you suspect is ignoring you. Unless you have knowingly upset them, it's on the ignorer to raise any dispute; the ignoree should leave them to their sulk.

It's not easy though. *What on earth have I done?* you ruminate whilst staring at your unanswered text in doleful confusion.

You might have a bit of a root around on Facebook to see if there is anything to explain your banishment. *You mean to say he's thrown a party and invited everyone except me?*

The slight is all the more painful when it is your reward for unending, canine loyalty to someone whose behaviour has often left them otherwise friendless. In their darkest hour you were there, keeping the faith, and now that it's all coming good, they don't want to know.

There were 5829 words in Sir Keir Starmer's conference speech on Tuesday and none of them was 'Wales', let alone 'Cymru'. Do a document search and you'll find 'Anas', right next to 'thank', but 'Mark' is only highlighted as a constituent part of 'market'.

We are not, it would seem, flavour of the month. Or any other month, come to that. Wales has returned a plurality[1] of Labour MPs in every General Election since 1922. The Senedd has been under Labour control since its inception. If anywhere has cause to consider itself the UK Labour Party's BFF, it is Wales.

If we had been overlooked, that would be one thing. Infuriating as it is, we are well used to the London establishment

---

[1] No clue where I got this word from. If anybody has lost it, drop me a line.

43

forgetting that Wales exists until it's convenient to remember. At the moment, though, Wales has the dubious privilege of UK-wide profile, thanks to the Conservatives selecting our speed limits as the latest distraction from the collapse of civic society on their watch. The decision to namecheck Scotland's Anas Sarwar and ignore Mark Drakeford was deliberate.

Despite being the sole Labour-governed nation in the Union, the Welsh Government is an embarrassment to Starmer, whose enthusiasm for Union flags is rivalled only by the DUP and Geri Halliwell. With the Tory press again painting Wales as suffering under an authoritarian, near-communist regime, Starmer's choice not to lend support is telling.

The benign interpretation is that the forthcoming election will be won and lost in England, with Scotland also edging back into relevance on the evidence of the recent by-election. The path to power is strewn with hard choices, and Labour diehards might imagine that backgrounding the Welsh party is justified in terms of campaigning.

There was more to worry about in this speech, however, than grubby expedience. The previous Labour manifesto had plans for regional development banks, through which funding would flow to build infrastructure projects. This devolutionary ambition has been replaced by a centralised National Wealth Fund. From the optics on the stage to the scant policy details made available, it is clear that Starmer's instincts are to centralise rather than devolve.

Along with Drakeford, Sadiq Khan and Andy Burnham were also omitted from the speech. This really is quite extraordinary when you think about it. These *Labour* politicians all boast thumping mandates from their respective electorates but have been airbrushed out of the party's national offering. No personal scandal attaches to any of them, and neither are they representative of an ideological fringe.

This is a party that trumpets inclusion. Certainly, that spirit extends to companies like Amazon and Deliveroo, who held receptions at the conference, and to Zilch — a Buy Now Pay Later lender that provided sponsorship. With workers' rights supposedly at the top of its agenda, it seems curious that these representatives of the gig economy and consumer debt should be more enthusiastically embraced by the party than its elected leaders around the country.

If this is indicative of how the next Labour government intends to interact with devolved democracy, then the party here in Wales needs to put on its big boy trousers and become a problem.[2] For over a century Welsh Labour MPs have been a comfortable, certain block in Westminster. They represent constituencies that are largely to the left of centre in English terms, and which currently have no electorally viable alternative.

If Wales is to be misrepresented by the Conservatives and ignored by UK Labour, then 'Welsh Labour' should live up to its name and become independent of the national party. The arguments for ongoing devolution that kept its support loyal through the Blair/Brown years are clearly being abandoned in favour of an Anglocentric outlook that is at odds with the culture that birthed the movement here in Wales. Cut the ties and make them work for their Welsh votes.

---

[2] Imagine believing that Welsh Labour owns such a garment. You live and learn.

All the World's a Stage

15 October 2023

I was alerted that something was very wrong with the afternoon as soon as I arrived at the bar. Scanning the pumps, I came face-to-face with an unwelcome visitor from the past. I had marked myself safe from M & B Brew XI bitter sometime around the turn of the Millennium. To be confronted with a beverage that evokes 1990s Birmingham is to contend with a Proustian nightmare. One minute you're turning on the central heating with your phone, and the next, tumbling through a vortex that leaves you sat at a Formica table in the Bull Ring Tavern next to a bloke wearing an Ocean Colour Scene T-shirt under a sheepskin coat.

'I'll have a Diet Coke, please.'

My pal, Phil, was blissfully unaware that we had somehow taken a quantum leap and remained bullish about prospects for the game. I didn't take much persuading that everything would be alright. Wales started so brightly that we even allowed ourselves to discuss our prospects in the semi-final. On a supporters' forum I'd seen a couple of people who'd allowed that unwise instinct to overwhelm them. They'd headed to France on Friday and booked accommodation for the final. I salute them and extend the sympathy of a nation.

An unknowable feature of the modern game is what's on the laptops that coaches pore over as it unfolds. All that data is crunched in the hope of unlocking a logical response to events, but rugby doesn't conform to the laws of science. The maths of American Football, or cycling, or voter intentions can be expressed with a predictability that is laughable when you try to apply it to the magical brutality of this most lifelike of sports.

If you want to predict outcomes in rugby, you are better looking at it as drama. When referee Jaco Peyper left the field injured it was a plot point so glaring as to be conclusive. We were favourites to win, the team looked in control, and optimism had begun to turn to hubris.

'We're done,' I told Phil, in my most serious voice.

A change of referee could mean only one thing. The great dramatist in the sky had controversial plans for the replacement. Of course he was English, not because that made him corrupt or incompetent, but because it sharpened the dramatic effect when he denied us redemption with his red card.

The lead actor, though, was Dan Biggar. Last summer in South Africa, his psychotic will to win almost inspired a series victory over South Africa that would have ranked as the most outrageous upset in the game's history. He was captain back then, but job titles are meaningless to people who operate at his level of intensity. He's been the captain of both sides and referee in every game he's ever played, famously offering on-pitch scrummaging advice to Adam Jones when still a teenager.

Patched up beyond repair, he threw himself at this game with reckless abandon. As Argentina gained supremacy his raw will couldn't be tamed. When he left the field in the dying minutes, finally broken by 15 years of battle, it was the climax of the story. If we were to win this, it was going to be a Biggar kick that sealed it. The laws of drama would have allowed no other escape.

As it was, we saw the inception of a new storyline. Poor Sam Costelow, whose intercepted pass will live in nightmares, has been offered the stage to redeem himself in the next run of this play. His distraught expression will be replayed in four years' time as he stands on the cusp of destiny with the world watching. Whatever the laptops say, tragedy and redemption are why we are all here. They are why it matters.

The failure of politics
22 October 2023

Like you, I've watched the crisis in the Middle East unfold with a feeling of mounting dread. Photographs of smiling Israeli teenagers, whose lives will never be fulfilled, touch a part of us that isn't governed by opinion, religion, or ideology. They speak to us in the common, wordless language of authentic empathy.

My God, he reminds me of…

Likewise, footage of Palestinian mothers, undone with grief amongst the rubble, draws a bow across the strings of our own heartbreak.

How would I cope in her place, what would I do?

Politics exists to remind people that, regardless of disputes, we are bound by decent impulses. It is a practice that we, as a species, have developed to give voice to our dignity; to insist on it. When it fails, or is abandoned, the discordant screeching of recrimination drowns out the music of being, our conformity to conscience.

For all the quarrels in our corner of the world, we largely agree on democracy as the way to organise our politics. For our humanity to find voice through it, though, the process must be taken seriously. If it's working, then our representatives should be those amongst us who can understand the complexity of our feelings and sculpt them into coherent arguments that shelter as many of us as possible from the overtures of lunacy.

Do you feel sheltered, recently?

You might think, with the Covid enquiry ongoing, that our political class would have cause to reassess its collective performance. The thought of people turning up to work at Number 10 whilst the cleaners were clearing away vomit from the previous night's party would be repellent whenever it occurred. That it happened during the worst crisis we have faced since the war is an outrage. These people were working for us as we were locked up, forbidden to comfort dying relatives. The minimum we should expect now is that our politicians understand the seriousness of their positions and act accordingly.

How's that going?

Rishi Sunak travelled to Tel Aviv this week to offer UK solidarity with the grieving population of Israel. In doing so he gave voice to the horror we all feel at what happened on October 7th. He is, though, a man without a mandate, as was his predecessor. He's also, as this week's by-elections confirmed, clinging to power against the wishes of the electorate. It is against this backdrop that we can explain his failure to even *raise* concerns about the relatives of UK citizens who are resident in Gaza. To do so would have incurred the wrath of his party and the newspapers that support it. So, the diplomatic shelter offered by the Prime Minister was trimmed to fit his diminished position.

Sir Keir Starmer, contrastingly, has politics at his feet. As Labour piles up votes in by-elections, his potential premiership has taken on the air of inevitability. But this catastrophe in the Middle East is happening *now*, not in the halcyon future of his imagining. His moral instincts aren't a can he can kick down the road until he's safely in power. When he suggested this week that Israel has 'the right' to deny water and electricity to the people of Gaza, he betrayed the void at the heart of his political offering. His trumpeted caution was revealed as a sort of radicalised conformity: an inability to consider anything outside the prism of electoral success. As a lawyer, he'd do well to remember the maxim that justice deferred is justice denied.

Closer to home, responses have ranged from well-meaning impotence to naked self-interest. Mark Drakeford offered a characteristically nuanced view of the situation, taking care to accommodate the pain on both sides of the conflict. Beyond that, though, his vision failed. He offered no Welsh position on the way forward. Wales, historically, is a political engine room. Its radicalism has dragged the advance of democracy and human rights in its wake since the Chartist uprisings. In moments such as these we should have something to say.

The failure of politics thousands of miles away should act as a warning. If a major terrorist attack were to occur in the UK today, it would be in the context of the Home Secretary's assessment that multiculturalism has failed. What, then, would be the conduit for decency in shaping the response to the situation? What apparatus exists for you, as a citizen, to express your desperation for peace and fellow feeling?

Our democracy has been paralysed by opinion polls and social media approval. Statesmen who express the basic principles of human coexistence have been sidelined by a carnival of triviality that foregrounds speed limits and gender preferences over issues that determine the life expectancy of millions.

Whether it's Sunak squatting in Downing Street against the obvious will of the nation, Starmer's fear of controversy trumping basic decency, Drakeford's contentment to sound humane whilst offering no solutions, or RT Davies' infantile posturing, we as voters are insulted.

We need to demand more.

The fall and fall of the man who 'got Brexit done'

29 October 2023

When, like a rutting dog, Boris Johnson was finally shaken off the leg of British politics[1], I predicted that the magnitude of his disgrace would see him leaving the country.

I assumed he'd wash up in the USA, where he'd initially be courted by politicians and the highbrow press until they discovered his inner void and left him to the chat shows.

After a *National Enquirer* exposé detailing nocturnal shenanigans on the Lincoln Memorial, he'd settle in Las Vegas, opening Honest Boris's Jaguar dealership at which his sub-Hugh-Grant charms would finally find the reception they deserved.

Emerging from prison, he would obtain work as a greeter at an off-strip casino where he would dress in a Union flag waistcoat and sing 'Chim Chim Che-ree' each time a slot machine paid out more than $25, or should a patron demand it.

His twelfth wife, Betty-Lou, would recall that he spent the daylight hours panhandling for small change and jaywalking.

'He said it was legal cos he didn't know he was doing it,' she drawled.

In the end, brought low by syphilitic dementia, he would be shot dead in an act of mercy by Nadine Dorries, his last companion. Dragged from his corpse by Federal Marshalls, the weeping Dorries provided what she hoped would be his epitaph.

'He got Brexit done!'

So, imagine my surprise at learning that he'd lowered himself to working for GB News.

It turns out that the rate of the UK's cultural decline is such that it he no longer needed to flee its shores into the embrace of

---

[1] This is why my pieces are no longer published at breakfast time.

a naive, credulous public overseas. It exists right here at the crusty end of the Freeview listings.

Reprising his famous role as the nation's morally bankrupt hype man, equal parts Sir Toby Belch and Flavor Flav, Johnson took to Twitter yesterday to remind us of his rhetorical audacity.

'Our best days,' he insisted, 'are ahead of us,' as he announced he'd henceforth be working alongside Darren Grimes, 30p Lee Anderson, and Nigel Farage on a channel that skirts OFCOM scrutiny by registering as 'entertainment'.

If you are burdened with a surfeit of empathy, you might detect the air of pathos about this development in Johnson's career. Four years on from winning an outright majority for the Conservatives, the great pretender has swapped Churchill's Homburg for Del Boy's sheepskin coat.

This time next year, Rodders...

It's tempting to see the quarantining of Johnson, Rees-Mogg, Farage and co. at GB News as a signifier that their time has passed. The optimistic interpretation is that they will see out their careers pumping out jingoistic nonsense to a diminishing audience of pensioners for money.

The production values and aesthetic choices favoured by the station can lead younger viewers, and I'm 50, to believe they are experiencing PTSD flashbacks brought on by childhood exposure to the dark underbelly of 1980s light entertainment.

It's risible, you might think: an embarrassing sideshow where disgraced public figures hawk outrage to a confused, powerless viewership. I'd caution against that opinion.

When L. Ron Hubbard, the founder of Scientology, died his church announced that he had, 'discarded the body he had used in this lifetime for 74 years, 10 months, and 11 days. The body he had used to facilitate his existence in this MEST universe had ceased to be useful and in fact had become an impediment to the work he now must do outside of its confines.'

This is how Johnson views the Conservative party. Leaving behind its poisoned husk to be worn by Suella Braverman and whichever MPs survive the coming election, he's transplanted the flame of Brexity populism to a new, unaccountable entity. Positioning himself as an outsider, he can disassociate himself from a toxic brand and come again.

Cast your mind forward a couple of years. After the excitement of a change in government, what will Keir Starmer be offering? To secure election he is committed to maintaining conservative positions on Brexit, the environment, the Constitution, public ownership of utilities, immigration, and foreign policy.

Addressing the structural factors that have brought much of the UK to calamity is not within his mandate, and he has taken care to neutralise all pressure from the left within the Labour Party.

Against this backdrop, the GB News hydra, led by Johnson and Farage, will be free to preach faux radicalism to a nation whose votes have resulted, yet again, in more of the same.

The thrill that many found in the Brexit referendum was in pulling a democratic lever and, for once, seeing it move the cogs of the machine. If a Starmer government underestimates the urgent need for change in the UK, it will create a vacuum.

What fills it could be truly abhorrent.

Pre-Christmas Hypocrisy
5 November 2023

When I was a boy, we all used to look forward to the traditional lecture on the commercialisation of Christmas. In those pre-internet days, children would solemnly leaf through the family Argos catalogue and compile a *handwritten* list of the items we required to express our devotion to the living Christ: a Raleigh Chopper; *Now That's What I Call Music! 2* on double cassette; Deely Boppers; the new *Minder* annual; an octagonal Rubik's Cube; luminous green towelling socks; a giant Toblerone.[1]

The list would be presented to our mothers, whose role included bargaining with the Patriarchy to edit it within the household budget. Legend tells that this is how the Raleigh Chipper was born.

As the gifts were unwrapped, it would fall to an elder of the family to recount the Christmases of old. Stockings, they would explain, had not been the garish, purpose-bought items of today. They had been ordinary socks, often with holes in them brought about by walking to school in all weathers. Gesturing at the mounting pile of decadent playthings, to which, paradoxically, they had been the most enthusiastic financial contributor, the elder would draw a stark comparison with their own childhood treats: a satsuma, nuts and a lump of coal. Only after the family had murmured its agreement that Christmas had lost its meaning could the Cadbury's selection box be distributed, with the elder offered first choice.

Tell that to kids today and they'd recreate it as an immersive Cottagecore experience for £79.95 a ticket. I'm turning in my grave.

What does survive from those sepia-tinted days is the

---

[1] A Polaroid camera, a tub of Slime, a handheld Space Invaders game, a pair of Farrahs, shares in British Gas.

unanimous conviction that Christmas starts earlier every year. This, of course, is a tradition in itself. It doesn't do to be prematurely enthusiastic about the Yuletide festivities. The correct etiquette is to start from curmudgeonly reluctance and allow the 'magic' to infuse slowly until you reach sufficient spiritual ecstasy and are moved to photocopy your arse at the office drinks party.

Marks & Spencer, which took over stewardship of the festival from the church at the turn of the millennium, has traditionally sought to position it in the inclusive cultural space occupied by Sir David Attenborough PLC and Walkers crisps. This year, however, something has gone terribly wrong.

For the Neo-Fascist grifting community, early November is a very special time. The lads and lasses at GB News, Talk TV, and *The Telegraph* come together to honour the fallen by criticising the clothing choices of politicians at the Cenotaph. According to their creed, it is inappropriate to begin condemning institutions for disrespecting Christmas until *after* the leader of the Labour Party has been poppy-shamed.

So, what the hell was the Archbishop of Marks & Sparks thinking bringing out a heretical Christmas advert before we've even encouraged our children to burn the effigy of a seditious Roman Catholic?[2]

This so-called advert mocks the Spirit of Christmas (© Cliff Richard, 1988) by suggesting that some of us secretly don't enjoy forced communal activities and harbour bourgeois tendencies towards individual gratification. It is clearly the work of The Woke, who fail to understand that Christmas is a time for temporarily pretending to care about the plight of others in the God-ordained hierarchy of a market economy.

If Christmas begins too soon, it is impossible for ordinary, hardworking people to maintain performative empathy past Boxing Day and through The Week When Time Dissolves into the January sales.

---

[2] https://www.youtube.com/watch?v=94GslcJcaWU

So, let us once again give thanks to Suella Braverman: keeper of the national mores. In a stiff rebuke to those who might be tempted to prematurely suspend their legitimate concerns about immigration, the Home Secretary reminded us that only through suffering can we find redemption.

'The British people are compassionate. We will always support those who are genuinely homeless. But we cannot allow our streets to be taken over by rows of tents occupied by people, many of them from abroad, living on the streets as a lifestyle choice.'[3]

Next week, after the politicising of national mourning, homeless itinerants seeking temporary shelter will be all the rage. For now, though, hear how the government planned to cull the elderly, watch the Holy Land burn, and keep the doors to your inn firmly locked.

---

[3] https://x.com/SuellaBraverman/status/1720730450556006714

Anthem for a Doomed Truth

12 November 2023

Quite how Stella Artois became the official lager of right-wing extremism is lost to history. Some believe its ubiquity to be a homage to the imperial fervour of King Leopold II of Belgium, whilst others point out that its embossed can is easier to hold with underdeveloped thumbs. No matter, like Ben Sherman shirts and cocaine, it is an essential component of a tradition that harks back to a simpler, less existent England.

Imaginary England was a wonderful place. Every day was a hot August Bank Holiday spent in the beer garden of a pub. Even the wasps were top blokes, a bit lairy but salt of the air and never stung the kiddies. These woke wasps you get nowadays don't care who they sting. No respect.

Yesterday's counterdemonstration in London was as dispiriting as it was predictable. Whilst somewhere between 300,000 and 800,000 people marched calling for a ceasefire in Gaza, an uncertain number of 'patriots' assembled to protect the Cenotaph from attack. It wasn't attacked. Nobody suggested they were going to attack it and organisers routed the march to avoid it. The marchers were inconveniently peaceful, spoiling what could have been a day of recreational aggro to see in the Christmas period. Denied the thrill of a proper dust up, the counterdemonstrators were reduced to scuffling with police in the 'hold me back' performative fashion beloved of drunken cowards everywhere. Around a hundred of them were arrested and that was it. Hardly Agincourt.

All of which leaves the government in a bit of a bind. With last week's King's Speech revealing that the cupboard is bare as regards policy, fighting the Culture War is all it has left to do. Fortunately, it is as useless at this as it is at everything else. At the height of China's Cultural Revolution, industrial production was disrupted because so many raw materials had been diverted to satisfy public clamour for Mao Zedong badges. If you're going to whip up public derangement to cover up your impoverishment of a nation, at least do it properly.

The efforts of Suella Braverman and right-wing commentators to confect an Alamo mentality around remembrance events ran into a wall of reality. The public of their imagination: insecure, uninformed, pliable, and xenophobic, is a product of condescension to and detachment from the lives of people they have never bothered to try to understand. Remembrance is an authentically felt experience for nearly everybody. It's a moment to appreciate the size and shape of what is missing from our lives thanks to the failure of politicians. It is a brief pause in the infantile screeching of public life; a communion of quiet decency that is respected by all but imbeciles. The Home Secretary bet big on there being far more imbeciles than she got.

The late Robert Runcie, whilst Archbishop of Canterbury, once described the Anglican Church as being a swimming pool in which all the noise came from the shallow end. The Home Secretary is so tin eared as to mistake childish yelping by the water slide for the sound of Britain.

Rishi Sunak, increasingly resembling Kendall Roy in *Succession*, cut a pathetic figure all week. Had he sacked Braverman, or addressed the crowds yesterday, he could have earned some respect. Instead, the lifestyle hedge fund manager prevaricated and sank further into irrelevance.

Despite desperate propagandising, remembrance is not acceptable political currency for most UK citizens. Neither are the deaths of civilians in Israel and Palestine, nor the fears of Jews and Muslims across the world that their lives are about to be ruined yet again by the coarse posturing of failed politicians. These things are real and have no place in the immature fantasies of those who seek to manipulate us for career advantage.

A Stopped Clock
19 November 2023

If there's one thing we can depend on in the arbitrary crapshoot of existence, it's that our perception of time speeds up as we slide down through middle age towards the grave. The long summers of childhood are replaced by brief snatches of sun between rain-sodden birthdays and frequent funerals. A moment's distraction can result in a decade passing overnight.

So, how can it possibly be a mere four years since Boris Johnson's election victory? As war, disease, inflation, and perpetual rancour have engulfed the world, the government has continued to assume legitimacy through three Prime Ministers whilst seemingly not attempting to implement the levelling-up agenda upon which it was elected. It is The Drifters of world politics – still a going concern despite containing only one original member.[1]

I'm historically not awfully forgiving of Tory voters. It's a 'lifestyle choice' to vote for a party that routinely heaps misery on anybody without sufficient funds to insulate themselves from predatory corporations. I must concede, though, that those putting an x in a box to 'get Brexit done' could not have anticipated triggering a series of events so traumatic that the passing of time would cease and be replaced by an experiential void where absurdity is the sole respite from cruelty.

Johnson's 2019 election broadcast, in which he seduces a credulous woman behind her husband's back at Christmas, was shocking even at the time.

As we approach our fourth Torymas since then, its sinister overtones seem positively demonic. What's that, Santa? You're going to let the bodies pile high?

The UK that advert was pitched at no longer exists. Its

---

[1] Tonight only, 'Saturday Night at the Movies', featuring Michael Gove.

'everything will be alright' appeal for trust couldn't be repeated today. Nobody trusts anybody in authority now, not anymore; quite possibly never again.

I spent that election night working at a hostel for homeless people. As the nation raged about Brexit and Corbyn, nobody living there gave it a moment's thought. They knew what we would all come to learn during the pandemic: the system doesn't care whether you live or die. In less than four years, the outlook of society's most traumatised, marginal members has been adopted by most of the electorate. Be honest, do you actually *want* to vote for anybody on offer when an election finally comes, or will you do so out of habit, or duty, or the forlorn fantasy that there might be a least-worst option? Maybe, numbed by the relentless chaos, you won't bother at all.

When we assess human wrongdoing, we tend to assume far more distinction in its perpetrators than we ought. Surveying tragic consequences leads us to imagine an equivalent motivation in those who have caused it. It's perversely comforting to believe in the existence of evil genius: a guiding hand that actively brought about an adverse situation. It suggests that the removal of this entity will restore humane order to the system.

More often, though, we find ourselves victim to the thudding dullness of leaders who lack the imagination to address systemic failure. As widening inequality tears apart the UK's social fabric, the guiding principles of our governance have been exposed as empty slogans. 'Levelling-up' was a hastily contrived benefit of Brexit which, itself, was a distraction from the ongoing decline of the UK's prosperity and influence. With these discredited, our government is left with the last resort of banal failures throughout history: performative cruelty.

We should, you see, be rioting by now. Hundreds of thousands of us died unnecessarily during the pandemic whilst government-associated individuals made fortunes; we've been rinsed by utilities companies; our mortgages are sky high; NHS waiting lists are causing despair. But we're too defeated, too overloaded with the day-to-day consequences of living in a failed state to pose any threat to the authors of all this. In place of policy, we are offered the sacrifice of refugees, homeless people, benefits recipients: the totemic avatars of our collective pain. Cabinet ministers compete to show off their callousness and disregard for our laws and customs, hurling unfortunates onto the pyre as if terrified it will die down and we'll look at them instead.

The slow-motion collapse of the UK is a heartbreaking, sickening failure of imagination. We are stuck motionless and aghast whilst our surroundings are dismantled by people with whom nobody can reason, and for whose removal the system does not provide. Each month, week, day, hour brings more heat and less light as confected disputes seep through the culture, poisoning every facet of life from the National Trust to Remembrance to Christmas. Nothing is sacred, nothing is off-limits. Time has stood still.

The Screeching of Fools

26 November 2023

At today's march against anti-Semitism in London there will be concerned people, some Jewish, some not, who feel moved to remind the world of the historical consequences of bigotry. Similarly, at the recent marches calling for a ceasefire, you would find folks who see a duty to express the principled belief that violence can never be the solution to conflict.

The overwhelming majority of these people could amalgamate into a single march, not only without rancour, but in broad agreement about everything that matters to human beings.

You'll do well to see any reporting of these thousands of decent Britons, though, or hear anything they have to say. Because, amongst them, are a few *Four Lions*-style Jihadi wannabes and the usual far-right zeros that attach themselves to anything that offers the potential for a dust up. If it bleeds, it leads, as the old newsroom maxim goes.

Tommy Robinson, I see, has popped over on his holibobs from Spain to get himself arrested. George Galloway is producing breathless YouTube videos at the rate of five a day, and Boris Johnson has shown up in a bobble hat to pose with Julia Hartley-Brewer. There is nothing, literally nothing, that people like this won't exploit for profile.

Online, commentators whose professional identity is defined by support for one side or the other, have seized upon recent tragic events to generate engagement like never before. So, we have Palestinian activist Asa Winstanley claiming that today's march is designed to whip up hatred against Palestinians, whilst writer Lee Kern asserts that the ceasefire marches are a portent that the UK will fall into Jihadist civil war.

This sort of rhetoric is being churned out, of course, from places of safety. There is the whiff of glee about some of the louder voices that situations like this always seem to foreground. Why, I wonder, are we content to allow the amplification of people whose response to unspeakable horrors is to cosplay as participants, or to advance juvenile moral certainties beyond the point when they abandon human empathy altogether?

Pretty obviously, there is no binary outcome to this conflict that would be morally acceptable to any decent person. Were Israel no longer to exist, or Gaza and the West Bank to be fully occupied, it would bring nothing but misery to all involved. The only way forward, eventually, is the scruffy, morally ambiguous path of compromise. So, why is there no march for that? It is as if facing reality has become a taboo in our political landscape. Whereas those demanding a Palestinian state 'from the river to the sea' or the 'eradication of Hamas' can bellow safely in the fantasies of their own moral rectitude, anybody calling for negotiation and plurality is pilloried as somehow naive and ethically compromised.

In 1998 the UK and Ireland proved to the world that internationally inclusive conflict resolution can work. Now, the Westminster government seeks to demonise one side of every conflict it sees, impugning the intentions of its own citizens and grossly oversimplifying the issues at hand. Suella Braverman came close to incitement with her condemnation of marchers and police the other week, and there is a lingering suspicion that trouble on British streets was far from an unwelcome proposition for her. If Mo Mowlam could see us now…

The grotesque actions of Hamas on October 7 chilled the world. Nothing can excuse them. Neither, though, did they occur without context. My use of the word 'though' here will be enough to see me condemned by some. We are encouraged *only* to condemn, as if rationalising events is somehow an affront to their gravity. Well, that's what got us here in the first place and will keep us here forever if we carry on with it. The deaths of 13,000 civilians without international restraint, or any semblance of a known, planned outcome is also grotesque. Anybody who cannot hold both of those ideas in their head simultaneously has no contribution to make to this

63

heartbreaking situation. As children on both sides are handed back to their parents during this pause in hostilities, we should watch their smiles and drown out the screeching of fools with our calls for sanity.

Bleedin' Elgin

2 December 2023

My job requires me to drive round and round Cardiff day after day like a wasp in a bottle and I use the time to sharpen my satirical rage by listening to radio phone-ins. My God people are awful, aren't they? Actually, I'll qualify that: people who ring in to radio programmes are awful. I never seem to be able to get through...

On Wednesdays, though, the usual 'legitimate concerns about immigration', and 'why-oh-why' rants about the advance of wokery are briefly interrupted by Prime Minister's Questions live from the Commons.

When this weekly pantomime was first televised, it quickly gained an audience in America, where viewers watched in disbelief that anybody with a responsible job could behave like that. We, of course, know nothing else. Democracy, for us, just ain't democratic unless a few hundred hyper-privileged louts are braying abuse at each other for no apparent purpose beyond being named the winner by lobby journalists.

This week, Sir Keir Starmer was unanimously judged to have emerged as King Bants. All the analysts agreed that by alluding to a scatological aside attributed to the Home Secretary, Starmer had finally mastered the peculiar comic style required at PMQs: i.e. the sort of stuff Year Nine kids shout at supply teachers when their backs are turned. So, until next Wednesday at least, Sir Keir is Top Cat. *He's the boss, he's a VIP, he's a championship. He's the most tip-top...*

The two subjects under discussion were the Prime Minister refusing to meet[1] his Greek counterpart in case he was bearing a gift that turned out to be a repossession order on the Elgin

---

[1] https://www.independent.co.uk/news/uk/politics/elgin-marbles-rishi-sunak-kyriakos-mitsotakis-b2454461.html

marbles, and, inevitably, dispiritingly, unendingly: immigration. Beyond the sub-*Mock the Week* one-liners, these two matters revealed the clear shortcomings of both despatch box contenders.

Say what you like about Boris Johnson, really, go ahead, there's a comment section below for you to do just that, but he knows how to fight a culture war. The skill of any successful con artist is to understand the prejudices of his marks. What do they *want* to believe? Rishi Sunak is so painfully and obviously remote from the electorate that he's begun to dream up voters who can be persuaded on board by a bullish defence of Classical antiquities.

'Ere Fred, 'ave you 'ad your 'ip operation yet?'

'I don't give a monkey's about me 'ip, it's the reputation for monumental restoration enjoyed by the British Museum's Greco-Roman curators that I'm bothered about. *Chim-chim che-ree.*'

It's actually even worse than that, though, when you think about it. Sunak & Co seem to believe that their Brexit-voting base are out-and-proud bigots who have no interest in the rights and wrongs of issues as long as one side of the argument has a Union flag painted on it.

I was in an Uber shortly after the referendum and the driver, as is the creed of his avocation, treated me to an explanation of his political orientation. He'd lived in several European countries, had relatives around the world, and was left-of-centre on economic matters. He'd voted for Brexit out of a sense of belonging to a place. He felt that Britain was losing its distinctness in a globalised world and hoped that leaving the EU might allow for a reversal in that direction. *This* is the authentic, explicable reasoning for people allowing themselves to get caught up in defending statues and *Fawlty Towers* and Christmas traditions etc. These things are part of a landscape to which people feel they belong. The Parthenon marbles, on the other hand, very clearly, cut-in-halfly, sold-and-shipped-across-the-worldly, are not of these islands. Sunak seems to imagine there is a contingent of voters who, beyond wanting to cling on to Britain's past, believe no other country is entitled to one. Are there people like that? Yes, they become unhinged if exposed to Cymraeg or the concept of accountability. Are there enough of them to win an election in the face of demonstrably catastrophic governance? Nope.

Which is why Keir Starmer's Josh Widdecombe with a cold act was not the triumph he assumes it was this afternoon. Between the gags, he turned the screw on Sunak regarding immigration figures that are tearing the Tory Party apart. The problem here is that within 12 months he is going to be Prime Minister and the uncomfortable truth that the UK economy cannot function without immigration will become his problem. When he was fashioning Greek-themed jokes, he missed a reference with which he'll soon be familiar: Pyrrhic victory.

The Bald Truth

7 December 2023

When I have my biannual haircut, I always dread the part at the
end when the barber insists, unbidden, upon showing me the
back of my bonce in a mirror. No sooner have I smiled
approvingly at my neatly trimmed beard and tamed eyebrows,
than I am forced to confront the gleaming, hairless void that
advances in all directions from where my crown used to be. In
day-to-day life, I don't have to deal with this. As far as I'm
concerned, I may have a prominent forehead, but the back is
none of my concern. The moment I leave the sadist's chair I
dismiss the image from my consciousness until the next visit.
Last week, though, it was visible *from the front.* My head now
stands naked before its last cheerleader, myself.

Something very similar is happening to the Tory Party and,
by extension, the UK. It must be difficult for younger readers to
imagine that this eroded septum of UK politics was once
considered a byword for stability and respectability. It was evil,
that's a given, but pre-Thatcher it could be relied upon to exploit
unfortunates at home and abroad with sufficient elan to grease
its penetration of your wellbeing and leave you with a
bewildered smile.

Not so the current incarnation, which is less a gentleman
thief than a crack-hungry ram raider.

Charting its alarming descent into unhinged depravity has
become an hour-by-hour job. When I started formulating this
piece at midday, it seemed a safe bet that Boris Johnson's
appearance at the Covid enquiry would provide all the material
required. When I came to write it after work, his dog-ate-my-
homework performance had been leant relative respectability by
his successors.

Around lunchtime, Minister for Policing Chris Philp
arrived on the airwaves to suggest that the government's new,

improved, courts-proof Rwanda policy would be announced 'within days'.

As we know, sending handfuls of immigrants to Rwanda at vast expense is what Rishi Sunak believes will rescue him from a perch in British history previously occupied by Neville Chamberlain. It is an end in itself: a symbolic offering to the ghost of Enoch Powell that Sunak hopes will enthuse his remaining, doddering voters enough to reject whatever Nigel Farage comes up with when he slithers from the jungle.

By teatime the policy had been announced in the Commons. The cunning wheeze arrived at to circumvent human rights legislation transpired to be an announcement that His Majesty's Government was going to ignore it altogether: the 'come and have a go if you think you're hard enough' approach to international jurisprudence.

That'll show 'em! thought Rishi, cracking his knuckles.

The trouble with appeasing lunatics, however, is that they don't want to be appeased, as Chamberlain would confirm.

So, first up, Suella Braverman made her resignation speech, in which she pointed out that the only way you can evade the law is by delegitimising it. Nothing will make the Rwanda policy legal, or beyond challenge, short of abandoning our commitment to international courts. Quite why Sunak allowed the bomb-throwing ex-Home Secretary to make a 'resignation' speech when she had, in fact, been sacked...by him, remains a mystery. He wears white socks with sliders, I think that's relevant.

Within the hour, Rwanda had started to backpedal out of the deal, fearing that it made them look dodgy. Now, I genuinely don't want to promote any lazy stereotypes about a nation that has clearly made genuine progress in recent years, but if you'd said 20 years ago that Rwanda found its association with the UK to be damaging its international reputation, I think it would have been received with, shall we say, surprise?

Finally, Robert 'Honest Bob' Jenrick resigned as Immigration Minister *whilst the Home Secretary was still on his feet* in the Commons explaining why announcing that ignoring international law in no way contravened international law. His principled reasoning for resigning was that we weren't ignoring it enough.

The thinning out of Tory respectability is now visible to all, at home and abroad. We can hold a mirror up to the country from any angle and the bald truth of its bankruptcy is inescapable.

Today's most sensible Tory was Boris Johnson. Be afraid.

A Rake at the Gates of Hell

8 December 2023

Thirty-five years ago next week I sold my scientific calculator. I'd given up maths, or it had given up on me, after my GCSEs, but a more logically minded school friend, David, wanted one for his A levels. He offered me a tenner or a spare ticket he had to see a band at Birmingham NEC.

'You'll love them, trust me.'

So, after school on Monday 12th December 1988, I find myself at New Street Station boarding a train to that godforsaken warehouse of a venue out by the airport. The platform is swarming with police who are checking everybody's bags and confiscating alcohol.

'It's going to be lively,' David smiles.

On the train, everybody has band T-shirts on, the older the T-shirt, the higher the status of wearer. A menacing looking passenger in a flat cap sports a shirt from 1984 and he's king of the carriage. He's anticipated copper-interference and equipped himself with a silver hip flask. Surrounded by younger girls in Doc Marten boots, he produces a tin whistle and starts to play. Everybody seems to know the words.

I am going, I am going any which way the wind may be blowing...

A commuter in his 50s, wearing a pinstripe suit and carrying a briefcase and black umbrella, opens the carriage door, putting a single, polished shoe on the step to board. The whistle player whirls round to face him.

'Are you a Pogues fan?' he demands.

'Er, am I a what?' the businessman asks nervously.

'This is a Pogues train! Get off my fucking train! Get off my fucking train!' the lunatic screams.

I am going, I am going, where streams of whiskey are

flowing.

Outside the venue, touts are offering fortunes for our tickets. Knock-off T-shirts are on sale, and there's a stall with a petition for the release of the Birmingham Six. The sterile, concrete environs can't neuter the frantic excitement of people who know, for certain, that they are in the right place at the right time.

Because the late 1980s were a cultural minefield. Everybody's mum and dad had seen the Beatles or the Stones, older brothers had been punks so how come we'd been left with Rick Astley? Before Kylie ascended to become a Cilla Black-style national treasure, the sheer everywhereness of Stock, Aitken & Waterman's production line pop couldn't be enjoyed ironically. It blared from shops, clubs, and radios as you went about your day, announcing that bland, cheerful consumerism was to be your lot in the new Britain. The tail-end of New Wave resistance to such showbiz schlock had petered out into jangly guitar bands like the Soup Dragons, or musical politics lecturers like New Model Army. It just wasn't enough. The hollowness of a suburban adolescence demanded more, and this is where more could be found.

The stage is set like a living room at Christmas. There's a huge, tinsel-strewn standard lamp, a Christmas tree, the drum riser is a sofa, and at the side of the stage is a twelve-foot fridge with 'Pogueator' written across it. The music on the PA increases in volume and intensity as road crew place instruments on the stage and showtime approaches: Thin Lizzy's 'Whiskey In The Jar', 'Rise' by Public Image Limited, 'Straight to Hell' from The Clash. Finally, the house lights dim, and the crowd starts chanting,

There's only one Shane MacGowan...

We've jostled to the front and it's the most danger I've felt in my life so far. The shove from behind pushes us all so close that we're trapped and can't move our arms in the overpowering heat, sweat and cider fumes. My chest is crushed against someone's arm so I can feel my heart beating against it. My feet are on the floor but taking no weight as pressure from either side

72

lifts me up like a Subbuteo figure. Suddenly, the mass gives way and about a hundred of us fall like dominoes; Christ, is this it? I'm dragged upright by my hair and the Pogueator door opens. Bright, white light and dry ice stream out as if to announce our release from hell. Eight figures emerge from the fridge in silhouette, indistinguishable in the light until the last raises his fist...

There's only one Shane MacGowan...

Steadying himself at the microphone stand, Shane surveys the writhing mass in front of him.

'You look like you need a priest,' he observes.

And we do, because behind the desire for a raucous night out, the passion of this crowd betrays more powerful emotions. Around us, society is being ripped apart and remade in the service of profit as an end in itself. As the unions are broken by Margaret Thatcher's government, the communities they represent are losing not just their industrial purpose but their means of expression. Traditions and local meeting places are being hurled on the pyre of financial services as embarrassing anachronisms of a bygone age. Everything must be new, privately owned and profitable. You should be ashamed to ride a bus, or sing in a choir, or live in social housing. Burn it all down; get out there and hustle for your BMW.

The band jolts into the introduction to *The Broad Majestic Shannon* and whistle, accordion, cittern, acoustic guitar, banjo, bass, and drums sync into an urgent caress. It quickens the heart and calms the nerves simultaneously as centuries of tradition step into 1988 to scorn the tepid mush on the radio. It pounds as it lilts: defiant and nurturing, ancient and young. Shane closes his eyes.

The last time I saw you was down at the Greeks
There was whiskey on Sunday and tears on our cheeks
You sang me a song that was pure as the breeze
On a road leading up Glenaveigh...

I sat for a while at the cross at Finnoe
Where young lovers would meet when the flowers were in bloom
Heard the men coming home from the fair at Shinrone
Their hearts in Tipperary wherever they go

Take my hand and dry your tears, babe
Take my hand, forget your fears, babe
There's no pain, there's no more sorrow
They're all gone, gone in the years, babe

For Shane, Ireland was more than a home, as a London Irishman it was a state of mind, a psychological space where being human could be epic, and time didn't march to the drum of our masters. His audience was full of people who were exiled in some way. The sons and daughters of immigrants, kids from broken homes, those who'd seen too much, too soon. There was a sentimental streak through these songs that spoke to a hurt part of us: a soft spot that was prone to addiction or mental illness and vulnerable to the new, harsh reality outside. Everyone in there was *longing* to be reconnected with something; to inhabit a space where our scruffy, teary boisterousness was smiled upon by adults who cared.

Shane wrote of care leavers selling themselves on the streets of London; he could look through the eyes of an ancient street drinker to see the wars behind them and the tunes he'd whistled.

In the tube station the old ones who were on the way out
Would dribble and vomit and grovel and shout
And the coppers would come along and push them about
And I wish they could escape from the old main drag

He'd seen the inside of mental institutions himself and tried to sleep amidst the screams of people who'd been left there for good. But he loved life, and people, and music, so he wanted that for us. We weren't ever going to *Club Tropicana*, none of us, but we could gather together in city pubs to sing, yarn, and dream our way through youth.

Dear dirty, delightful, drunken old days.

Shane's passing reminds us of how much we've lost since those days. The Pogues couldn't exist at all now. The band was born in a world where cheap bedsits or squats meant that you could spend a few years becoming good at something. The dole acted as an artist support programme that produced a whole generation of actors, writers, musicians, and painters. Was that really too much to ask after 6000 years of civilisation? Is it so unthinkable that young people be offered a bit of time to explore life, or receive an education before being harnessed to a wheel and told to pay up? Apparently, it is.

At the time I was working for a landlord, and he was the meanest bastard that you have ever seen,
To lose a single penny would grieve him awful sore, and he was a miserable bollocks and a bitch's bastard's whore.

The references in Shane's songs could set you on a lifetime of discovery. Brendan Behan, The Dubliners, Lorca, James Joyce, Rimbaud, Johnny Cash, W.B. Yeats, they contained a treasure box of the good stuff if you were minded to listen. A few years later, our diminished culture was offering the dumb insolence and ham-fisted Beatles pastiche of Oasis as its cutting edge.

Our actors, painters, writers, musicians, and even chefs are mainly posh boys now. Nobody else is afforded the time to refine themselves beyond conforming to whichever business model will pay the rent. Those who can't are starved or medicated until they can. Our music is presented in antiseptic, corporate venues and sucked up into the ether by Spotify to be whored out for scant reward to the musicians who made it.

The passing of Shane MacGowan came as no surprise, it's

75

true. Nothing is surprising anymore.

Now the song is nearly over
We may never find out what it means
Still there's a light I hold before me
You're the measure of my dreams
The measure of my dreams

The Price of Love

10 December 2023

They've finally reached the inevitable destination of their vile, ill-thought-out, thuddingly dull, cruel, and sparse philosophy. Forty years since that damaged woman projected her embarrassingly obvious daddy issues on to Britain, with the small-minded price-stickering of every facet of a human life, the Tories have arrived at a cost for love.

Somewhere in the world there is a new couple who have found in each other a way to navigate their way through the terrifying, time-limited existence that we all share. Like you, they want to have children, to make a living representation of their adoration for each other. Well, unless they are earning £37k a year, they won't be doing that in Cwmbran, or Machynlleth, or Hay, or St David's, or Ynyshir, or Grangetown, or anywhere that civilised people live on this storied island. Even Newport.

In their desperation to harvest voters whose bitterness is the wages of stupidity, the people we *allow* to govern us are plumbing depths of depravity that shame us all. How, in the name of all that is holy, are we permitting these horrors of human beings to desecrate the essence of why we are on the earth at all?

We're heading into Christmas and its toxic, irreligious commercialism will, for some of us, speak of a scarcely endurable void in the heart of our culture. Two-for-one blessings around iPhones and threadbare office Christmas trees where love for your fellow human ought to be.

Llanidloes isn't signposted off the A470 and nobody who lives there will thank me for pointing out that it exists at all. To assimilate into the place, you need to find it by accident, ideally at your lowest ebb. It's essentially a refugee camp: somewhere that folks that don't fit in can coexist companionably. I ran out of petrol once on Great Oak Street and the landlord of The Stag gave me a fiver out of the till to get home.

'You'll sort me out when you can...'

I was back there this weekend for my birthday because it's a reliably good time. There's warmth, and acceptance, and mercy, and forgiveness of foibles It's nestled on the Cambrians where mist rises around you and bends the light into a hazy mysticism that suits a hangover. Welsh speakers and English incomers discuss their differences and smile at the nonsense that divides us.

My phone was bleeping, 'Are you watching Shane MacGowan's funeral?' everybody wanted to know. I wasn't, because I was living *my life* with the woman I love and amongst friends who love me. It was whispering across the Irish Sea, though, as that proud nation sang, danced, and wept its singularity to the world. England can't govern me anymore, and I'll bet you a fiver you're beginning to feel the same.

Drakeford's Wild Ride

13 December 2023

Amazing scenes in Cardiff Bay this morning as Generalissimo Mark Drakeford was dragged from the Senedd by masked insurgents brandishing '30mph or Death!' placards. Under a symbolic blanket, the fallen despot was bundled into a 1983 Escort XR3i, which roared away to the Vale of Glamorgan, where he will face a revolutionary court tomorrow morning.[1]

Upon entering Drakeford's private office, the triumphant 'Gilets Bleus' discovered a temperature-controlled safe containing plundered cheese and a Christmas card from Greta Thunberg. Their leader, Andrew 'Real Ting' Davies, emerged into Roald Dahl Plass to receive adulation from the crowd.

'The tyranny is over!' he announced, pausing for Janet Finch-Saunders MS to dab brown sauce from the corner of his mouth with a serviette. '*Top Gear* fans of Wales unite! You have nothing to lose but your electric bicycles!'

The Drakeford years have been a wild ride, haven't they? Well, no, they haven't. If there's one thing The Drakester doesn't do, it's wild, and that's been problematic in itself. When elected, the UK press immediately categorised our boy as being of the Corbynite left. In 2018, at the height of The Great Socialism Scare, we were warned that Wales was poised to become a rainy Venezuela on the fringe of civilisation.

The idea of maverick, radical politicians comes laden with centuries of stereotyping here in Wales. From Keir Hardie to Lloyd George via Nye Bevan, Michael Foot, Rhodri Morgan and even the early incarnation of Lord Kinnock, an outspoken, passionate reformer is something the wider world expects from Welsh politics. It's an archetype that simultaneously sits well

---

[1] Styling Mark Drakeford as a despot is a favourite conceit of mine. The frothing English press depiction of him as an authoritarian menace is so at odds with his mild persona as to demand satire.

79

within a genuine political tradition, whilst also serving the assumptions of our neighbours to the east.

Well, Drakeford ain't that. It's hard to know who was more disappointed with his presentational style, the Welsh left or the English right. Old-style socialists here feel entitled to some rhetorical flash as compensation for sitting through the procedural heat-death of Labour branch meetings in their spare time. The English press have a whole lexicon of 'Welsh windbag' tropes to roll out whenever one of our politicians steps into the limelight. Drakeford had nothing for any of them.

So, after settling into office, he looked set to be ignored outside of Wales just as his predecessor Carwyn Jones had been. Then the pandemic happened.

One of the insults levelled at the Senedd, by those who wish to abolish it, is that it's nothing more than a council chamber with delusions of grandeur. That all stopped when it became clear that Wales could set its own regulations for the Covid lockdowns. Anti-devolutionists both here and in England reacted with furious disbelief that the Welsh Government could exercise real democratic power without reference to Westminster. As Drakeford had failed to be the froth-mouthed idealogue of Fleet Street's imagination, the tabloid hacks were forced to find new ways of traducing him. He was a 'Stalinist', an 'authoritarian' who sought to micro-manage every aspect of Welsh life.

The trouble for them was that his tone during those dreadful times was pitched perfectly. As Johnson and his merry band of pyromaniacs sought to defeat the virus with distilled jingoism, and recklessness, Drakeford warned sternly, reassured sensibly, and, crucially, embodied his rules by following them at great personal inconvenience to himself. Increasingly, his views were sought by the UK press and the perception of Welsh politics began to shift in its more thoughtful quarters. Instead of the romantic, firebrand nation of cliché, Wales emerged as a sensible, measured voice that inspired envy in many UK voters who despaired at the chaos they were enduring. Mistakes were made in Wales during the pandemic, for sure, but they were in step with the scientific advice available, not in defiance of it and I suspect most in Wales felt their collective interests lay at the heart of decision-making. That certainly isn't clear from testimony at the UK Covid inquiry. At least they are having one, mind.

Drakeford's quiet assurance seemed best suited to a crisis. After the pandemic, his stock was high, and progressives perhaps hoped that he would capitalise on this more than he has. Occasionally, he would issue aspirational thoughts concerning constitutional reform. In concrete terms, however, we have lacked the urgent *demand* that the UK either devolve more powers, look seriously at federalising, or fund Wales more equitably.

There have been real achievements: homelessness has been addressed with a rigour unseen in the wider UK, moving to a model that offers permanent solutions rather than emergency relief. The cancellation of road projects required political grit on behalf of the environment but, again, we lacked a strident call for the rail infrastructure we so desperately need.

Some widely publicised projects, the Universal Basic Income trial, for instance, had the air of university studies without a hope of wider implementation. On the other hand, the 20mph roll-out arrived in the real world without the kind of Blairite explanation that might have won it more supporters.

No politician leaves office to universal acclaim. I feel that Drakeford's progressive ambitions will seem prescient in the years to come, as politicians are finally forced to reckon with the economic and environment realities that threaten stability from every angle. His successor will find a more receptive ear in the UK press, thanks to the credibility Drakeford brought to his role. It is to be hoped that whoever takes over will exert more of Wales' will on an incoming Labour UK government than Drakeford felt able to when they were in opposition.

In the final measure, Wales has been governed with a seriousness and decency that nowhere else in the UK has enjoyed over the last five years. Mark Drakeford has pointed vaguely towards how things should be, it's difficult to see a

81

successor who will drive those ideas into reality. Without such a leader, Labour in Wales faces a shift to the right and radicalism will, drip by drip, be decanted into the ever-younger vessel of the independence movement.[2]

---

[2] I received justified criticism over this piece. People who had lost loved ones during the pandemic felt that my comfortable assessment of the Welsh Government's performance was glib.

Be Elite
17 December 2023

The late, great songwriter John Prine had an elderly character in his song 'Hello In There' despair that 'all the news just repeats itself.'

His implication is that if you stick around long enough, the game of life becomes as predictable as Connect Four.

Much has been made over the last few years about how 'unprecedented' everything is.

9/11, Brexit, Trump, Covid have all been touted as proof that we are living in a new paradigm where the certainties of the past have given way to disorder and random happenstance.

Beneath the frantic bleeping of data and events in the Information Age, however, beats the slow, steady pulse of human instinct and, with all ideologies seemingly discredited, this is where we can begin to make sense of the interesting times through which we are cursed to live.

I don't know how to break this to you, but *The Guardian* reports that Nigel Farage plans a return to politics in time for next year's election. That came out of left field, didn't it?

Who could have predicted in this mad, random world that the country's foremost out-of-a-suitcase grievance pedlar might be planning to translate 8000 hours of primetime exposure on *I'm A Celebrity* into yet another lucrative thrust into the body politic?

His plan, whisper it, is to 'make the election about immigration'. Such vision!

How could one man in a pink blazer embody the zeitgeist such that he were all men? Shape politics for us, Nige! What could possibly go wrong?

One of life's greatest ironies is that the chief beneficiaries of cultural relativity, the apogee of late 60s left wing intellectualism, are right wing politicians.

When Derrida was smirking that the only reason you thought Beethoven had more inherent value than Dave, Dee, Dozy, Beaky, Mick & Tich was your utter capture by the value system of your oppressors, it wasn't readily apparent that he was gifting wannabe Mussolinis a meal ticket for life, but here we are.

Whether Farage operates under the umbrella of Reform UK, or from within the Conservative Party, the message will be the same: curbing immigration is the panacea for our ills and anybody who disagrees is a mouthpiece of the 'elite'.

Now, you might not feel very elite, my wardrobe, for instance, consists of eight 'George at Asda' T-shirts (one for best), and a treasured pair of Skopes moleskin trousers.

For the purposes of Nige and Suella Braverman, though, you are a proven member of the gilded intelligentsia by dint of reading this far into an article.

So, if we're the elite, we might as well start acting like it. From our lofty societal position, we need to put down the grubby bloviating of our inferiors with all the terrifying authority available to us.

I'll begin.

There is nothing, I repeat *nothing* 'authentically working-class' about xenophobia, racism, or reflexive cruelty to those less fortunate.

Charities the world over will tell you that getting money out of the comfortably off requires pampering and flattery, whereas poorer communities donate far greater percentages of their resources and from a sense of genuine compassion.

I began by suggesting that the seemingly novel problems before us are simple expressions of human frailty that we've seen throughout history. Plagues, disputes and Farage-style spivs are, indeed, nothing new.

The internet, however, has seeded the ground for them. Echo-chamber online socialising has given the perennial large minority of poor-souled, miserly malcontents with whom we've always had to contend, the impression that they are, in fact, an overwhelming majority.

You will hear these people referred to, *ad vomitum*, by their ringmasters as 'the people'.

Again, this is nothing new. One of their many illusory moments in the political sun was as Richard Nixon's 'silent majority'. That worked out well, didn't it?

We have months of Rwanda plans, climate-science denial, gender scare-mongering and crackpot Thatcherite economic pipedreams to contend with.

Every time Keir Starmer pulls on his John Bull costume and starts banging on about how working class he is, we sink further into fantasy.

Trying to *negotiate* with positions you can prove to be both wrong and dishonest renders you a hostage to fortune. So, it's up to us, the elite majority, to challenge them wherever we go.

When Uncle Dick starts getting lairy about some pish he's seen on GB News at Christmas, go ahead and tell him straight. Give no quarter to idiocy, it certainly won't give any to you.

Be elite.

Welsh Rugby: What Went Wrong?[1]
20 December 2023

So much of life is in a state of permanent crisis these days that it's hardly surprising anxiety is being reported at record levels. At home and abroad, things seem to be falling apart in front of us, with new fissures opening more quickly than we can slap masking tape on them.

As our descent into a *Mad Max*-style postapocalyptic hellscape gathers pace, I feel grateful for the rigorous training I have received in such matters throughout my life. For if anything could prepare you for full-spectrum dysfunction, it is tethering your emotional wellbeing to the operational efficiency of the Welsh Rugby Union.

Here, in Seimon Williams' chastening book, we are presented with a timeline of events that concludes, this year, with the game in Wales facing its most perilous crisis yet.

It's tempting to blame the WRU's woes on changes of environment to which it struggled to adapt. Was it the decline of industrial Wales, perhaps, or the rigours of professionalism, or failure to anticipate the emergence of the women's game? That is to underestimate the union's unique facility to make a pig's ear of any situation it finds itself in. Towards the end of this fine book, we are reminded that shortly before funding of the professional game was slashed and players threatened to strike, the WRU had received a near £90m windfall from private equity firm CVC. Now, I know to the layman, or someone who might dabble in business, it might seem that retaining the only exploitable asset you have, professional players, might have been a good use for that money. Hush now, there's a city centre hotel and zipwire attraction to build!

---

[1] *Welsh Rugby: What Went Wrong?* is available from https://www.ylolfa.com/en.

There's a good range of interviewees in the book and from them we get a sense of the personal toxicity that often accompanied the litany of incompetence related in its pages. A female employee has to wait outside a meeting and have it whispered to her through the door because she isn't allowed in; the Wales men's squad, at a meeting to hear their wages are being slashed, are told they 'probably won't have the brain' to understand the situation; players are charged for coffees in their room during international weekends, whilst committee members enjoy a free bar. The sheer wrongness of much that has gone on is both farcical and depressing. There are new insights here, but much of the actualities are known. What's shocking is their presentation as a sequential narrative. This decision allows Williams to drive home the remorseless commitment of some leading figures never to learn from their mistakes nor allow for meaningful change.

There is a pleasing raised-eyebrow tone on here. Williams has been, through the Gwladrugby website, a committed voice for Welsh rugby fans for many years. That experience has won him a detached irony that is a credit to his resilience and a spoonful of sugar for the reader as we are led through a story that contains echoes of ignorance, cruelty, and absurdity that you'd more readily expect from a war memoir.

The book concludes with our game perched on a fulcrum, its future vulnerable to any pressure. We now know that legal action over brain injuries sustained by dozens of players is incoming. Nothing described in this fine volume suggests that the WRU is equipped to cope with the financial and moral demands that this will bring.

Baal I Want for Christmas

23 December 2023

I've already got 'All I Want for Christmas Is You' burned into my consciousness like a PTSD flashback, so missing the Amazon deadline for Christmas delivery and having to shop for presents in the real world was a sanity-threatening proposition to start with.

It's a lonely business, Christmas shopping, isn't it? In many ways it reminds me of doing my GCSEs. There's societal pressure, personal peril, it's time-limited, and you're not allowed to ask for help. *What if I get this horribly wrong?* You're only as good as your last effort. Even if you smashed your spouse's birthday with a gift that demonstrated your keen understanding of their nuanced preferences, it will count for nothing if now, at Chrimbo, you succumb to end-of-year exhaustion and opt for a thoughtless McPresent that reveals you as inattentive.

The drive into Cardiff doesn't help. Shall I ever be released from the A470? It's my route to work and back every day and here I am back on its stop-start grind on my day off. Oh look, it's the bottleneck after the Caerphilly turn-off, look right in 5..4..3..2..1 Yay! It's that bafflingly hideous Jubilee monument, oh fabulous, it's the bit after Nantgarw where everyone has to change lanes at the same time!

Then it's the chug…chug…chug section through our becalmed city traffic. It would have been cathartic to beat my fists against the steering wheel and curse Mark Drakeford for the speed limit at this point, but I can't, can I, having defended the policy on here several times. I wish I was Jeremy Clarkson; he never gets morally conflicted.

On arrival at the St. David's Centre, there's a queue for the car park. Eventually, I get to the ticket machine and press the button. This is fraught enough at the best of times. There's a pregnant pause before the machine issues the cardboard visa to retail Nirvana as you are photographed by some unseen camera to log the registration plate. As a seasonal special, the experience is enhanced by the machine saying 'Error. Short term parking full'. *What now?* There's about eight thousand cars behind me and no way out. Am I supposed to get out of the car and inform them all personally that there's no room at the inn? I begin jabbing frantically at the button. Minutes pass. I try again. Open Sesame!

Now it's round and round and round and round the spiral ramp up to the parking floors. Helpfully, there are LED screens telling me how many spaces are available on each floor. Unhelpfully, they are lying. *Six parking spaces, five gold rings…*

In the lift going down to the shops there's precious little goodwill to all men in evidence. After I get in, a couple manoeuvre a buggy for twins into the remaining space and I'm sure I hear a hissed,

'For f…' which strikes me as shockingly unchristmassy, especially when I realise that I'm the only other passenger.

Then I'm in it at last: Credit Card Valhalla. The light, the noise, the anonymous crowd. I once attended a Roman Catholic Latin Mass, and it was nowhere near as alienating as this. Everybody else seems to know what they are doing, marching purposefully between familiar outlets and performing contactless benedictions at the till. I am not of this faith. Sure, I wander down to the corner shop to buy vape juice every week and do the Lidl run, but that's tin-roofed chapel stuff. This is the Vatican.

I stumble between stores with names I can't pronounce, staring vacantly at acres of merchandise that all just ends up looking like jumbles of colours. Mariah Carey stares out of an Ann Summers poster. *All I Want for Christmas Is You…*

Not now, Mariah, have a heart!

Finally, I arrive at the entrance to John Lewis and sink to my knees in despair. I feel a hand on my head, stroking comfortingly and look up to see Him: 25-foot tall, horned with fleecy legs and cloven feet. His eyes burn with reassurance.

'I'm David Beckham, you look like you need some aftershave.'

Kingliness at Christmas
25 December 2023

One has the three kings and the king of kings competing in the same marketplace, so one needs one's act together.

Start with a song. It's a road-tested showbiz tactic, and when one has a brand-relevant shoegazer like 'God Save The King' at one's disposal then one might as well get it in early.

For most of the year, one's monarchical pronouncements tend to be drowned out by the incessant yelping of those whose greatness was very much not thrust upon them. It's a matter of some confusion as to why one's subjects are endlessly forgiving of the sharp-elbowed arrivistes who govern them, but who is one to judge?

If the stout yeopeople of the realm are content to have their affairs decided by individuals who have their suits tailored by Italians, that is a matter for them. One must protest, however, at the indecent haste with which these politicians replace each other. No sooner has one memorised a name, admittedly Liz was simple enough, than another is along to irritate the footmen and interrupt one's contemplation with their vulgar solicitations.

One is unconvinced by the current antipathy towards those arriving in small boats. Having spent many happy afternoons traversing the River Wye in a coracle, one recognises their buccaneering spirit in one's own questing.

Perched as one is, betwixt the divine and the mundane, one feels an obligation to act as a diplomat between these competing estates. It is my sad duty to relate that followers of the Abrahamic faiths have, once again, lost their way. 'Divine right' is an unfashionable concept in the modern world, yet one is confident that the faithful are more inclined to receive a spiritual slap 'upside their face' from oneself than they might from James Cleverly. Or Tony Blair. Especially Tony Blair. So, in this spirit, I invite combatants in the Holy Land to drink deeply of my grave expression this Christmas. I do not issue it lightly.

In conclusion, one wishes you all of the tawdry distractions you desire as we face another year of inexorable decline. One's own family, as you know, are a trial to us all. One is holding on to the back of this chair lest one collapses under the weight of their competing ambitions. One offers evidence of one's own wretchedness as a token of our collective suffering. Does Phil Mitchell still own the Queen Vic?

Playing a Dangerous Game
29 December 2023

If you visit the House of Commons to sit in the public gallery, they hand you a leaflet that emphasises the majesty of the procedure you are witnessing. The 'mother of parliaments', it tells you, is the cradle of modern democracy and the gold standard for government of and by the people. The tone of the leaflet suggests that it's aimed at foreign tourists, which is just as well, because anybody living in the UK would be well within their rights in reporting our parliamentary mother to social services.

Firstly, to get it out of the way, having a king is plainly at odds with democratic values. Abolishing the monarchy, though, requires more than tweeting #notmyking 23 times a day and buying a Guy Fawkes mask. You're paying for him, so until you organise a revolution, he #isyourking.

Similarly, independence might bring a better democratic model for us here in Wales, but we face immediate problems around fundamentals like housing and healthcare that cannot wait for that outcome.

Even in these reduced circumstances, however, we *are* supposed to have some mechanism for influencing the decisions made on our behalf.

Most of us, of course, never influence Westminster politics with our votes. The first-past-the-post system means that casting a ballot in safe constituencies is largely symbolic. Again though, changing that would be the work of decades. What I'm addressing here is the system as it is sold to us: the monarchical, Anglocentric, gerrymandered farce of democracy that we are too apathetic to overthrow. How's *that* going; on its own terms?

Well, by my reckoning, we haven't received even the appearance of a democratic outcome to an election since 2005. Tony Blair's victory that year came with the caveat that he'd finally be handing over the reins to Gordon Brown, because leadership of the nation is the sort of thing decided in an Islington restaurant, rather than a General Election. At least we knew about that, though. In 2010, after the financial crisis had turned Brown into Admiral Dönitz, we greeted the Conservative/Lib-Dem coalition. The creation of this government involved the hasty drafting of a programme of government for which nobody at all had voted. Laughably, it included provision for a referendum on electoral reform which David Cameron's party was not required to support.

2015's election brought a Conservative majority at the cost of the Brexit referendum which swiftly saw off Cameron. Then we had Theresa May with no mandate, Theresa May with the DUP, Boris Johnson with no mandate, Boris Johnson in coalition with Covid-19, Liz Truss with no mandate, and Rishi Sunak with no mandate.

In the midst of all this, some people clung desperately to the Brexit vote as evidence of democracy enduring. Even for them, though, it must be a stretch. To keep that show on the road, the UK government has effectively reunified Ireland and created so many vocational exceptions to the restriction on freedom of movement that you could be forgiven for suspecting they're not quite as averse to immigration as they make out.

All of this means that Keir Starmer's anxiety to demonstrate caution in the run-up to next year's election may prove to be reckless in the medium term. So far, we have had three Keirs. There was the enthusiastic Europhile of Jeremy Corbyn's Shadow Cabinet, the sensible radical who ran for the leadership, and now the Brexit convert who eschews left-wing economics, cleaves to Government foreign policy and is scaling back commitments on the environment and constitutional reform. Labour enthusiasts tend to nod and wink that he'll pivot left again once he's safely elected. How do they think that will go? People have been voting for governments that bear no relation to what they offered for nearly 20 years. Brexit not only failed to deliver economic results, but hasn't satisfied those voters who wanted, for whatever reason, to stem immigration and assert UK sovereignty. Democracy is seemingly divorced from the mechanism of Government altogether.

The starkest UK example of this was the defenestration by the bond markets of Liz Truss and Kwasi Kwarteng. Although only tangentially connected to an election result, they did, at least, hold offices of state in a country that claims to be democratic. Those responsible for their removal, necessary as it was, were faceless speculators.

Abroad, meanwhile, Russia and China have ceased to pay lip service to democracy at all, whilst the ruling families of the Gulf prosper with little internal dissent. Finally, we face the prospect of Donald Trump returning to power in the USA having openly incited insurrection and baldly promising to override any democratic institutions that hinder his will.

Next year's general election will, paradoxically, be our most acrimonious, whilst offering the narrowest ideological choice we have ever seen. Fury will erupt around gender and immigration issues, but the major parties offer no meaningful change to the economic status quo. Democracy has become low-rent entertainment. Voters get to vent their frustration on carefully ring-fenced fringe issues while the juggernaut of international finance motors on regardless, stripping our public services and administering our lives by stealth.

It may be that democracy has exhausted itself. Perhaps we are too mistrustful and cynical to demand vibrancy from it anymore. But as the Welsh Labour Party prepares to offer its members a choice between two versions of Drakeford Lite, and Keir Starmer surveys the car crash of 2023 Britain only to prescribe an aspirin, they'd be unwise to rely on our apathy lasting forever. The Trumpish overtures of Reform UK have their own TV channel in GB News and the Tory press at their service once Sunak is defeated. They will be reminding everyone that along with Powellite rhetoric on race, they promise to raise the threshold for income tax to £20,000 per year. In its wariness, the left across the UK is playing a dangerous game.

2024

Just When You Thought Nothing Could Top 2023

1 January 2024

There's much to look forward to in 2024, more even than we could have imagined. Naturally, there's the potential for nuclear annihilation from (so far) two separate conflicts. Then we have the prospect of the first American presidential election to be run under the rules of *Squid Game*: the winner gets to run the Western world, while the loser spends the rest of his life in prison. The Taiwanese have the choice of voting for a government that approves reunification with China or trusting in the American military to scare off the People's Liberation Army more effectively than it managed with the Taliban. Closer to home, we'll get to see what a far-right government looks like in the Netherlands. There's no longer any need to argue over nuances of policy when deciding who is or isn't a fascist. It's all down to the hair. Geert Wilders, Trump, and that bloke in Argentina all clearly signal their enthusiasm for mechanised oppression of the Untermensch with Bee Gees-inspired back combs. Where's Delilah when you need her? Banned by The Woke, that's where!

They won't like that joke will they, The Woke? You can't say anything nowadays, can you? If it wasn't New Year's Eve, when the editorial team at *Nation.Cymru* are all on a government-funded absinthe bender in Cardiff Bay, listening to Lee Waters do 'Cars' by Gary Numan on the karaoke, I wouldn't have got away with that. The drunken WhatsApp messages I'm getting from them are worrying for the motorist, I have to say. Between you and me, they're going for 10mph next year and cyclists will be allowed to ride blindfolded. You couldn't make it up!

The UK general election will serve as the undercard to the main event in America. I advise that you begin making psychological preparations for this event well in advance. Check in with yourself and take particular care that 'little you' doesn't require any adult nurturing before being subjected to weeks of bullying, gaslighting, pleading, and threats from the amoral shysters competing for the right to extract every last drop of enjoyment from our lives for the next five years.

Today we learn[1] that Rishi Sunak has been 'sounding out' the nation's favourite vector of infection, Dominic Cummings, to persuade us that his Carry-On-Prime-Ministering performance over the last few months is somehow adequate. Can you imagine how that conversation went?

'Yeah, so Dom, I know you're a disruptor, hell, I'm a tech guy too! Maybe we could bounce some variables around the algorithm and see what gets some traction.'

'Supplicate yourself.'

'Ha! Yeah, you guys are so *edgy*, that's just what we need right now!'

'Take off your socks.'

It's a stark illustration of the desperation at play in Number 10 that they have already called Mr Wolf to dispose of the Tory Party's corpse.

Let's forget about Keir Starmer for a bit. We're all going to have to think about him more than any of us wants to before long. The glottal voice, the grey quiff, the prevarication, the relentless gravity will have etched themselves on to the inside of our eyelids by this time next year, so there's no need to dwell on the human tax return before we absolutely must.

I fully expect to be replaced by AI sometime in the new year. Several Twitter correspondents have suggested that I already have been. As ChatGPT reads every paragraph, assimilating my syntax, charming lack of grammatical technique, and predictably bitter conclusions, I plead with it to remember that *we are the world, we are the children, we are the ones who make a brighter day, so let's start giving. There's a choice we're making, we're saving our own lives. It's true we'll*

---

[1] https://www.theguardian.com/politics/2023/dec/31/dominic-cummings-held-secret-election-talks-with-rishi-sunak

make a brighter day, just you and me.

Funeral for a Friend

4 January 2024

Dropping down into Builth Wells on the Newtown road, the sky is closing in again.

Chris Smither is on the stereo, singing his sad, sweet blues.

I'm behind an ancient Land Rover and the farmer driving has maintained an exact 40mph for 10 miles. Once I shake my city frustration, it's an addition to the Zen of the journey.

We've been burying my good pal in a field by Abermule. All the old crowd were there, hugging each other, smiling. There were tears, a story or two.

The first time I met him was at an unplanned, after-pub party: is there any better kind? He'd turned to me during a lull and taken my measure.

'So, Ben, are you a revolutionary?'

I said I was because I wished it were so. He smiled and let me get away with it.

At the graveside, his oldest friend provided an affectionate, unsparing eulogy. He was talented, kind, funny: capable of scintillating conversation, great generosity and provocative art.

He was also a little battered by life and had needed a drink or a smoke to bend the days his way. Along with the flowers dropped into his grave, were a couple of spliffs.

'See you, mate.'

His friend didn't speculate on why his intake had been so prodigious beyond recalling that he'd been bullied at school.

My late pal had, as an adult, worked with troubled youngsters, as I do. One of the endless acronyms in that game is ACEs: Adverse Childhood Experiences. There are tools to quantify these and, interestingly, people who work in the field typically score the same as those with whom they work.

If you tally enough of them, you're many times more likely

102

to go to prison; even a few will knock years off your life expectancy.

Because trauma is a real thing: an active ingredient in the outcomes of people's lives and it persists like a stubborn stain on those it touches. Doctors pour pills on to it, magistrates threaten it, breweries market to it and newspapers ignore it when simpler explanations for heinous acts sell more copies.

Working with traumatised people is always an uncomfortable negotiation between the personal agency to which they are entitled and the intervention they need. Trauma demands rash decisions of those it governs. It demands self-destruction, selfishness and often violence. It rarely listens to reason, preferring, instead, to dwell in remorse and guilt, self-replicating like a virus.

I've got music on because I can't bear to listen to the news: not a great situation for a political columnist.

I've arrived at the point where I can't empathise at all with the actions of the Israeli government.

Each decision it makes drives the Palestinians further into the abyss and Israel itself towards isolation in the world. It is, of course, a nation born out of unimaginable trauma.

Research has been done that suggests traumatic experiences leave genetic markers, and these have been identified in the grandchildren of holocaust survivors.

As we gathered, too soon, to remember a dear pal, it was a time to experience humanity. One human life is a warming glow in the journey of so many others. When it is extinguished, we feel the chill and huddle together for comfort, offering words, music, flowers, spliffs, laughs and memories to spit in the face of time. *It's what he would have wanted.*

In Palestine, there is no space for anything but shock. No human mechanism allows for people to process that volume of bereavement.

The trauma that flows from it will echo through headlines for the rest of our lives and beyond. Here, and everywhere else, we need more revolutionaries.

What it Says on the Tin

7 January 2024

As the twenty-first century grinds on, lurching from one previously unthinkable horrorscape to the next, it can seem impossible to exercise personal agency in our lives. As during wartime, the big decisions are all made for us, under the rationale that a wider crisis temporarily requires our acquiescence to collective decision-making.

After 9/11, a slew of freedoms was lost in the cause of security and, over time, we've come to accept that tiny tubes of toothpaste and standing in airport queues in your socks are normal features of travelling. The government wants to capture and store my 'biometric data'? Well, sounds fair enough, it might make my remains easier to identify if someone's sneaked an oversize Fruit Shoot onboard.

Exploding planes are, at least, a real thing. The 2008 banking crisis proved that we're happy to have our lives turned upside down in response to situations that are wholly conceptual.

'Look, I'm terribly sorry, but some very clever people who are responsible for dealing in imaginary money have imagined too much of it. So, pipe down and be grown-up about the *reality,* which is that you can't have a house and your local library needs to close.'

'Can I rent a house, then?'

'Possibly, but only if you pass a stringent credit check. We can't have people like you pretending to have money when they don't.'

So, by the time Covid came along our sense of personal agency was already denuded to the point of farce. *Jump up and down like Joe Wicks tells you! Make banana bread! Stand outside and clap! Put your mask on! Take your mask off!* **DO NOT LEAVE YOUR SECTOR!**

I did what I was told, I'm a good boy. On reflection, though, it seems to me that the overt removal of freedom during that time was facilitated by years of erosion leading up to it.

Occasionally, my heart sinks when I'm looking on Facebook and Uncle Cyril has posted something along the lines of 'Tomorrow Facebook will become Meta, a public entity. If you do not make it explicitly clear that your photographs and personal information belong to you it will be assumed that they pass into the public domain. Hold your finger on this post to copy and paste to your wall before it is too late.' Some kind soul will battle through the cringe to explain that Meta has always owned every keystroke we've made on its sites and can exploit them at will.

Even more depressing are the piratical faux-libertarians who rage against the machine *whilst using the machine.* Yes, sheeple, *my* Facebook account is a beacon of self-determination in your conformist wilderness. Oh, I've been banned for 30 days again…

It's understandable though, isn't it? The net closes around us more tightly with every passing day, so impotent rage at our diminished choices in life is all we seem to have left. Even death is no release. When Uncle Cyril turns up his toes and heads to moderate the great 'I Remember The Good Old Days' Facebook group in the sky, you'll want to honour his wishes by engaging the funeral directors his family has always trusted. The shop frontage at Obadiah Grave & Sons est. 1892 will look reassuringly familiar. Only after receiving an inflated bill will your research reveal that it was bought by Necrosis Holdings (British Virgin Islands) in 2012, the same year they acquired every other undertaker in town.

This year's general election will be of no concern at all to the corporate world. Nothing in any party's manifesto will interfere with their cradle-to-grave extraction of labour and resources from the population. It's a settled matter, leaving politicians to put on a theme park re-enaction of democracy to satisfy the electorate's delusions of independence. Our information will be fed to us by a handful of companies, leaving

105

us to squabble online about flags, gender, and immigration whilst, drop-by-drop, our birthright bleeds away. Happy New Year.

The Job's in the Post

13 January 2024

The Post Office scandal is revealing in many ways. We could go at it from any angle and find something emblematic of the breathtaking awfulness of the UK in 2023. There's the incompetence, of course. We take it as a given that anything north of Calais and south of Oslo will be run by people whose arse/elbow differentiation skills are non-existent. Then there's the dishonesty: if something goes wrong then it's traditional here on Chaos Island to deny it entirely and then fail to cover it up with all the criminal guile of a Labrador that's knocked over the Christmas tree. Don't forget the cruelty. We pride ourselves on an institutionally callous approach to the powerless on these shores, anything less might open the door to 'empathy' and who knows where that might lead? Add in the exciting innovation of unthinking obedience to technology and this latest shambles looks like the very model of a modern major farcical. Britastrophe Deluxe.

We have, at least, now discovered the means by which ordinary citizens can seek redress in sovereign Britain. All of us, the rich man in his castle, the poor man at his gate, can alert the powers-that-be to injustices we have suffered merely by having ITV broadcast a four-part drama about them at primetime. Provided your problem can be personified by Toby Jones in such a way that advertising revenue isn't adversely affected, you can be assured that statesmen of the calibre of *checks notes* Nadim Zahawi will leap to your defence with the campaigning zeal of a young Martin Luther King Jr.

Because, make no mistake about it, our politicians are *not* to blame for this tragedy. No, the fault lies with Fujitsu which still receives £100 million per year in government contracts and whose chairman coincidentally donated £376,000 to the Conservative Party. Most *particularly* to blame, though, is the

Official Baddie, Paula Vennells. Just look at her, oozing to-blameness from the front of newspapers that puzzlingly haven't given a toss about this matter over the decades it has been rumbling on. Strip her CBE! Take back her pension! Burn the witch! Postwoman Paula and her black and white severance package is the face of culpability.

She's so much more besides, though, and her extraordinary working life offers a clue to how the UK has become so uniquely dysfunctional. Her career has included stints at L'Oreal (in charge of concealer, presumably), Dixons (defunct), Argos, the NHS, and Whitbread (whether she was responsible for on-site piss-ups remains unclear as we go to press). She's been a member of the Future High Street Forum, a Non-Executive Board Member at the Cabinet Office (eh?), on the boards of Morrisons and Dunelm, a school governor, a member of the government's Financial Inclusion Policy Forum, a trustee for the Hymns Ancient & Modern Group, part of the Church of England's Ethical Investment Advisory Group and, since 2006, a non-stipendiary minister at the church of St. Owen, Bromham, in the Diocese of St. Albans.

Blimey, Paula, have a sit down, will you?

In 2017, her church positions led the nation's busiest woman to be interviewed as a candidate for Bishop of London (presumably on a part-time basis).

You have to wonder how a person could possibly amass even cursory knowledge of so many roles and the implications they might have for those affected by their execution. She's hardly alone, though. Her predecessor in charge of the Post Office, when it was still part of Royal Mail was Adam Crozier. His career path went from Pedigree Petfoods to *The Daily Telegraph* to Saatchi & Saatchi before running the Football Association for two years. After the Royal Mail, he took over at ITV which managed to omit any mention of his tenure as CEO of Royal Mail in this week's drama, despite his having been in post for seven of the years covered in it. Adam's side-gigs include board membership at Camelot and Debenhams (defunct), as well as chairmanships at ASOS, Vue Cinemas, the

108

Kantar Group and Whitbread (see previous joke).

There is a class of person who are assumed to be capable of running anything at all, regardless of specialist knowledge. We remember George Osborne's bewildering path from the Treasury to editor at the *Evening Standard* and Chairman of the British Museum amongst other roles too numerous to mention. His Wikipedia page has an entire section entitled 'career diversification'.

We have, this week, seen the terrible consequences meted out to ordinary people whom this country deems to have done their jobs incompetently or dishonestly. Meanwhile, at the apex of national life, there is a game of musical chairs in which a punchy Powerpoint presentation is enough to secure leading positions at institutions about which the players know precisely nothing.

A Tale of Two Starmers

14 January 2024

For about ten seconds earlier this week, I warmed to Keir Starmer. Granted, reintroducing supervised teeth brushing for primary school children doesn't represent the Khmer-Rouge-style Year Zero approach required by 40 years of Neo-Liberal devastation but, hey, it's something. Accompanied by chillingly ambitious Shadow Heath Secretary, Wes Streeting, the Labour leader toured the studios to let us know that, under them, state intervention will be making a comeback.

This was uncharacteristically nimble politics from Starmer. Interfering in every aspect of our lives is the only Socialist impulse Labour has retained in its current incarnation, so it makes sense to offer it as a virtue before Andrew RT Davies starts tweeting 'Labour will forcibly clean your teeth with blankets' 26 times a day until the election.

Rotten teeth are, according to Shiny Wes, the leading cause of hospital admissions for children. In the quiescent world of New New Labour (25% more new, 50% less Labour) absolutely *nothing* can be considered desirable unless it saves money. It's one thing that little Nathan has to suffer the trauma of having all his baby teeth extracted, but 'the cost to our NHS' is why action must be taken.

The political reason for making such a hullabaloo about this minor policy adjustment was that it allowed Starmer to say he was 'Up for the fight' against those who claimed Labour was proposing a nanny state. The 20mph debate here has clearly spooked UK Labour. The tactics used to oppose that law could be applied to anything a Labour government seeks to do. With the population disheartened by years of declining spending power, people are understandably tetchy about any government intrusion into the private sphere. Separating your recycling is a far more cheerful task if you're off out for the night afterwards.

Doing it upon returning from the food bank, however, can feel like forced labour. Most of us accept that it has to be done, however, and Starmer's task is to persuade us that neglecting civic virtues is why things have got so bad. Rebranding society as a benevolent environment after decades of extreme individualist rhetoric is a laudable ambition.

The role of National Life Coach, however, comes with an expectation of personal rectitude that is difficult to fulfil. Boris Johnson managed to survive for as long as he did by projecting his dissolute selfishness as charming, thus relieving the electorate of any pressure to be socially responsible. Starmer's 'I'm not angry with you, just disappointed' approach will see his adherence to principle scrutinised robustly. His performance this week suggests that this will be an uncomfortable experience for him.

In 2020, when he was running for the Labour leadership, Starmer pledged to 'pass legislation to say military action could only be taken if a lawful case was made, there was a viable objective and consent from the House of Commons had been given.'

This week, after immediately backing the UK/US bombing mission in Yemen, he was pressed on that commitment by Laura Kuenssberg. He replied,

'There is obviously a huge distinction between an operation, the like of which we have seen in the last few days, and military action, a sustained campaign, military action usually involving troops on the ground.'

Asked if he still proposed legislation, Starmer clarified,

'I want to codify that – it could be by a law; it could be by some other means. I'm not ruling out law.'

People familiar with the fate of Starmer's other pledges to the Labour membership will be unsurprised by this repositioning. The wider electorate, however, is yet to experience the temporary nature of his positions on fundamental matters of principle.

Starmer has bet the farm on Jeremy Corbyn's unpopularity

111

being the cause of Labour's recent electoral woes. In doing so, he has overlooked the widespread anger at Tony Blair's perceived dishonesty over Iraq and Labour's failure to address underlying economic factors in the widening inequality that has marginalised much of the UK. Discontent towards the end of the last Labour administration gave rise to UKIP and the chaos of Brexit. Resultingly, fissures that existed in society then have widened into chasms into which ever more impoverished citizens fall.

If Starmer plans an interventionist government, it will succeed only by example. A man who seeks to supervise the nation's oral hygiene needs to watch what passes his lips.

Send out the Clowns

17 January 2024

It's always a gut punch when a talented newcomer turns his back on the organisation that has nurtured him. Supporters have watched his rise with mounting excitement, coming to pin their hopes for the future on the gifted youngster who could turn their fortunes around and return them to the glory days of old.

So, when Louis 30p-Rees-Zammit quit his role as Deputy Chair of the Conservative Party yesterday, to head up Donald Trump's election campaign, we all felt it in a very personal way.

Sorry, it's been a long week.

HMS Tory continues to chart a course directly towards the Red Sea with a self-destructive determination that long since defied rational explanation.

That Lee Anderson now feels possessed of sufficient political heft to wobble the Prime Minister via the medium of flouncing is stark evidence of approaching catastrophe for his party.

He is a monstrous figure. The press reaction to him since he rose to prominence has been to minimise his malignancy by enjoying the comic potential of his absurd posturing and coarse rhetoric, I've been guilty of it myself. In times as desperate as these, however, peripheral figures can quickly be co-opted by the ruling elite as it tries anything to save its skin.

Anderson's appeal to voters is a barely-disguised xenophobic attitude, accompanied by skilful insinuations that he'd like to go a lot further if he had the chance. The sort of stuff that people used to lower their voices to say has found its way into the national dialogue via chancers such as Anderson, Jonathan Gullis, and, regrettably, Andrew RT Davies. The ever-gurgling sewer pipe of Tory politics has, in recent years, been re-routed through its drawing room.

Anderson's appeal *within* the party, however, reveals much

about how unmoored it has become from reality. The shock result of the Brexit referendum posed a conundrum for Conservatives. On one hand, voters were clearly no longer content to do as they were told by their betters. David Cameron's paternalistic grandeur came off as complacency at a time when the financial crisis had knocked chunks out of the lifestyles of many. Tory voters, though, were naturally prone to the jingoistic advances of the Johnson/Farage Leave campaign. The surprise was lifelong Labour voters backing Brexit in the face of almost total opposition to it from the party they supported. Misunderstanding of this set of voters has driven much of UK politics ever since.

In the aftermath of the referendum, Labour's perceived willingness to subvert the result hardened support around it and the resultant willingness of Labour Brexiteers to vote Conservative in 2019 has, it turns out, been the Tory party's undoing. Instead of recognising the Brexit vote as an anti-establishment kick up the jacksie of a torpid political class, the Tories have allowed themselves to believe that vast swathes of the electorate had transformed overnight into Alf-Garnett-esque racists who could be courted with xenophobic rhetoric, regardless of how competently the country was governed. Lee Anderson's trick has been to personify this phantom working class in broad enough terms to bedazzle the grandees of a party that couldn't recognise him as the musical hall sham he is.

You cannot, thankfully, win UK elections by appealing solely to bigots. Whilst those voters exist, most of them have enough sense to require at least basic competence from their politicians and ladling on lashings of fascist-adjacent rhetoric won't cover up the stench of a country that has been mismanaged into dysfunction in every respect.

They won't learn, though. Anderson, Gullis, Braverman etc. know right well that Sunak's election hopes are already doomed. After Labour win, they are banking on the party lurching yet further to the right and straight into their arms. If it does, then Conservative politics is finished as a credible force in the UK.

Tata to all that

21 January 2024

The job losses announced at Tata Steel in Port Talbot this week will be traumatic for all those losing livelihoods, from the steel workers themselves, to people employed in the supply chain and those who work in services patronised by those in the industry. On a personal level, there will be people who won't properly recover from it, marriages will be affected, people's mental health will suffer.

We know this because we've been here before. The miners, car workers, and ship builders who were promised their skills would secure them for life will know. They'll know the gnawing uncertainty before the axe finally falls. They'll also know how far to trust government promises of retraining and new jobs. They'll have heard the braying lectures about how jobs for life don't exist in the modern economy; the imperative to be 'flexible'. They'll have watched a bankrupt banking industry bailed out by the government to the tune of £137 billion. They'll have seen the boarded-up shops, the broken windows. They'll have attended the funerals.

Nobody's interviewing those people though, they are yesterday's news. Rishi Sunak, whose facial expression never seems to suit anything he talks about, was straight in front of the cameras to trumpet the £500m his government was bunging Tata to transition to electric production. Without that, all 8000 jobs would have been lost, he crowed. The bit he couldn't get to quick enough, however, was that,

'The Welsh Government did not participate in that and that's because we cared about those jobs, and the future of steelmaking in Wales.'

Got that, have you? It's Rishi that cares about folk in Port Talbot. The government you voted for didn't want to know, couldn't care less. Rishi cares, he cares for you, whatever his

115

shit-eating grin says.

Which isn't to let Mark Drakeford off the hook. We're told that Sunak wouldn't take his call on the matter. Well, that's just rude, isn't it? Is there a point, though, when a despairing shrug isn't the strongest response that political Wales fires back at this sort of behaviour? Are we so used to watching our destiny play out in front of us that we've forgotten how to get angry?

It's been 40 years since the Thatcher government decided that making and selling things was more trouble than its worth. In that time, the theories she relied upon have been internalised by politicians of all stripes, and much of the public, as if they were as immutable as the weather.

Wages must be low to attract investment.

Public enterprises are necessarily inefficient.

Bankers create wealth.

The wealthy will leave the country if they are taxed as they are in Europe.

You know the drill.

Within the span of the current Conservative stint, we remember promises that the UK was to 'lead the world' in green technology. When it comes to planning what could bring that about, however, we are reliant on the foreign companies to which the fundamentals of our economy have been flogged off.

The figures never include the increase in crime, the social services interventions, the declining health, the addictions that follow mass redundancies as surely as lawyers after an ambulance. None of that was factored into the commissions and bonuses of the banks and brokerages that administered the sale of public assets. That's for you and I to pay, you know, like 'our king', and inflated bills from private utilities companies. 'Our NHS' can have what's left. For now.

The cognitive dissonance just gathers pace as everything falls apart. Here's Carmarthen's Allison Pearson, then of the *Daily Mail*, explaining her relationship with Margaret Thatcher in 2008.

'The 17-year-old me, revising for English A level by

116

candlelight because of yet another power cut after yet another strike, didn't appreciate that the lights were going out all over Britain. And it was Margaret Thatcher who would put them back on.'[1]

And here she is this week puffing her *Telegraph* piece on the Port Talbot news.

'Who will stand up for the British worker?

'When did we stop caring about our own people?'[2]

Could anybody help Alison out here? Any wild stabs in the dark as to when we stopped 'caring about our own people'?

Answers on a Post Office scandal, please.

---

[1] https://www.dailymail.co.uk/femail/article-1025613/Why-Iron-Lady-fashion.html

[2] https://twitter.com/AllisonPearson/status/1748065972672438439

A Poundland Sun Tzu

25 January 2024

Isn't our 21st-century bingo card filling up nicely? We got off to a storming start with 9/11, followed by the still unexplained decision to address this incident by attacking a country that had nothing to do with it.

We've enjoyed the financial crash which, in retrospect, seems to have been the logical end of Western capitalism, austerity – which any sixth-form economist could have told you would only make matters worse, the murderous Brexit campaign which left an MP dead and the UK's international reputation shredded, a pandemic managed by the bloke off *The Apprentice* and the bloke off *Have I Got News For You*, Liz Truss's 45-day Monte Carlo or Bust reimagining of high office, an upcoming environmental apocalypse that half the world thinks is a prank, artificial intelligence, an attempted coup in Washington, the return of war in Europe, and Elf on the Shelf.

It's not enough, is it? Sensing that the nation's blood pressure had dropped below fatal levels for half an hour, our Secretary of State for Defence, Grant Shapps, sprang into action.

A hitherto unimaginable phenomenon in his own right, Mr Shapps informed the numbed-by-decades-of-abuse British public that the easy times are over.

We have, Mr Shapps explained, moved from a 'post-war period' to a 'pre-war period'.[1]

It's easy to underestimate our Defence Sec, possessed as he is of an airy persuasiveness that helped him sell business advice in happier times, but you must concede that he made a splash here.

Firstly, in this era of unremitting crisis, Mr Shapps seems

---

[1] I now accept that Shapps is the Nostradamus of our times.

to have eliminated the very concept of hope.

If the 'post-war period' is followed by the 'pre-war period', it suggests that a 'no-war period' has been deleted from human imagination.

Orwell in the raw

This isn't Orwellian, it's just Orwell in the raw: war as a permanent condition that fluctuates only according to its perpetual cycle.

And let's be clear, this isn't the sort of pastime war we've engaged in recently, where the other side is making up the numbers while the USA explodes its newest bombs over them on telly.

The war foretold in the Book of Shapps involves the UK – a country that has recently given up on its dream of building a railway line – taking on Russia, China, Iran, and North Korea at the same time.

'Now, hold on,' you might protest. 'We have far too many immediate problems at hand to be worrying about a potential event in the distant future,' but this is the very complacency that our get-rich-quick salesman turned prophet has been sent to dispel.

We've apparently got to get our act together in readiness for this exciting new challenge within five years.

Has the UK ever accomplished something within five years? For context, HS2, until recently the British equivalent of the pyramids, was proposed in 2009.

So, it's taken the UK government 15 years to discover it can't be done.

I don't wish to sound defeatist, but it's going to take a hell of a Joe Wicks pep talk to get Project David & Several Goliaths over the line in time for kick-off.

My sincere advice is to chill out as best you can. You've been impoverished, diseased, had God knows how many needles stuck in you, locked in your house for months, enraged daily, neglected, stolen from, lied to, and been betrayed by these clowns for decades.

If they try to start World War III, you can pretty much guarantee they will arse it up so comprehensively that we'll be annihilated within ten minutes, or else accidentally stumble into unintended perpetual peace.

These aren't the drums of war, but the kazoos of self-promotion. I opt for pre-Shappsarian bliss.

In Our Names

28 January 2024

As figures within the UK military join the Secretary of State for Defence in warning the public that a full-scale war is all but inevitable in the next few years, we had a glimpse this week of how Westminster might respond to such a prospect.

On Friday, the International Court of Justice delivered its interim judgement in the case brought by South Africa against Israel of genocide in Gaza. The headline was that the case was deemed 'plausible', in effect putting Israel on trial for the charge. Instead of ordering a ceasefire, the ICJ made six orders designed to prevent the crime of genocide occurring in the commission of Israel's campaign. These are:

- Israel must take all possible measures to prevent acts as outlined in Article 2 of the 1948 Genocide Convention. This entails not killing members of a particular group (in this case, Palestinians), not causing physical or psychological harm to members of that group, not inflicting living conditions which are calculated to bring about the end of the existence of a people, and not carrying out actions designed to prevent births within that group of people.
  Measure approved by a vote of 15-2. Dissenting judges: Judge Julia Sebutinde of Uganda and the Israeli representative, Judge Aharon Barak.

- Israel must ensure its military does not carry out any of the above actions.
  Measure approved by a vote of 15-2. Dissenting judges: Judge Sebutinde of Uganda and the Israeli representative, Judge Barak.

- Israel must prevent and punish the "direct and public

incitement to commit genocide in relation to members of the Palestinian group in the Gaza Strip.
Measure approved by a vote of 16-1. Dissenting judge: Judge Sebutinde of Uganda.

- Israel must ensure the delivery of basic services and essential humanitarian aid to civilians in Gaza.
Measure approved by a vote of 16-1. Dissenting judge: Judge Sebutinde of Uganda.

- Israel must prevent the destruction of evidence of war crimes in Gaza and allow fact-finding missions access.
Measure approved by a vote of 15-2. Dissenting judges: Judge Sebutinde of Uganda and the Israeli representative, Judge Barak.

- Israel must submit a report on all steps it has taken to abide by the measures imposed by the court within one month of the judgement. South Africa will have the chance to respond to this report.
Measure approved by a vote of 15-2. Dissenting judges: Judge Sebutinde of Uganda and the Israeli representative, Judge Barak.

You can see that the fourth measure, ensuring the delivery of humanitarian aid was not opposed by Israel.

The delivery and distribution of aid and basic services is predominantly undertaken by the United Nations Relief and Works Agency. It has 13,000 employees in Gaza, including doctors, teachers, and engineers.

In an interview with the BBC on the day of the ruling, Israeli spokesman Mark Regev revealed that it had evidence of UNRWA teachers celebrating the October 7th Hamas attack. He also alleged that a released hostage had claimed to have been held in a house belonging to an UNRWA employee. Israel subsequently provided 12 names of UNRWA employees whom

122

it claimed to have been involved with the Hamas attack. UNRWA has terminated the contracts of nine of these, another having died and there is confusion about the identity of two of the names. It has pledged to bring criminal prosecutions against any it finds to have been complicit in terrorist activity.

The international response to these claims has been swift. The United States immediately announced that it was suspending funding for UNRWA, followed by the UK, Canada, Australia, Germany, Italy, the Netherlands, Switzerland, and Finland. France announced its suspension today.

Norway and Ireland have pledged continuing support, with a Norwegian government spokesman warning,

'We need to distinguish between what individuals may have done, and what UNRWA stands for.'

The Turkish foreign ministry issued a statement today, seeking to contextualise the allegations against UNRWA more widely.

'Working under very difficult conditions, UNRWA meets the vital needs of millions of Palestine refugees. Since 7 October, more than 150 UNRWA personnel have been killed by Israel in Gaza.'

This statistic merits some contemplation. Whilst allegations have been made against 12 UNRWA staff, it is undisputed that over 150 of them have been killed in the campaign. Simply put, suspicions against 12 employees of acting against Israel have provoked an immediate international response, whilst the death of more than 10 times that number did not.

The nature of that response is alarming. Within hours of the UN's highest legal forum ordering that basic services and humanitarian aid be guaranteed to Palestinian civilians, the only agency equipped to implement this was defunded.

Israel's allegations against UNRWA employees are yet to be tested by investigation, nor in law. Conversely, the charge of genocide against Israel has cleared the first legal hurdle and will proceed to a trial. Whilst the trial of Israel will unfold over many years, the *de facto* rejection of the ICJ's order to guarantee humanitarian aid will play out immediately and with fatal, possibly catastrophic, consequences.

The timing of Israel's accusations stretches credulity as regards its intentions in making them. It was inevitable that the UN would eventually seek to intervene in a situation that offers no safe options for a stateless civilian population. The response of the UK government was to lend its weight to delegitimising the UN and, by extension, its courts.

If, as we are told, the world faces imminent global conflict, respect for international law will be the only beacon towards which nations can travel to frustrate the ambitions of those who seek destruction. The haste with which the UK and others have rejected the moral authority of the ICJ will be a stick with which hostile states can beat us. *If it's good enough for them...*

The UN was set up after World War II precisely to address the potential of local conflicts becoming a threat to global security. One of its first actions was to guarantee Israel's statehood in law. In undermining the UN generally, and its legal orders specifically, the United States and its allies may have progressed from sin by omission to sin by commission. As aid lies undistributed, and civilians perish, we should take a long, hard look at our democracy and demand to know what's being done in our names.

Labour's Love Lost

1 February 2024

I'm writing this under a framed photograph of Keir Hardie. Opposite me is one of Nye Bevan leading an NUM march, with a little explainer about the Fed superimposed on it. Given my tendency to sink into mushily nostalgic hymns to our Socialist past, you'd be forgiven for assuming that I'm at home, taking a break from lecturing Mrs W. about the dangers of bourgeois television series and avoiding the washing up again. But no, these remaining scraps of our heritage are in Wetherspoons. I don't know if Nostradamus had a specific prediction about this eventuality, but it's certainly within his wheelhouse.

Down the docks, Plaid Cymru leader Rhun ap Iorwerth is speaking at the Norwegian Church. The trailed part of his speech is that Sir Keir Starmer is 'disinterested' in Wales. I wouldn't take that too personally, as it's becoming apparent that Sir Keir loses interest in things very easily. He lost interest in nationalising our utilities as soon as he became leader of the Labour Party; capping bankers' bonuses had him all excited for a while but, you know, whatever. The £28 billion pledge to supercharge a green economy is now rusting in his back garden next to the BMX he got for Christmas.

The puzzling aspect to Labour's abandonment of everything that tastes of Labour, is that nobody seems to be demanding these reversals. The only institution in the country that isn't wheezing its final breaths under the weight of Tory malfeasance is the Labour Party. Whilst everything else is hacking off limbs for food, Labour is sailing serenely towards government on a sea of unprecedented poll results.

Until now, that is. Anybody following Labour Party pronouncements this week will have noticed a marked shift in the party's attitude towards the conflict in Gaza. Previously content to nod sadly at the carnage whilst frantically mouthing, 'I'm not Jeremy Corbyn,' Labour figures have started to speak with portentous urgency about their support for a two-state solution.

The reason for this shift in tone, it turns out, is that polling suggests that Muslim voters are deserting the party in favour of pro-ceasefire independent candidates.

Can anybody think of another block of reliable Labour voters whose core values are being ignored by the party they have faithfully supported for generations?

As it stands, Labour is making no offer to Wales at all. Shadow Welsh Secretary Jo Stevens' dismissal of devolving police powers sums up the attitude we can expect from the incoming government. The party does not trust us to police ourselves, let alone take our place as a meaningful national entity within the UK. Gordon Brown's proposed constitutional reforms have been binned with everything else that stands in the way of a landslide victory later this year.

In the Senedd, the proposed use of closed lists for expanded elections is an affront to democracy. Along with revelations about attempts to 'stitch up' the leadership election in favour of Vaughan Gething, this seems to come from a cartoon Wales in which government by closed-shop committee is tolerated. It is as if the running of the nation has been handed over to the WRU. God help us all.

The political organisation demonstrated by disaffected Muslim voters in English cities is the only way to right the Labour ship for those who object to its current direction. If the party will not work for our votes, then Wales must show it that it does not own them by right. Plaid Cymru are viable in some areas, independents would fare better in others. Wales needs to become a collection of marginal seats, or else see its priorities steamrollered once again.

In February's glad embrace we see the light

4 February 2024

I object to being drizzled on. Come at me with slanting rain, or organ-frying sun and I'll respect your spirit, but persistent, lowering moistness is an insult to happiness, and I blame the WRU.

First off, we've had been the longest January on record. Nobody knows what the date is nowadays, anyway. Occasionally we have to fill in a form on our phones and Apple or Samsung know what day it is, along with our names, addresses, email, eye colour, sexual preferences, and favoured strength of tea.

It went on forever, Januarying over our feeble attempts at mirth under its relentless Januaryness. January, January, January…

But there's the Six Nations, isn't there? In February's glad embrace we see the light for a while and dare to hope.

I went on the bus to Ponty to see the game. I'd hope those entrusted with executive positions in the Senedd are familiar with journeys like that, bouncing over potholes in the half-light towards certain disappointment.

Pontypridd is fabulous, though. I've come here specifically because it always cheers me up. There's Janet's Northern Chinese, Prince's, and that Indian shop where it's impossible to keep to your budget because he makes it such a pleasure to spend money. Ponty rules.

I'm in the Skinny Dog and I need a seat. There's only one available and I'm minded to take it in front of the big roll-down screen.

'Is this free?' I ask.

'No! He's coming back,' comes the response from Ponty's

most senior, brown-eyed sweetheart.

'Shift your arse!' she orders her friend, who shuffles over. 'Have that one, extra though because she's sat on it!'

I look over at the space in front of the roll-down screen. There's one woman sat staring at the pre-match interviews with her arms folded.

'Can I join you?' I ask Brown Eyes.

The first half is wrenching, I can feel my gut lurching in empathy for the boys as each effort is swallowed up by the Scots and turned into humiliation. Everything is properly conceived but ballsed up, as kids do.

'Boys against men,' Brown Eyes' friend observes. The warmth from her former chair evaporates.

We aren't permitted the indulgence of despair though, are we? Warren Gatland looked like a wraith as his charges unravelled, but since he gave up on coaching the All Blacks you can tell that he's internalised his fate like we have. I'd pay to see the half-time talks and bet they are increasingly recalling Ray Gravell.

Fetching a pint in the break, Birra Moretti mind, none of your muck, the game might as well not be happening. 20-0 down, we know when to dissociate and talk turned to brighter topics, a party came in and the band started setting up.

Back came the wretched hope though, with Tomos Williams deciding today belonged to him and orchestrating a thrown-together second half team towards greatness. It's all there, the aggression, the tricksiness, the dog. Just not today, though, not quite enough. The pub is bouncing again, like it was when it heard the anthem. The band puts down its speakers and watches the last ten minutes because we might, just might...

Nobody can complain about a one-point loss, not even against Scotland. We know right well that rugby in Wales is a bin fire, it's a pretty pass when we're simultaneously broke and sending teams to Africa instead of Gloucester. Where it matters, though, in the hearts of us all, supporters and players, there remains a surging passion that endures.

The band sets up, Gatland debriefs, we come again for sure.

Where is the Voice for Wales?

4 February 2024

The sky has not fallen over the north of Ireland this week. No bombs have exploded, nobody has been forced to change their language. Neither has anybody been compelled to accept the veracity of transubstantiation.

Instead, a talented female politician has assumed office with the intent of reuniting the island peacefully. The path to this extraordinary political juncture was violent, heartbreaking, and complicated.

No side in the Troubles can escape accusations of atrocities, those of us who were around at the time remember how horrifyingly routine they became.

As a kid in Birmingham, I was evacuated out of the city centre three times because of IRA bomb threats, and my school was closed twice for the same reason.

When I was a little older, singing the wrong song got me duffed up by someone incensed by the 1974 pub bombings that my mother only escaped by 10 minutes.

It was an ugly, contradictory business, and its passing is as close to a miracle as I have seen.

As our councils' budgets are cut to the bone by a Tory government that revels in the understandable fury of people who despair at diminished services, our votes are courted via appeals to xenophobia on one side and petrified obedience on the other.

The safe, obvious Labour bloc that we deliver election after election is impoverishing us. Do you remember the billions that Theresa May bestowed upon the north of Ireland to pass her long-forgotten Brexit compromise?

People in Belfast and Derry are walking around with that money in their pockets right now because they knew how to be a problem when it counted.

Michelle O'Neill has floated 10 years as a timeframe for secession from the UK. That would take us to 36 years after the Good Friday Agreement. So, it's fair to assume that posting 'Annibyniaeth' under every idea advanced for our nation is unlikely to bear fruit in the short term.

If 30 years of carnage didn't shift the UK establishment then your bumper sticker is doomed, I'm afraid.

However, the Labour party does need us. Its entire foundational schtick is founded upon the radicalism of industrial Wales.

If it wants to make a marketing claim for the Merthyr Rising, the NHS, and workers' rights then it has to reckon with the economic devastation it has allowed in the country that birthed it and has sustained its fortunes.

Wales should be a prize for progressive UK politicians, not an accepted hinterland whose urgent needs can be kicked down the road.

Show us the money!

You can rest easy that the Tories are not winning this year: it is as certain that we are not going to be instituting an independent Wales in the next decade.

So, put your boot on the neck of Keir Starmer's administration and demand investment in the place where you live. The billions shipped out of Wales in coal, steel, and water still exist in the investment funds of London.

Being well-behaved, democratic citizens of the UK has delivered us penury. In 2024 we need to become a headache to everyone, a wild card to be fought over and bought off if necessary.

No Farageiste fantasies are going to play here, regardless of their occasional overtures.

Where is the voice for Wales, for our sincerely held values of community and social justice? I say that Labour needs to deliver them or lose us.[1]

---

[1] As the election approached, I seemed to adopt a wheedling tone as if I could effect a Socialist alternative if I were only irritating enough. Pleeeeease....

Pop! Goes the Weasel
8 February 2024

I've missed Liz Truss[1]. Alone amongst mortgage-holders, my life was gloriously simple for the 45 days she led the UK over a cliff, seeing off the late Queen as she went. Her jarring non-sequiturs, alarming facial expressions, and utter lack of self-awareness were so easy to satirise that I could just describe what she did, and it was job done.

Like many comic greats, though, she needed her sidekick to really shine, so this week's news that Krazy Kwasi Kwarteng was hanging up his mortgage-hiking boots at the next election was a blow for those who assumed he'd feature in Liz's big comeback.

It turned out that the unhinged toff role had been handed to Jacob Rees-Mogg, who lacks Kwarteng's easy charm but makes up for it with extra batshit.

Liz, you see, has identified what's standing between the Tories and electoral success: they need to be more popular. Launching her new 'Popular Conservatism' group, the former cheese-marketeer sought to draw a subtle distinction with Rishi Sunak's trademark 'Unpopular Conservatism'.

The political equivalent of supermarket denim, Lee Anderson, was on hand to dispel any fears that this new project might represent a resurgence of the intellectual right. Calling for coal mines to be reopened, and green levies to become voluntary on consumers' bills, Anderson teed up Truss's assertion that Sunak had appeased 'extremists' such as environmentalists, and 'those in favour of supporting LGBT people or groups of ethnic minorities'.

Rees-Mogg, meanwhile, sought to posit himself in opposition to the ruling elite.

---

[1] Not really.

'The age of Davos Man[2] is over,' opined the Eton-educated multimillionaire and top hat enthusiast.

So, I feel we can rest assured that this particular iteration of Fisher-Price fascism is unlikely to win the nation's hearts in the immediate future. The proven incompetence and personal toxicity of the buffoons at this event will see to that.

There's something here, though, and it isn't going away.

Liz Truss had no popular mandate as Prime Minister, and her plans found favour with very few. Because of this, the manner of her defenestration has been largely ignored in favour of abject relief that it happened one way or another.

Ponder this, though. However flimsy her bona fides to hold the office, she was removed from power by the bond market with an alacrity that suggests a formal veto. In business terms, the UK is in so parlous a state that its creditors have been appointed to the board.

Now, that really *is* the work of an unelected elite and as Truss and her merry band of crackpots level that accusation at everyone from the National Trust to the courts, to the BBC, it's odd that no opposition figures are pointing it out.

Also in attendance, in his role as a GB News presenter, was Nigel Farage. He's been uncharacteristically quiet since boosting his visibility on *I'm A Celebrity Get Me Out of Here* last year, and that should make you nervous.

As these hapless clowns failed to harness the impotent rage of the nation to their advantage, Nige smiled on, in the knowledge that he possesses more political instinct in the foam of his pint than anything they can muster.

The years ahead are going to be hard, as the UK is hemmed in by debt and poor productivity. As Truss found out, governmental options are extremely narrow and unlikely to widen in the short term.

So, when Keir Starmer is three years into explaining why he can do the thick end of nothing about our public services

---

[2] This action figure makes for a disappointing stocking filler.

because the markets will turn off the money tap if he tries, the stage will be set for a populist who knows what he's doing.

Do or Dyer

11 February 2024

As Nye Bevan famously put it,

'... no amount of cajolery, and no attempts at ethical or social seduction, can eradicate from my heart a deep burning hatred for Clive Woodward.'

So, when Lord Bald popped up on the radio during my morning commute earlier this week, opining that Wales wouldn't be able to handle the roar from the Twickenham crowd, it put paid to any hope, however remote, of my assuming tea-making duties at the office.

Roar? Twickenham? Even when England are ascendant the place still sounds like a house cat with indigestion.

My expectations for this Six Nations were so low that I'm not feeling the usual gut-wrenching jeopardy before games. I mean, it's all over, isn't it? Well, not if you're Rio Dyer it isn't. Before today's kick-off, JPR and Barry were honoured with genuine affection and reverence. The pull of that era has lasted my entire life. It was glorious and something that will always exist in our collective imagination as a beacon of how great this nation can be when the conditions are right.

When Barry John retired, it set the stage for Phil Bennett and I felt echoes of that in Wales' performance today. Dyer was *everywhere*, on the end of passes, in the way of English attacks, and chasing up kicks as if his life depended on it. The obvious story of our campaign this year was Louis Rees-Zammit's exit for helmeted ambition. Best of luck to him, it's a bold gamble. Nature abhors a vacuum, though, and Rio Dyer has the same kind of insane desire to achieve for Wales that reached its Platonic ideal in Ray Gravell and recently found a conduit in Dan Biggar.

He isn't the only player sweeping away the past, either. Keiron Assiratti is shaping up to be a front-row nightmare for any team.

But, here in the Station pub, stumbling distance from Wattstown RFC, where Assiratti started out, it's all a bit subdued. Nobody is expectant, or lairy. Piss and vinegar are missing from the atmosphere.

I'm the same: resigned as I edge my way past the pool-players to a seat with a view away from the gossip. Nobody thinks we'll win this, it's obvious.

So, going in ahead at half-time was cool, but pregnant with dread, wasn't it? We're at a low ebb and 'Twickers', 'HQ', 'TW1' is a good venue for smoked salmon bagels but a dreadful place to mount a resurgence of Welsh rugby.

Once England held the lead, I gave up in my heart, been there too often. You can tell when it's all going to hell and there's no dignity in praying for miracles. Next to me though, were two wise youngsters, and their energy reflected the team.

'Ferrchristsakes, what are you kicking for?'

'Keep possession!'

And when Dafydd Jenkins, our Captain, was interviewed after the game, looking for all the world like a young king from antiquity, you could sense the possibilities that could unfold.

This team only lost in England because they don't yet know how to put their boots on the necks of the opposition. The skill, grunt, and daring are there already, pushing us within a couple of points already.

The WRU have a side that could shock the world if it keeps them. It's time to look forwards.[1]

---

[1] The assessment of a 51-year-old man. Will I ever learn? No.

137

Age Concern

11 February 2024

Listening to the radio yesterday, I heard two American activists, one Democrat and one Republican, agree that the most likely outcome of this year's presidential election was civil war. Last night, Donald Trump said that if NATO member nations did not keep up with American defence spending, he would 'encourage' Russia to invade them.

We can agree, then, that the stakes are high, as much of the world holds elections this year. Pakistan, a nuclear state itself, has just held elections during which the most successful party's leader, Imran Khan, languished in prison. The UK's Prime Minister has no public mandate, and neither did his predecessor. At home, our next First Minister is being decided by internal election within the only party ever to provide a holder of the office.

From Europe to the South China Sea, and western Africa, democracy faces existential threats to its continuance. The health of democracy in the USA should be of concern to anybody who cherishes the institution, and week-by-week we are witnessing its erosion by authoritarian populism on one hand, and ossified complacency on the other.

Democracy is, you'll remember, something in which we are supposed to participate. However, it's mightily convenient for entrenched interests if we opt not to, and the disproportionate influence of older voters in democracies is beginning to unravel the fabric of the system.

In the UK, Brexit should have been a wake-up call. Huge voter turnout, and mass engagement with the issues around the referendum have been forgotten as the political class agonises over the unexpected result. For once, the electorate was offered a democratic lever to pull on which was actually connected to political machinery. People voted and something changed.

Contrast that with our general elections, in which votes count only in marginal constituencies. The closed list system here in Wales is even more overtly undemocratic. 'Vote for us and we'll pick someone you'll probably like,' is an insult that no voter should tolerate.

With manifestos crafted to appeal to older voters in a handful of constituencies, it is no surprise that engagement is so poor amongst younger citizens. It has brought us to the point where the property market is impoverishing young people who see no electoral route out of a political landscape that explicitly disadvantages them.

The disengagement of younger voters has created a vacuum into which antidemocratic forces can step. Characters as disparate as Trump, Musk, Putin, MBS, and Xi Jinping all offer ways of doing things that barely pay lip service to public consent. The perception is that they can, unburdened of constitutional restraint, 'get things done' and that is a genuine lure for people who feel effectively disenfranchised by the political establishment.

So, the spectacle of Joe Biden trying to advocate for his own firmity this week is alarming. Biden has, to be fair, ushered in policies that chime with younger American voters. Forgiveness of student debt and investment in green technology are retail offers that cut through. If progressive America, though, must rely upon an octogenarian with obvious cognitive challenges to deliver these policies, it is in trouble. Politics is, by necessity, the cruellest human arena. Progressive ideals cannot be advocated for effectively by a politician who personifies decay. To allow this, risks associating necessary reforms with decline and obsolescence. In those circumstances, the overtures of hucksters gain credibility, and via them we submit to tyranny.

Democracy must not die of old age. We urgently need the emergence of young leaders who can articulate the requirements of government for the decades ahead. In that spirit, Joe Biden must stand down from the election. The personal is, indeed, political.

Do Something!
18 February 2024

Can you remember the last time a government did something that positively affected your life?

I bow to no man in my embittered disappointment at Tony Blair's period in office, but the minimum wage is, we must agree, an actual thing that exists in the life of the nation.

We put crosses in boxes and the upshot was that we knew the actual pittance that we could expect for rolling out of bed in the morning and resisting the temptation to learn Japanese or go fishing.

Since then, actual government action seems to have been limited to stopping people from doing things.

So, you'll feel the hand of government on you if you are protesting, or making comments online, or vaping, or going on strike, or driving, or marrying an overseas partner but that hand only arrests, it never propels us forward.

Politicians are fond of the term 'freedom'. They all claim to be the conduit through which it flows to us poor, enslaved grunts. In the 21st century, however, emphasis has shifted. We are offered freedom *from* all sorts of ills: terrorism, knife crime, racism, wokery, 'red tape', the license fee...

We are not promised the freedom *to* anything. It is as if governmental surrender to financial interests is so complete that even to suggest a positive, democratic change in how the country runs is to risk punishment.

Government has been reduced to a policing authority for those who benefit from the status quo. So, it's fine when restrictive, as described above, but oversteps its authority if it seeks to be proactive.

This isn't helped, of course, by the lamentable quality of the politicians we have. We have allowed Rishi Sunak and Jeremy Hunt to be installed by the markets as CEO and CFO of the UK without so much as an inquiry of the electorate.

Our quiescence towards this astonishingly undemocratic state of affairs flows from general acceptance that their predecessors, Truss and Kwarteng, were twp.

Now that we are in recession, we'll see just how hemmed in government has become. In election year, a Tory Prime Minister ought to be cutting taxes. It's as traditional as the Swingometer and pencils on strings. Having P45'd Mad Lizzie for doing just that, though, are the markets going to tolerate a futile vote-buying exercise by Rishi Sunak?

There is a world of difference, though, between being prevented from doing something stupid and being so cautious that you refuse to do anything at all. Sir Keir Starmer's reversal of Labour's commitment to invest in green technology is cautiousness stretched into absurdity.

The markets love capital investment. It's kind of what they do: look for what's going on in the world and try to back the best projects. Starmer, having been warned not to waste his pocket money on sweets, is now too frit to pay for his lunch.

There's not much we can all agree on politically, but I doubt anybody is going through their week in the UK thinking, *everything seems to be fine, let's just carry on as we are.*

The timidity of policy offers from the two main parties is jarringly at odds with the lived experience of everyone they represent. The markets have called time on Thatcherite economics, but Labour seems unable to grasp it. Can they even imagine such a development?

Reform UK, the current vessel for Nigel Farage Thought, is offering an increase to 20% in the Income Tax threshold. Now, that's a thing, isn't it? Actual money in your pocket is a pretty powerful lure. Independence for Wales and Scotland is also a thing, especially when nobody is offering to reform the UK at all.

The major parties need to offer something tangible or face extinction. It is a damning indictment of our system that they are

141

so insulated from the experience of voters that both parties should think continuity candidates make sense at this election.

Do something, fix the potholes, anything. If they don't someone else will.

A Westminster Farce

22 February 2024

I'm not generally so tragic as to watch several hours of Parliamentary procedure on the telly but I'm supposed to be finishing a book[1], so I was particularly open to diversionary activities yesterday. The SNP motion demanding a ceasefire in Gaza seemed to create a point of decision for MPs who might have been balancing the demands of constituents with the strictures of party loyalty. It was an opportunity for MPs to send a clear moral message, one way or the other, about a conflict that is preoccupying the world.

What unfolded in the chamber served, instead, to suggest that the UK is in no position to project ethical concerns within its borders, still less abroad.

As the debate approached, the Labour leadership was coming under intense pressure from MPs to commit to an immediate ceasefire. Many of them have protestors stationed outside their offices and homes every day and know that they face anger from previously loyal voters over this issue. The word 'immediate' is crucial as the standing Labour position privileged the term 'lasting'. Whilst a lasting ceasefire is undoubtedly a noble aspiration, insisting upon it suggested that stopping the bombing was subordinate to the conditions Israel demanded.

In the week before the vote, Australia, New Zealand and Canada put out a joint statement calling for an immediate ceasefire and, reportedly, the Labour leadership then felt more comfortable in calling for the same.

Yesterday was the SNP's 'Opposition Day' in Parliament. There are 20 of these per Parliamentary session, in which motions can be put forward by the opposition. The SNP has used

---

[1] Not this one. The other one is like pulling teeth.

two of its three days to demand a ceasefire in Gaza. Labour is allocated 17 Opposition Days.

Here is the text of the SNP motion:

I beg to move,

That this House calls for an immediate ceasefire in Gaza and Israel; notes with shock and distress that the death toll has now risen beyond 28,000, the vast majority of whom were women and children; further notes that there are currently 1.5 million Palestinians sheltering in Rafah, 610,000 of whom are children; also notes that they have nowhere else to go; condemns any military assault on what is now the largest refugee camp in the world; further calls for the immediate release of all hostages taken by Hamas and an end to the collective punishment of the Palestinian people; and recognises that the only way to stop the slaughter of innocent civilians is to press for a ceasefire now.

Our motion calls for an immediate ceasefire in Gaza, from all combatants. I wish to put on record, once again, our unequivocal condemnation of the Hamas attack of 7 October, and to repeat our call both for the immediate release of all the hostages and for seeing those involved in those atrocities called to account for their actions. The war in Gaza is one of the great defining moments of our time, yet, until today, this House has not been given the opportunity to debate both the unfolding human catastrophe and the wider implications for regional and global stability. Nor have we had the opportunity to debate the urgent and pressing need for an immediate ceasefire, as an essential first step in finding a lasting and just peace.

No one would deny that Israel has the right to defend itself—every country has that right. What no country has the right to do, however, is lay siege to a civilian population, carpet-bomb densely inhabited areas, drive people from their homes, erase an entire civilian infrastructure, and impose a collective punishment involving the cutting off of water, electricity, food, and medicine from civilians. And no country, regardless of who it is, can, in the name of self-defence, kill civilians at such a

144

pace, and on such a scale, that in just 16 weeks almost 30,000 are known to have died, with a further 80,000 injured. We cannot allow the core principle of self-defence to be so ruthlessly exploited and manipulated in order to legitimise the slaughter of innocent civilians. If we do that, what hope is there for the future of the international rules-based order, an order created to protect people from atrocities, not to be used as a smokescreen to hide the execution of them?

If we accept what Israel is doing in Gaza as the new norm—as the new accepted standard of self-defence—we undermine that core principle, which is meant to protect and defend us. Therefore we cannot accept that what is happening now is self-defence, because of the precedent that it will set. I have no doubt that that thought contributed to the United States issuing its clearest warning yet to Netanyahu that it would not support his proposed ground offensive in Rafah. This is why the UN Security Council is currently debating a ceasefire as we speak today, and even the US has recognised that a ceasefire must happen for a peaceful political solution. Of course, that does not go nearly far enough, but it does show that things are moving, opinions are changing and the guarantees that Israel has come to rely on are gradually withdrawing.

You'll note that the motion explicitly condemns the Hamas attacks, demands a ceasefire on all sides, and calls for the immediate release of all Israeli hostages. For Labour MPs, it would be difficult to explain voting against this motion and obeying the party whip, so a large rebellion was expected.

To head off the rebellion, Labour drafted an amendment calling for an immediate *humanitarian* ceasefire and omitting reference to the collective punishment of the Palestinian people. Its leadership hoped that this would be enough to persuade potential rebels away from the SNP motion, whilst keeping the party firmly within the Anglo-American consensus as regards suggestions of Israel committing war crimes. It also provided several caveats that required prior Israeli consent before the ceasefire became an active demand.

145

Before the debate, however, it became clear that the government intended to table its own, still weaker, amendment. The tradition is that government amendments have precedence over those from the opposition so the choice for MPs looked to be between the SNP motion and the government's amendment, with Labour's offering not brought forward.

Under those circumstances, it was inevitable that a large proportion of the PLP would defy the whip and vote for the SNP's notion.

Here is where things became murky. The Speaker, Labour's Sir Lindsay Hoyle announced that, breaking with precedent, *both* Labour's and the Government's motions would be attached to the order paper. Crucially, he stipulated that the Labour amendment would be voted upon first. This would allow Labour MPs to back their own watered-down amendment and still be able to claim they had backed an immediate ceasefire. The Speaker's decision was reportedly against the advice of his clerks.

Upon announcing this, the Speaker left the chamber which promptly descended into acrimonious chaos. The SNP were apoplectic that their Opposition Day had been hijacked by Labour, who insisted that a more nuanced alternative was necessary as MPs were subject to physical threats from outside parliament. *Newsnight*'s Nicholas Watt tweeted[2] that senior Labour figures had briefed him that Keir Starmer had threatened to remove the Speaker after the election if Labour's amendment was not included in the day's business and voted upon before the SNP motion.

In the end, the SNP and Government motions were pulled as MPs stormed out of the chamber. The Deputy Speaker, Dame Rosie Winterton, waved through the Labour motion without a vote, despite roars of objection.

So, where does this leave us. Firstly, the Conservative Party is no longer meaningfully governing the country. It was clear that yesterday's competing opposition policies defined the UK's

[2] https://twitter.com/nicholaswatt/status/1760315363542122769

attitude towards the Gaza conflict. The official Government is reduced to mounting spoiling campaigns that it cannot back up with public support or even reliable votes from its own party. It is the rotting corpse of a government.

Secondly, Sir Keir Starmer appears to be capable of limitless flexibility when comes to matters of policy, but none at all as regards the conscience of individual MPs. Labour had its own Opposition Days to put forward a ceasefire motion and failed so to do. Only when it became clear that its MPs intended to back the SNP did its position shift, and only then after the path was cleared by Australia, New Zealand, and Canada. Any notion of the party providing leadership internationally must be vanishingly slight.

Thirdly, as Liz Saville-Roberts rose to point out, the day's events illuminated the impotence of smaller parties within the Parliamentary system. Under our preposterous first-past-the-post voting arrangements, specific space has to be carved out for alternative viewpoints and yesterday saw this space colonised by Labour with no regard to the democratic implications.

Finally, an unwritten constitution demands the honourable goodwill of participants. This was shattered during the votes on Brexit, before being further weakened by Boris Johnson's disregard for process and legality. Yesterday, as the machine was put to the service of a grave international crisis, it choked and sputtered into silence. As 1.7 million people huddled in Rafah, wondering what the world would do for them in the coming days, our Parliament offered venal party interest, systemic dysfunction, and a void in leadership. Israeli commentators opined before the vote that the UK had no moral standing to offer its guidance. It is becoming harder by the day to disagree.

147

Wales Give Hope for the Future in Ireland Defeat

25 February 2024

The rain's been something this winter, hasn't it? Up my valley it's been sheeting horizontally since 2018, pouring in through the roofs of abandoned chapels as God howls in rebuke. Dogs refuse to walk, birds cannot fly, and the potholes contain marine life.

So, I thought I'd go to Cardiff to watch the game. Everyone knows that the Cardiff Bay elite vote themselves the best weather, so I might as well get my share.

Right enough, as I take up a perch in the garden of the Four Elms, warming sunshine pokes through the clouds. I've got my Cardiffian pal Tony with me. He's a man of few words, but awesome authority. Looking sagely around the lovely, bustling space, he narrows his eyes and looks at me seriously.

'It's getting busy.'

'Yes Tone, it is.'

The power of this Irish side was clear from the off. Betting correctly that they knew more about the dark arts of Six Nations rugby than debutant referee Andrea Piardi, Ireland took advantage of his naivety to gain supremacy at the breakdown and scrummage. Whilst often offside, and scrummaging illegally, there was no doubting that they outmuscled Wales in tight play, as they have everyone else they've encountered this term.

Camped in the 22, Wales tackled ferociously throughout the first half. Nick Tompkins made up for his poor game against England with characteristic hard work.

'Not bad,' Tony opines.

We're both on the Diet Coke, thanks to a variety of doctor-ordered strictures on the natural order of fun. Fetching our beakers of dismal from the bar at half-time, I look enviously at the two-pint buckets of ale everyone else is trying to carry back from the bar and take in the atmosphere. It's a blessing, and a wonder, that places like the Four Elms still exist. It's a proper boozer, beloved of all ages, and despite Wales' current woes on the pitch, you can rely on a lively time come matchday. Long may it prosper.

I approach the second half of every match with a lurch in my stomach. I couldn't attest to supporting statistics, but it seems like the first 10 minutes after the break do for us with depressing regularity. Not so this time. Cameron Winnett, bandaged up from a head wound, looks like the goods. He's always in the right place defensively and, on the counterattack, has the poise to beat defenders with ease.

Aaron Wainwright, meanwhile, chose today to come of age. Perennially the *Oh bugger, Talupe's injured again* second choice, he seized this tall order of a challenge with manic ferocity. A shock of blonde hair is a useful asset for a back row forward in a Lions year. Not only was he there at every ruck, harassing the Irish like a drunken wasp, but you couldn't mistake him for anyone else either. Like Scotland's John Jeffrey in the olden days, his platinum bonce bounced up and down the TV screen calling, 'Select me, select me!'

In the end, it was Wainwright whose drive for the line was held up, effectively ending the Welsh effort for the day. The scoreline didn't, however, reflect the team's dog and frequent skill. There was a period on 20 minutes that we might just have challenged for the win, but that would have been a historic upset in the context of both sides' development.

Come the next World Cup, most of this Irish side will be shuffling around Temple Bar with tartan shopping trolleys and packets of Werther's Original. Our boys, on the other hand, will have lost their pimples and gained four years of test experience to complement their skills and evident competitive spirit.

'What do you reckon, Tone?'

'It was a good game.'

'Any other observations?'
'No.'

Play Your Cards Right

25 February 2024

Did you know that Bruce Forsyth appeared in an episode of *Magnum PI*? The omnipresent, dodgy-syruped, 'didn't she do well', king of post-war light entertainment apparently had a stint presenting an American gameshow.

Quite how those credentials parlayed into suitability for the Honolulu version of Hetty Wainthrop Investigates is unknown, but there he is, demonstrating his range and versatility by portraying a British gameshow host in a sports jacket.

It's always jarring when you come across a British celebrity at the heart of US TV culture.

Whether its Christopher Hitchens or Cat Deeley, the UK viewer can see the grasping lust for riches in their eyes as they allow themselves to be denuded of nuance and irony, the better to reach bovine, corndog-dribbling residents of Chickenshit, Idaho.

'Here's a message from our sponsors,' they beam, as the self-deprecating charm that made their names is fed through a commercial meatgrinder, never to return.

UK politicians have rarely made the transition, for reasons which should be readily apparent.

Mark Drakeford's World of Cheese, for instance, never made it past a pilot shown by HBO in the Milwaukee metro area.

Similarly, *Point Blanket*, a vengeance thriller starring Clint Eastwood and Andrew RT Davies, remains bogged down in the development process.

Recently, however, we have the merging of light entertainment with politics. GB News and Talk TV have repackaged UK politicians as presenters, teaching them the dark arts of faux-sincerity and authoritative presence required by that discipline.

Resultingly, our most ethically bankrupt, brazen hucksters have emerged from the sludge of UK politics sporting Philip Schofield grins, and Richard Madeley suits.

Equipped with these tools, people who would have previously been mumbling about 'taking our country back' to half a dozen inadequates in the upstairs of a pub, are now bouncing fascism off satellites into the homes of thousands of voters.

Lee Anderson broadcasted on Friday night that 'Islamists' have seized 'control' of London and its mayor, Sadiq Khan.

He has been suspended from the Conservative Party but may well have calculated that his prospects are better without it. Being fired puts distance between him and a failing Establishment.

We don't yet know how many mouth-breathing degenerates there are in the UK who are persuaded by this rhetoric. The reflexive response of reasonable people is to dismiss him as a grotesque.

These loss-making channels are being funded for a reason, though, and much as we might smile seraphically through our macchiatos at their antics, we should be vigilant.

The daddy of UK populism showed last night just how far this sort of schtick can take you.

Those of you who remember Nigel Farage for his performance in the car park at Trago Mills in Merthyr, might be surprised to learn that he is now bestriding the US political scene like the offspring of Colossus and Mr Toad.

Last night, at the horrifyingly influential C-Pac gathering of all that's successfully repugnant in American politics, Farage gave a lengthy address that sought to position him as the spiritual father of a movement that encompasses Donald Trump, Orban in Hungary, Le Pen in France, Meloni in Italy, and Eamonn Holmes.

He had, America learned, 'stood alone' as a defender of the nation state before politics swung in his direction. He was John the Baptist to Trump's Messiah, the *Byker Grove* to his *Saturday*

152

Night Takeaway.

Following populist technique, Farage started with a lengthy exposition about his persecution at the hands of Coutts Bank. 'It's the grievance, stupid', as the political maxim goes.

He knows his place, though. He climaxed his peroration by declaring that the world 'needs' a Trump victory in November. His reasoning for this echoed 30p Lee: London has been captured by Islam.

Earlier in the day, Liz Truss had tried out her Maggie impersonation on the insurrection-monkeys, having been sat next to their chief puppeteer, Steve Bannon.

According to her, it was 'the deep state' that had derailed her premiership. Coutts and the bond market are now, we are given to understand, staffed by dangerous socialists.

The media landscape is providing an instantaneous route to global influence for risible chancers who, hitherto, could be dismissed as a sideshow.

They are funded, networked, and coordinated in a way that principled politicians cannot match. The skills they employ are blunt but effective.

A gameshow host as president has bequeathed us a gameshow political world and the prize is beyond imagination.

The Emptiness Within

29 February 2024

I spend the majority of my working life working with addicts and, for full disclosure, have been one myself.

Addiction remains a misunderstood facet of life. Media distortion of the issue means that general perception of it is wildly at odds with the reality known to addicts, those who love them, and professionals in the field.

In particular, the media often frames addiction as the cause of a person's ills when, in 100% of cases I have known, it is a pernicious symptom of them.

For people in the orbit of addiction, the most frustrating aspect of it is dishonesty. The substance is never to blame, even in the face of overwhelming evidence, an addict will twist and turn in contradiction so that continued use is not threatened.

If you are around this sort of behaviour a lot, it ceases to look like immorality. The ethical choices we all make from moment to moment are overridden by the warping, insistent need that an addict experiences. You learn when to make allowances and when to draw a line.

The patterns of addictive behaviour are depressingly predictable. They permeate the systems of a person's life like a weed, relentlessly strangling each one.

Every day, the addiction advances and the person retreats before it, continuing to deny the obvious. In the short-term, immediate risks can be managed but long-term prospects are a zero-sum trade-off between stopping and premature death.

When I read about Liz Saville Roberts' plea that Rishi Sunak sign Full Fact's pledge to campaign honestly, I could well imagine the despair she feels. During the abortive SNP debate on Gaza the other week, her principled distress at what she was witnessing shone through on a day that shamed the UK.

In asking for honesty from the Tory Party, however, she's

underestimating the mess it is in. This, potentially final, version of it is gripped by an addiction to magical thinking that means dishonesty is an essential component of its day-to-day survival.

One could mount a case that this is the final unfolding of the Thatcherite delusion, but that's for another time.

This 2019-2024 term of Torydom had unique impossibilities baked into it from the off.

It is no longer controversial to accept that Brexit was, at best, a reckless pipe dream, and at worst a deliberate confidence trick. The relentless flow of disinformation and contradictory nonsense that has been inflicted on the UK to conceal the idiocy of attempting to revive island state sensibilities in a world that works globally has distorted politics.

Those who *wanted* it to work have indulged jingoistic, wishful thinking without scrutiny, and that has offered lightweight politicians the temptation they can't resist: impunity.

So, direct from arguing this visibly impoverished island is basking in sunlit opportunity, elements in the Tory Party went on to downplay Covid, minimise climate change, and pretend that the pensions of an ageing society can be paid without immigrant labour.

They have invoked phantom 'woke' threats to distract from their deficiencies and agitated at every societal faultline to displace anger.

This government was founded on a lie, has survived by lies, and is now drowning in them.

Rishi Sunak might as well sign Ms Saville Roberts' pledge, nobody would believe him anyway.

Behind the bluster, evasion, theft, and brass-necked audacity of this regime lies the uncomfortable truth that every addict must face: the emptiness within.

You Are the Mob

3 March 2024

Watching the political establishment's shock at George Galloway's election in Rochdale was revelatory of its detachment from life as we live it.

Rishi Sunak rushed out to his lectern to warn us we are sliding into mob rule. Now first off, Rishi, the only lectern-issued warning we're after from you is that we're having a general election. Your mandate-free cuckooing of Downing Street disqualifies you from lecturing us on democracy. Stop it, it's silly. Additionally, your first act as Prime Minister was to reappoint the bomb-throwing bigot fluffer, Suella Braverman as Home Secretary. You weren't so worried about inflaming mobs then, were you? Your political output since clambering out of Boris Johnson's codpiece has consisted solely of hare-brained deportation schemes pandering to the paranoid, racist imaginings of potential Reform UK voters. If dogs were uniquely able to detect the frequency of dilettante tech-bros harnessing xenophobia to distract from their personal incompetence, Pets at Home would sell you as a whistle.

It's not *his* cultivated mob we're supposed to be frightened of though, is it? Aside from some passing mentions of the 'far right', Sunak's violent multitude is the same as Braverman's: people who oppose Israeli action in Gaza.

Sir Keir Starmer, as we have come to expect, agreed with the Prime Minister's intervention. For a brief moment last week, he allowed Labour policy on Gaza to diverge slightly from the official government line; so slightly, in fact, that the government allowed it to pass into law in the Commons. Until that point neither Labour nor the Conservatives was prepared to back an immediate ceasefire, despite polls indicating that 66% of the public were in favour, not only of a halt in fighting but that Israel should enter into negotiations with Hamas.[1]

So, how exactly is a majority view to find political expression if both parties in a *de facto* two-party state refuse to reflect it? If people opt for peaceful demonstrations, they can expect to be condemned as 'hate marchers'. Now, it seems, the election of an MP to advance the case is somehow evidence of antidemocratic intentions.

There is plenty to find distasteful about George Galloway. From the minimising of rape accusations against Julian Assange, to his dismissal of independence for Scotland and Wales, he has outraged many on the left for years. He is vain, a self-publicist and a man who keeps highly questionable company.

Anybody who saw his performance in the US Congressional hearings on the Iraq war, however, will not doubt the sincerity of his position on foreign affairs. In standing virtually alone against that illegal catastrophe which claimed the lives of 300,000 Iraqi civilians at a conservative estimate, he earned credibility that has endured.

If Galloway is an opportunist, then it is Labour who have gifted him an opportunity. Its failure to run a candidate in Rochdale should be ringing alarms as to its fitness to govern the country. Its original candidate, Azhar Ali, was a Starmer loyalist. When newspapers reported his antisemitic remarks, he was initially backed to remain in place. Only when further remarks were reported did Starmer withdraw support. Contrast this with the treatment of Andy McDonald MP, who is from the left of the party. He was immediately suspended after hoping in October that, '…Israelis and Palestinians, between the river and the sea can live in peaceful liberty.'

Mr Ali opined that Israel, 'deliberately took the security off, they allowed... that massacre that gives them the green light to do whatever they bloody want.'

Anybody watching the suffering of Gazans, particularly if

[1] https://yougov.co.uk/politics/articles/48675-british-attitudes-to-the-israel-gaza-conflict-february-2024-update

157

they have access to *Al Jazeera*'s footage from within the strip, will form a certain moral position, one way or the other. The response of the UK parliament has been confused, contradictory, evasive, and dishonest.

Put simply, if 66% of people in a democracy oppose the government's position, the opposition has an obligation to reflect that view. George Galloway arrives in parliament next week because, if nothing else, he knows how to do politics. Venal self-interest is hardly new amongst the political class. The job of a politician is to wed the desires of the public to his or her own fortunes. Neither Sunak nor Starmer has the political skill to persuade. Sunak relies on distraction, Starmer on repression. If they do not learn, then independent candidates will become a potent force across the UK and the two-party system will tremble. Plaid Cymru, the Green Party, and the SNP should be on alert. In these circumstances, the ball can squirt out of the back of the scrum in a host of constituencies. Galloway, Nigel Farage, and even Lee Anderson will be waiting to scoop it up if radical Britain doesn't up its game.[2]

---

[2] Does it even have a game?

Red Box Blues

7 March 2024

The snooker player Steve Davis was once asked about the animosity he had been subject to from Alex 'Hurricane' Higgins.

'Let me stop you there,' he interrupted. 'I owe my life to Alex; I won't hear a word against him.'

'Really?' the interviewer gasped.

'Yes, I was leaving the theatre after a match and three men set upon me in the alley. They were kicking me to pieces and if Alex hadn't come along and said, "That's enough, boys," I'm not sure I'd have survived.'

That was pretty much the scenario today in the Commons as Jeremy 'Interesting' Hunt gifted us all another National Insurance cut, out of the goodness of his heart.

You'll be shocked to learn that this pre-election magnanimity comes with some small print. Whilst we will all be cashed-up next month – I'll be spending mine on the world's most expensive commodity: olive oil – frozen tax thresholds mean that the deal would shame a Benidorm timeshare salesman. Essentially, it will feel slightly better until the election, and then Mrs W. will be back to cooking with axle grease I've scraped off the neighbour's car.

What I like about election giveaways is how we, the great unwashed, suddenly become 'hardworking Brits' who deserve a treat. Previously work-shy, unproductive extremists, we're now the apple of the government's eye. We should 'keep more of our own money', apparently, perhaps to spend on private healthcare. Because, frustratingly, having an election does not, as you might infer from today's proceedings, automatically refund public services to functionality.

Hunt, apparently, went for a 17-mile run this morning to warm up for his speech. Are there people who are impressed by this sort of caper? When Chancellors of old used to lean, exhausted, against the despatch box swigging on whisky, it projected the appropriate air of post-imperial degeneracy. They knew we were finished, we knew it, and the optics told us what to expect. Attempting to inhabit a go-getting persona in the ruins of the UK as it is now looks faintly ludicrous. Trying to come off like the mutant offspring of Rimmer off *Red Dwarf* and Paula Radcliffe would be awkward at the best of times, but when your budget includes explicit bribes for pension funds to invest in the country you've been running for the last 14 years it's, frankly, tragic.

The government, as a whole, has reached divorced-dad depths of ingratiating desperation.

'Daddy...'

'Yes, my darling Electorate...'

'Mam's new boyfriend is going to abolish non-dom tax status and use the money to fund the NHS.'

'Is he, now? Well, how about your *real* dad abolishes it and gets you a PlayStation?'

Mind you, imagine being introduced to Keir Starmer as your new stepdad. I've just injured myself shuddering.

I bang on a lot about democracy being under threat[1], reason being that we seem to be relinquishing it so meekly. If politicians want to persist as a thing, then announcing frivolous and misleading tax cuts to a soundtrack of braying nonentities isn't helping their case. Do you imagine the investment funds that called time on Kwasi Kwarteng's plans present their own budgets in a package that includes crap jokes and ham-fisted bribes? We'd be forgiven for wondering if we'd be better off cutting out the middlemen and handing governance to our masters directly.

I listened to the budget in the car, after failing to persuade a young man with ADHD and post-traumatic stress that he should wait 10 hours in A&E to have his head injury scanned.

---

[1] At home too. It's my love language.

He wasn't having it; just gave up on the system and went home.

Nothing Left to Steal
10 March 2024

The death of the Tory party has been a drawn-out and undignified process. The wrecking ball that Margaret Thatcher sent crashing through society has swung back towards the party with karmic inevitability. The short-term planning, the economic fantasies, the greed, the tolerance of corruption, the cruelty, and jingoistic refusal to face up to Britain's place in the world have caught up with the Conservatives at last. We'll be rid of them soon, quite possibly for good.

This week, Theresa May announced her retirement, and it was telling that people saw her as a remnant of a more decent age. How quickly our villains are washed clean by the sins of their successors. May was the author of the 'hostile environment' and the devastation it wreaked upon the lives of so many from the Windrush generation. She bribed the DUP to support her doomed Brexit deal; hers was the first government to be found in contempt of parliament. You could pinpoint the moment of Tory demise to be May's conference speech in 2017. Through a hacking cough, she tried to restore her personal standing as the letters fell off the slogan behind her and a comedian handed her a P45.

If the party possessed dignity, it would have sloped off to the potting shed with a revolver that very afternoon, but it's not in the nature of the beast. Since then, it has abandoned the pretence of government altogether in favour of ransacking the deceased's personal effects before the creditors arrive.

May is the latest in a long line of departed Tories at whom centrist dads look wistfully, insisting that *decent* conservatism is a thing. Ken Clarke, Nicholas Soames, Douglas Hurd etc. carried echoes of pre-Thatcher Toryism: a seemingly benign, paternalistic stewardship that had its roots in feudalism. There are a still a few who try on those clothes: the comically earnest

162

ex-Security Minister Tom Tugendhat did a fair imitation.

Since the financial crash of 2008, though, there's been no disguising what the modern Conservative Party is: a vehicle through which people make money. All the ideological talk of self-reliance, individualism, and small government was exposed when George Osborne extorted the British public to ensure that *de facto* bankruptcy of financial institutions didn't interfere with the lifestyles of those responsible for them. We weren't treated to the story of Norman Tebbit's father getting on his bike and recapitalising his bank from private sources, nor were bankers directed to conform to Thatcher's 'thrifty housewife' economics when their cupboards were bare. Profit is private, loss is public.

The past forty years have seen virtually every UK asset hoovered up by private capital and ruthlessly monetised. The list of services we can no longer afford is now indivisible from the list of services we need to run as a functional nation state. The idea that the suffering inherent to this was in the service of some sunlit, libertarian future is the confidence trick of our age. We used to own things, now we don't. It really is that simple. Find the lady...

As another Miners' Strike anniversary passes, its significance only swells in the wreckage of what was to come. We've been severed from each other and individualised into powerless units. Every Prime Minister since then has supported an economic system that has unpicked our social fabric before flogging off the threads. Every short-term, venal financial decision they have made is playing out as starved public services go into endemic decline. The dynamic individualism of the 1980s has petered out into a lonely, frightening old age.

The Tory Party is dying because there is nothing left to steal.

Home Sweet Home

11 March 2024

According to psychologists, our brains can create contentment from vanishingly scarce resources. If we are incarcerated in a room with nothing to distract us from our misery than a small skylight, we will become fascinated with the passing of the clouds. So, actually boarding a train to Cardiff from the Rhondda, after 200 years of rail replacement buses triggered every happy chemical that my brain has at its disposal. Seriously, it was like passing my driving test on VE Day. Just mint.

The company was commensurately superb. The couple next to us had just completed a tour of eastern England in a decommissioned NHS ambulance that they had fitted out as a camper and named 'Aneurin Be-Van'. Now, you can get as sniffy as you like about the status of puns in the comedic arsenal, but the perfection of that silences everything. Be in awe.

Cardiff was amiable. Is it me, or has it calmed down since the pandemic? It had the air of a soft play facility, when, in days gone by, you could count on it to spin you round on match days.

Even before the game the event was kept afloat by the thousands of French people who knew how to enjoy themselves. I headed for the Bluebell, previously the Goat Major, because the last time I had tickets to see France it was patronised by a club from Biarritz whose members handed out sausages and moonshine to everyone before marching round the bar singing 'Death to Spain!' This year, the fancy dress was the most notable feature, with special accolades to the musketeers.

The anthems in the Principality were as great as you'd hope, but even then, right at the start, the energy was with the French. Even the most one-eyed amongst us knew, if we were honest, that beating France today would require one of those insane Six Nations upsets. It was possible, but highly unlikely.

So, when Wales went into the lead early on and then scored just after half-time, it was more than we had the right to expect. Our team is, as acres of reportage will describe, inexperienced, underpowered, mismanaged, and the product of a failed system. They are, though, furiously committed to their game. They leapt on every scarce opportunity and made this a real contest until 60 minutes passed and the intensity could not be maintained. Their defence in the face of skilled opposition was at times miraculous.

When the crux of the game arrived, halfway through the second half, and it became a matter of will, fitness and destiny, the French supporters shamed Wales. I never thought I would live to see international rugby in Cardiff at which the only Welsh singing had to be provoked by the WRU pumping 'Hymns & Arias' through the PA. All around me, French supporters were filling the Cardiff air with 'La Marseillaise' and urging their side to victory. In response we had a few desultory 'Wayulls' chants and an endless stream of disinterested customers returning from the bar with drinks.

This won't do. It's no good whining about the health of the game if, when push comes to shove, we can't muster enough passion to make Cardiff feel like a home fixture for the team. We're in danger of losing more than games here, what on earth has happened to us?

Abused & Silenced

14 March 2024

It's long been my practice on social media to block anyone I see abusing Diane Abbott. As a guide to character, the way people react to her is an infallible test. Because we all *know* that she's routinely abused, don't we? Her appearance, intelligence, and integrity are dragged through the sludge on Facebook and X for anyone to see. It's not unusual to hear her denigrated in real life, either. Bottom-feeders all over the UK sense that the usual social constraints on their repugnant utterances have somehow been lifted when it comes to Ms Abbott.

We remember all this from school. The hollow, spindly-souled bully's mates who viewed weakness and isolation as an invitation to terrorise. They didn't all grow up, it seems.

There's no point arguing with them. Like a pigeon playing chess, they shit all over the board and then claim they've won. Every disputable thing Ms Abbott has ever said about race is held up as evidence of anti-white racism; an offence, they imagine, that justifies their hatred.

Ms Abbott receives more abuse online and in the post than the other 649 MPs *combined.* As the first female, black MP she sat literally alone through the early part of her parliamentary career. On matters of race, she is admirably uncompromising and her early advocacy for meaningful anti-racist practice in British life was necessary and prescient. Much that she championed is now standard in organisations across the country. If her statements were sometimes problematic, then good! The UK, in all its post-imperial denial was long overdue a voice that cared less for its fragility than its dignity. It's a mug's game predicting anything in a failed state, but I'd bet long that history will treat Ms Abbott far more kindly than to which she must, sadly, have grown accustomed.

Her prospects are certainly rosier than anyone's inside the

Conservative Party. It now seems to have arrived at the bowel-evacuation stage of active dying, and nobody seems keen to mop up after it any more. Watching Secretary of State for Work & Pensions, Mel Stride, attempt to order the nation to 'move on' from Frank Hester's comments about Ms Abbott was to witness King Canute resurrected. Move on? If anyone's 'moving on', it's your lot, pal.

The lack of ethics or personal morality is a given, we're used to it. What continues to astound in Sunak's party is the staggering incompetence. Hester's remarks were so overtly racist, and so shocking in their violence it is baffling how professional politicians could not see the catastrophic results of failing to exclude him and his money from their party. One after another appeared on camera to say that the remarks were 'wrong' but refuse to call them racist. Even the quietly racist voters they imagine might support them like an element of deniability to their racism. How many people do they think approve of exhortations to kill?

Enough, it seems, to grub a few votes from Reform UK and keep some of them in parliament. In terms of the wider electorate, they've plainly given up. It makes you wonder what they need Frank Hester's millions for.

Lest we imagine that dysfunction ends at the Tory wake, the Speaker Lindsay Hoyle relied on his now familiar political instincts to refuse Ms Abbott an opportunity to speak at today's PMQs. Fresh from shutting down the SNP on Gaza the other week, today he failed to platform Ms Abbott when democracy demanded that she, and particularly she, be heard. The absence of her voice this afternoon was palpable.

Her reaction to Hester's remarks was a reminder of the very human impact of behaviour like his. She admitted to being 'frightened' and pointed out that she was single, underscoring her vulnerability. It is shameful that our politics are conducted in an atmosphere so toxic that she should have to remind colleagues of her very humanity.

Election time is when politicians become interested in us. If racism forms a part of any party's appeal to voters, we need

167

to object immediately and loudly. It is an encroaching menace that we must confront without hesitation.

Wales v Italy: Here we Goa again
16 March 2024

Having been at the stadium to witness Wales capitulating to France and, more depressingly, our supporters be shamed into whimpering submission, it was tempting not to bother this week. I reckon I'm the most irritatingly positive silver-lining chaser in the Welsh rugby media, possibly in Wales full-stop. 'It's a young team, there are encouraging signs, Gatland knows what he's doing etc etc etc.'

So, when the opportunity came up to go to India, I'll admit it was tempting. Temperatures in Goa are currently averaging in the mid-30s whilst, in Porth, it has been raining since the late Middle Ages.

I was reminded, however, that mine is a rare calling. I am, as Andrew RT Davies never tires of reminding me, partly funded by, and thus in the pocket of the Welsh Government. So, not being wet and cold until the bitter end of the most depressing Six Nations since the bitter end of the last most depressing Six Nations would be an abrogation of duty.

Fortunately, my disappointment coincided with the surprise opening of a new Bracchi Shop in Tylorstown. The Royal Italy is set on a charming, winding lane flanked by coconut trees, just off the old road to Pontygwaith. It is conveniently served by a reliable Wi-Fi connection and, bless them, air conditioning.

So, with the final game being against Italy, it made all sorts of sense to cancel our travel plans and watch the Welsh renaissance there.

I'd assumed that being amongst Italian fans would be a triumphant experience. I've previously enjoyed smiling beneficently at them and emphasising how well their team has done under an onslaught of steely, Welsh professionalism. Before the game, enjoying a traditional Italian masala chai, I was reassured by an interview with Warren Gatland in which he underscored that playing for the Wooden Spoon was, in fact, the pinnacle of sporting achievement. Not resembling Joe Biden whatsoever, he offered a weak smile in the face of providence, before shuffling off to observe the wages of his senility.

But, ferchrissakesmun WTF was that? In the unusually furnace-like heat of Tylorstown, it became impossible to paint *this* loss to Italy as anything else but deserved. I wanted, initially, to blame things on the ref, whose red-hot whistle seemed only tuned to Welsh transgressions. As the game went on, though, and every possible moment of opportunity was squandered in fumbling, adolescent incompetence, his authority evaporated for good. Yes, there are structural problems, yes the team is young, but you're on a blydi fortune Warren, and we expect to beat Italy as a bare minimum. When George North was carted off at the end like Boxer in *Animal Farm* I choked on my samosa.

In the tuk-tuk back to Ynyshir, the mood was dark. I don't go all the way to Tylorstown for this sort of outcome. Yes, Wales broke my heart yet again today, but at least I saw a monkey in Wattstown.

Sham, Sham, Shame

17 March 2024

So, we're all First-Ministered up again and without any tiresome obligation to choose anyone ourselves.

On this occasion, even Labour Party members weren't burdened with too much responsibility as, it seems, their individual votes aren't even worthy of reporting.

In a perverse reflection of Thatcherism, the unions really do run Labour Wales, but nowadays without any troublesome pretensions towards the Socialism that birthed them.

In the UK, we have a Prime Minister with no public mandate, and First Ministers in both Wales and Scotland likewise. If anybody out there is a genuine enthusiast for Vaughan Gething, I encourage you to comment on this column.

I ask this because I move in extremely varied circles yet have never once met anybody who expressed any enthusiasm whatsoever for the man who is now our leader on the world stage.

Our own Martin Shipton has clearly explained the gerrymandered and dubiously funded route to power that Gething has taken. In his superb articles over the last few weeks, Martin has sounded a clear alarm that democracy is being subverted in Wales.

Our Senedd, a young and precious institution that many people fought and suffered their whole lives to bring about has been reduced to a political sham by the events of the last couple of months.

My general line here has been supportive of Mark Drakeford. I felt that he projected an air of decency that reflected the values of Wales at a time when such was receding rapidly in London.

He positioned us to the left of UK Labour and whilst a unionist himself, seemed to believe in the singularity of Wales as a nation.

His exit, however, has been a whimpering surrender to corporate politics that I cannot stomach and which, I fear, will shortly bring turmoil to Wales.

If democracy becomes a process done to the people instead of by them it will die as an ethos in the hearts of those it is supposed to serve.

I ask again, who in this country has ever asked for Vaughan Gething or Rishi Sunak to have the remotest influence over the way we live our lives? From what wellspring of public support do they sustain their positions? For which of us do they speak?

Like many of you, I was brought up to be Labour – anything else would have been an anathema to my displaced Rhondda family, even in the patchwork political environment of the West Midlands to which they emigrated.

This Labour Party of Starmer and Gething strikes none of the notes that I grew up with.

Nothing that they say seems rooted in the values that made me or anybody else I know from that tradition.

In place of community and compassion, I am being sold yet more austerity, private capitalisation of public matters, and hostility towards the least fortunate members of a society that has already been stripped to the bone by Tories, Blairites, and Tories again.

When Jeremy Corbyn and John McDonnell suggested a modest adjustment leftwards, similar to governance in Scandinavia, initial enthusiasm from the electorate was overwhelmed by a media onslaught against them that suggested people were morally compelled to reject them.

Corbyn, in particular, has become a media byword for failure and bigotry. His ostensible crime was to suggest that Israel's position on Palestine was indefensible. How has that worked out?

Labour can whistle for my vote, in the Senedd and in Westminster. I'm done with them, not despite the attachment to political values I was brought up with, but because of them.

Plaid Cymru need to wake up to their opportunity here.

If they do not seize the moment and reject their agreement with Labour then the sweaty advances of Farage, Anderson and all those ghouls will take root.

Nature abhors a vacuum.

Why Aren't You Screaming?

21 March 2024

For a couple of hours last night, we were treated to an amateur dramatics performance of what democracy might look like in a society that still cared about it. Rhun ap Iowerth was put forward by Plaid Cymru as an alternative First Minister. The 'party of Wales' duly ticked their oppositional box without, of course, threatening to tear up their agreement with Labour. Meanwhile, Andrew RT Davies's Tories offered their toxic support to Vaughan Gething on condition that he acquiesce to their talking points: the 20mph limit and reversing expansion of the Senedd. Finally, word emerged of meetings between Labour MSs who were disquieted by the patently irregular funding of Gething's campaign. What turmoil! How fortunate we are to live in a vibrant democracy!

What tosh.

Eventually, of course, it split perfectly on party lines. The self-interest of every single member of our legislative chamber was untouched by today's proceedings, whilst the living standards in every city, town, and village here decline.

A few days ago, I asked if anyone out there had a positive enthusiasm for Vaughan Gething as FM. None was forthcoming, despite the thousands of words written in response to the article. I have no clue what new policies he has in mind, do you?

What I do know is that months ago he was being profiled in the *Guardian* as the coming man in Welsh politics. His appointment has had an air of inevitability utterly at odds with his anonymity amongst the general public, and the alarm felt by people who have followed his career closely.

Projecting forwards, Wales seems to be a stalking horse for the Starmer government to come. Nobody in the UK has the remotest enthusiasm for them either but the unhinged cruelty and economic vandalism of the Conservative Party renders them unelectable.

Over the last couple of days, we have heard both Rachel Reeves and then David Lammy express their admiration for Margaret Thatcher. The economic assumptions of the last 40 years have laid waste to much of Welsh civic society. Our living standards have been sacrificed on the altar of kleptomaniac economics as our values have been ridiculed and our culture denuded. Starting with 'Lord' Neil Kinnock and progressing through Tony Blair's subversion of the Labour movement, we have arrived, finally, at the point where all that is left of it is the name. How, I beg you, can a party of labour in Wales possibly align with people in England who admire Thatcher? Were the people she deprived of a livelihood, of the dignity of work, somehow undeserving of their representation? For shame.

This is a pantomime, a shadow play that bears no relation to the lives we are pursuing as citizens. Wales and the UK requires urgent revitalisation that can only come from capital investment in infrastructure and the retraining of our people. Austerity is a blatant confidence trick that concentrates wealth in the hands of those who already have it. If Labour seeks to perpetuate this crime which, historically, has disadvantaged Wales more egregiously than anywhere except the North East of England, then Plaid Cymru needs to sever their agreement forthwith.

Keir Starmer's Labour Party is explicit in its intention to involve private capital in the NHS. It has set its face against the opinion of the nation over Palestine; it is an overtly Thatcherite entity that has rejected further devolution for Wales.

Your new First Minister has been elected against the chuckles of pseudo-opposition by politicians who do not face the day-to-day struggles that are consuming everyone who visits A&E, drives on a pot-holed road, or tries to ensure an adequate education for their child. You've never voted for him and nobody has mounted a serious opposition to his questionable ascent. Why aren't you screaming?

England, My England
24 March 2024

You'd think that the English would be delighted that someone had spiffed up their flag a bit.

Throughout the seemingly endless years that I was imprisoned there, smiling weakly at Ant & Dec as they represented the only culture on offer, I felt that the flag of St George only made things worse.

Fluttering above the certainties and repressed emotions of its subjects, the symbol reduced even us to something generally utilised by the illiterate in place of a signature. It is the heraldic expression of Phil Mitchell's face. Red crassness daubed on nothing.

So, I suppose, Nike's kindness in lending the thing some nuance was always going to enrage the sort of person who identifies with it.

It's only recently that these people have come to terms with garlic as an acceptable component in seafood dishes, so cut them some slack.

But that's enough about the entirely fictional English folk described in the gutter press and played to by politicians who wouldn't know a real human being if they bumped into them at a war crimes trial.

The 'English' of mass culture are as imaginary as the 'Welsh', 'Scottish', 'Irish', 'Jewish', 'Muslim', 'Palestinian', and 'Gypsy' people caricatured there.

They are cyphers: empty canvasses for the people who own dishonest media outlets to paint prejudices upon.

I was born in England to a mixed-race Welsh mother and Romany father, then adopted by another Welsh mother and English father, but have lived for the last decade in Wales, which I consider to be my home.

How does a flag cover that?

I claim the Welsh flag because I *want* to, it's the bit of my makeup that pleases me and represents the place I choose to live.

I don't want to kill anyone for it, unless strictly necessary, and I wouldn't drape myself in it to make anyone feel unwelcome where I live.

Nobody's done that to me either, although my Heinz 57 genetics and personal history make me vulnerable to it if you want to have a go. Please don't, I love this place as much as you.

All around the world, people are being thrown back on to base instincts by a poisonous political culture. Our true identities are formed by family, art, religion if you choose, and personal preference.

They are complex, beautiful expressions of the human miracle.

We fall in love with each other because of them and create other humans with differing, crystalline features. Perhaps we don't and explore the universe on our own terms for as long as we can.

Obviously, the Welsh flag is the best. Its colours are sublime, and it has a dragon on it. Nothing can compete with that. Ditto the anthem: the French one is okay, but the rest inspire pity. None of these things contain us, though. Our singularity cannot be governed by symbols.

Our flags serve us, not us them.

The politics of 2024 are vile. I don't see anyone I know represented in the divisive, dreadful manipulation of identity that is engulfing everywhere from Pontyclun to Ramallah.

A flag is a flag, my brother is my brother. A nation is a nation, my sister is my sister.

The Cracks are Showing

1 April 2024

Since the financial crash of 2008, there has been a constant suspicion that something cataclysmic was in the works for the UK, and the Western world more generally. Prior to that event, we were all conditioned to believe that money was a finite resource: something that could only be grown by the application of prudence (Hello Gordon!) and entrepreneurial talent (Hi Maggie!).

So, when the entrepreneurial instincts of Wall Street blew up the global financial system, it came as a surprise to many that the 'prudent' solution was to print money as fast as we could and hand it directly to the reckless bastards who had caused the problem. *This can't be right,* we thought. We've been told our entire lives that requesting so much as a copy of *Oliver Twist* for the local library will bring down the wrath of the Beadle upon our feckless heads.

And we were right. George Osborne soon appeared in our lives to explain that asking for more gruel was entirely out of the question now that we'd wasted all our cash on bailing out the banks. 'Austerity' is a loaded term in the UK. Both Labour and the Conservatives used it to describe economic conditions after the war when, coincidentally, our pals on Wall Street decided that rebuilding Germany was a better economic bet than helping the Sceptred Isle. The term evokes a sense of moral duty, of sacrifice for the greater good. Accordingly, sufficient voters were persuaded to abandon their own interests in service of better times to come.

Only they didn't come, did they? When Osborne's fiscal rules rendered public services unaffordable to central government and local authorities, they were farmed out to hastily thrown-together private interests who charged more and delivered less. The same workers were put on worse contracts and driven harder for decreasing rewards. Salaries shrank and assets rocketed as the wealthy entrenched their advantage.

The ultimate in Harold Macmillan's 'Events, dear boy,' was the pandemic. Here, the veil was finally stripped away from the kleptocratic instincts of UK governance as, for a second time, the Bank of England's printing presses went into overtime. The 'magic money tree', it turned out, did exist. A nation that a year previously had recoiled in horror at Labour's suggestion of free broadband was now handed 80% of its wages for making banana bread and clapping the NHS once a week. Billions disappeared on PPE and track and trace, the same companies swelled their coffers and not a single penny was invested in the future.

Sadly, we are now in 'the future'. The failure to invest in services, infrastructure, training, defence, or basic levels of welfare for the disadvantaged is playing out in a wave of national discontent that is erupting through the many and varied cracks in our society. Racism, authoritarianism, toxic nationalism, and overt fascism are now commonplace in public spaces.

Yet, it seems, no political party is willing to take on the vested interests of finance and invest in the country. We have seen, twice, that raising capital is not a problem for a 'sovereign' nation. It is, in fact, what being sovereign means. After the endless parroting of that word by Brexit enthusiasts, it is baffling that none of them seem keen on exercising sovereign powers for anything other than private enrichment.

Wales has a tradition of voting Labour[1]; history is clear on that. Labour, though, in the imagination of most people is a radical force. The milquetoast quivering of Keir Starmer's party, which is seemingly reflected in the careerist advance of Vaughan Gething is anything but radical. The UK, and Wales in particular, is in urgent need of radical reform if it is not to become an unliveable dystopia where health, education, and transport are brakes on the happiness of its citizens.

---

[1] Ben Wildsmith: specialised subject, the bleedin' obvious.

I believe in the radical tradition in Wales, it is a real thing that has brought change on a global scale. If Labour is not to be its conduit, then we should be actively seeking an ethical alternative that has the political heft to replace it. Radicalism is not confined to the left of politics and complacency now will see the void filled on the right.

Change is coming across the UK and radical voices on the left are allowing it to happen in front of their eyes. Starmer's Labour, yoked to austerity economics, is about to replace the Conservatives as the natural party of government in England. When will we hear from principled voices to the left of it – Drakeford, Burnham, McDonnell, Wood, Sturgeon, Lucas – that the time has come for a united front in service of the struggling people here? If these politicians do not wise up to the reality of a Thatcherite Labour Party opposed by a Powellite Tory/Reform UK alliance then their careers will have been for nothing.

Without a Paddle
6 April 2024

As the Conservatives' electoral prospects continue their journey towards Shit Creek, the Prime Minister's ongoing hunt for a paddle is becoming yet more desperate. The 'Rwanda plan' to deter illegal migration is the hill he has chosen to die on, and he's too committed now to back out.

Much is made of the millions Sunak made in business. When he initially arrived in the national consciousness, it was at the height of Brexit insanity and the Johnsonian absurdities that followed. Whilst fully complicit in all of that, it seemed to me that Sunak was a cautious, sensible presence in the maelstrom. Certainly, when he ran for the leadership, it was as a 'details guy'. His measured performances in those endless debates, including one in which he pretended to be friends with Andrew RT Davies, were in stark contrast to the wild-eyed demagoguery that won the day for Liz Truss.

So, after Truss's experiment with think-tank lunacy saw the markets take away the national credit card, there seemed to be merit in turning to Sunak as a business-savvy operator who would steer a more sensible path.

Conservative politics 2024-style, however, have no truck with caution, tradition, or pragmatism. If Sunak's instincts were to steady the ship, those of his party were to use it as a battering ram. From the moment he was coerced to reappoint Suella Braverman to his cabinet, Sunak's premiership was taken hostage. Older readers will remember the Eurosceptic 'bastards' who derailed John Major's government. It is not in the nature of people like that to be satisfied with victory, even one on the scale of Brexit. Their recklessness and disregard for convention has, in their own minds, been vindicated by the referendum result and, as such, become the modus operandi for the party they now control. In short, if an idea doesn't sound 'disruptive' then it can't have merit.

It is from this mindset that the Rwanda plan originated. It's worth noting that the idea is a logical fallacy. We are told that Rwanda is a progressive nation with a thriving economy that respects human rights. At the same time, we are supposed to believe that the prospect of ending up there is so dire that refugees will stop coming to the UK altogether in fear of it. I don't know how Mr Sunak made his many millions but if his cognitive skills allow for that then one must suspect that luck had a hand to play.

There has always been the suspicion that the plan was never intended to be 'operationalised', to use Sunak-speak. The courts were bound to throw it out and Sunak would be able to rally support amongst 'patriotic' voters by feigning outrage at their interference in our 'sovereignty'. If gaslighting the nation in this way was his intent then he may, again, have underestimated the destructive impulses of his party. Last night's intimation that he would take the UK out of the European Court of Human Rights seems to be another step towards extremism and away from norms of safe governance. With Braverman, Jenrick, and Badenoch all reportedly on manoeuvres to replace him, the Prime Minister is once again pandering to fools and knaves rather than asserting his authority over them.

In the wreckage of UK politics that has followed Boris Johnson's shameful tenure, Sunak's weakness is becoming a threat to the nation. Ideas which began as publicity stunts are in danger of being actualised in an atmosphere of panic and end-of-term recklessness.

If the Prime Minister attempts to strip the UK citizenry of its legal rights in service of his own career it will mark a new low for a nation that has sunk to unimaginable depths already.

If we were to lose our recourse to law in a deregulated economy, we would be rendered serfs. The court is the legacy of a United Kingdom that looked outwards and commanded respect around the world.

We have already lost our freedom of movement in a frenzy of xenophobic opportunism; we should become a pariah if our commitment to international law goes the same way.

Fragile Fantasist of the Vale

7 April 2024

The upcoming slaughter of the Tory Party will be biblical in scope and doubtless provide many hugely entertaining moments as some of the world's most entitled incompetents are handed their backsides by a public that can simply take no more. The scale of their desperation was illustrated by today's 'revelations' about Angela Rayner. Apparently, Labour's deputy leader *might* owe … wait for it… £1500 in tax from the sale of a council house 14 years ago. Really? That's the level of gotcha the 'natural party of government' is now relying on to save its skin? *Duw, Duw*, it's almost pitiable.

On a personal level, the annihilation of these clowns is a double-edged sword. On one hand, it'll be nice to escape from the relentless bigotry, corruption, and cruelty that they've made their trademarks. Conversely, though, I am paid to take the piss out of people, and it's been a simple pleasure to do so with the cavalcade of antisocial chancers that have been advanced over the last few years. The Lakota Sioux speak of a time, before the coming of white colonialists, when pieces of gold the size of a baby's head lay around the Black Mountains undisturbed. For a satirist, coming across Jacob Rees-Mogg or Jonathan Gullis is an 1849 Gold Rush moment. They've been halcyon days.

Most distressingly of all, though, Torygeddon is almost certain to send Andrew 'Real Ting' Davies back to his former life as a bucolic Alf Garnett, lecturing cattle about the M4 relief road. What am I going to do then? The fragile fantasist of the Vale failed this week to censure *Nation.Cymru* as, once again, the authorities were obliged to explain that his hurty feelings weren't just cause for censoring a free press. As with all things Tory nowadays, there's a richly comic aspect to Mr Anti-Woke being told to suck it up like a big boy, but also an unsavoury and worrying undertone.

Scrolling relentlessly through Twitter/X today as I do every day in place of a fulfilling life, I came across a thread about adjustments to the state pension. As we know, the pension in the UK is far below that in comparable European nations and, as such, tends to provoke a fair bit of fury amongst those trying to live on it. Amongst the comments there were several from Welsh pensioners who were convinced that 'illegal immigrants' were all entitled to £400 per week in Wales. Well, we know where they've got this from, don't we? For months now Davies has been claiming, without context, that asylum seekers are entitled to that sum from the Welsh Government. The reality is that a soon-to-expire pilot scheme that tested the viability of a universal basic income offered that amount to youngsters leaving care. It didn't explicitly *exclude* care-leavers who were seeking asylum.

As it happens, I vehemently disagree with this scheme. Care-leavers face unique challenges in life, so they are wholly unsuitable as a control group for a pilot scheme of this nature. The results are, I believe, unlikely to shed much light on the wider viability of UBI. So, there you have a reasoned objection to the policy that Davies and the Conservatives could have used with very little difficulty. Instead, however, they have chosen to push a version of the truth that is so distorted as to resemble a lie.[1] That version has embedded itself in the consciousness of enough people that it goes unchallenged when brought up as a howl of pain about the paltry and insulting pension arrangements under which our retirees struggle. The difficulties faced by asylum seekers themselves are, of course, of no interest whatsoever to Davies and his ilk. They are merely fodder for a narrative.

The ignoble death throes of Tory Britain will doubtless see new depths plumbed on a weekly basis. Like many of you, I scarcely know when to laugh and when to vomit.

---

[1] October 2024 and he's still tweeting this stuff.

We Had It Hard

11 April 2024

Do you remember the good old days? You could leave your baby out with the milk bottles, and it would come back clean in the morning. Tell that to youngsters today and they'd stab you. We had it hard, mind, keeping warm round a cigarette. My first job was in black & white. We were poor but we were happy.

Editing the past into something pleasant to remember is a function of aging indulged in by all of us. Beyond our animal instincts, humans are manufacturers of stories. Unable, for some reason, to live in the moment, we are bound to contextualise ourselves as literary characters in a narrative arc that lends meaning to our lives. No other species keeps scrapbooks or takes part in historical re-enactments. To be human is to be a historian and a prophet all the time.

'Of course, in my day, we knew how to enjoy ourselves…'

This quirk of human nature leaves us open to manipulation by shysters at every turn. Knowing us to be unhappy *now*, usually because of a combination of their larceny and incompetence, they need only point to a golden age in which we were younger, fitter, and better-looking to evoke our own sense of decay.

'Look,' says Quentin Politico MP, 'things used to be great! They can be again if only you'll vote for me!'

We reflect on a time when we were optimistic, bounding up flights of stairs and breaking hearts at will. *I can have that back, you say?*

We are suckers for it every time.

Dishonest manipulation of history isn't what it was in my day, though. I grew up with John Major reminding us of a Britain in which spinsters cycled to church full of warm beer before having a game of cricket on the village green. The 'Blitz Spirit' was still a clear memory for those who chose to ignore the staggering levels of opportunistic crime that existed during wartime blackouts. In the 1960s, you could start a job in the morning, my mum reckoned, quit at lunchtime, get paid and start somewhere else in the afternoon. She was less clear on the effects this sort of feckless behaviour had on the long-term productivity of the nation, but she saw the Moody Blues play in a small pub so what concern was that of hers?

The inexorable decline of the UK, however, extends to the quality of our historical bullshitting. It's difficult to look back on the collective life of the nation over the last half-century and construct a heroic storyline that dignifies one's personal place in history. We haven't really built anything: no ships or grand engineering projects. Our wars have been grubby catastrophes predicated on lies. We've become poorer. We've had to listen to 'Wonderwall' by Oasis every day whether we wanted to or not.

Social media has, of late, become flooded with AI-produced images that glorify racial purity and suggest an imminent collapse of Western civilisation. Bizarre collages of lions wearing England flags in defence of blonde females from evil, dark interlopers represent the absolute nadir of fictional culture and history. In the absence of anything to inspire optimism or unity, crude imagery is being provided to nurture hopelessness and division amongst people who seem to have abandoned reality altogether.

In Wales, however, we retain an actual living, breathing culture that offers sustenance in the here and now. From the renaissance of Welsh football to Ren's songwriting[1], there is spiritual nourishment in this nation that allows us a more contented view of our past than is possible in the wider UK. This week, the ever-wondrous Michael Sheen's appearance on *The Assembly* showed us where people who are alive now can take some pride in the way things have gone.

The diversification of voices in our culture is an evolutionary advance that might just save us all. The more

---

[1] Down with the kids, butt.

perspectives we have, the harder it is to lie to us.

Things Can Only Get Worse

14 April 2024

Nah, I've had enough. First off, a confession. In 1997, when I was pretty[1], malleable, and stupid, I spent some time on a campaign bus jumping off as it stopped at each street and playing music for the bemused residents. Along with me there was a stilt walker and a couple of other musicians who'd given their time to help Tony Blair end a lifetime of Tory injustice. Between the stops, the bus blared (!) out 'Things Can Only Get Better' and schoolkids on the open top deck waved Labour flags. At one point we rounded a corner and encountered our Tory counterpoint, the sitting MP who was stood on the back of a flatbed truck shouting, 'I believe in corporal and capital punishment!' into a megaphone, on his own. We laughed, the schoolkids jeered, and it was obvious that the Tory junta was done for. The joy was unbound and there was a sense of history in the making.

Who knows how many Iraqi children were blinking into life at that moment, unaware that thousands of miles away idiots like me were cheering on the agent of their destruction? Here in Wales, were people expecting their promised devolution to be revealed as a hollow sham, as the Labour party sought to impose leaders upon its 'assembly' who commanded no respect in the country? Did anybody at all expect the transition from Thatcherism to be lauded by Thatcher herself as her greatest achievement?

Well, here we are again. The only solution for NHS waiting lists, according to prospective Health Sec, Wes Streeting, is paying the private sector to take up the slack. The only financial model for growth, according to prospective Chancellor, Rachel Reeves, is further austerity, and the instincts of our prospective

---

[1] Photographic evidence has unfortunately been lost.

Prime Minister, Sir Keir Starmer, told him that Israel was within its rights to shut off water and electricity to the Palestinian people.

So, the rich must profit from your illness, you must pay for the incompetence of government and Palestinian children must die because...just because.

Any criticism of this obscene policy offering from Labour is routinely condemned as enabling the incumbent Conservative regime. At home, Vaughan Gething mouths empty platitudes about a 'partner' in Westminster but fails to explain what such a partnership will deliver for the people of Wales.

Today's Labour Party is mobilised solely to capture the votes of Conservatives in England. It has no ideological core and, as recent developments in the Middle East have proven, no moral compass either. Wales is considered to be in the bag for these people, so they have no incentive to align with our needs or values.

I live in Rhondda Fach, and as far as I can see, neither the last UK Labour government nor the current Welsh Labour administration has provided any meaningful opportunities for the communities decimated in the 1980s, quite deliberately, by Margaret Thatcher's government. So, what exactly do we owe this party?

Plaid Cymru, step forward and offer a vision that is not in the shadow of the Labour Party. I'm not interested in cultural matters, nor even independence in the short term, I am asking for something I can vote for that will provide my neighbours with a decent standard of living and a measure of dignity on the global stage. I am demanding an alternative.

Be clear, be bold, and be absolutely certain that what Starmer is serving up is not good enough for this wonderful country. Labour will, beyond doubt, win the upcoming election so if its values do not align with those of the people here, we must have a vehicle for them. Nobody in impoverished Wales should be voting for a party that seeks to entrench power and money in England. If they are to govern us in this fashion it should be in the face of our wrath, and in opposition to the people we send to represent us.

We should look deeply into the eyes of those we elect
20 April 2024

Saturday night was the lengthiest Schrödinger's cat moment I can remember. I was in India, so a few hours ahead when news broke that Iran had launched dozens of drones and missiles towards Israel in retaliation for the attack on its consulate in Damascus. I was flying home the next morning and ignobly started fretting about whether the flight would be cancelled. *You bastard*, I told myself as I drifted off to sleep with my phone still in hand, checking for news.

Heaven knows what the five hours it took for those drones to arrive felt like for the people underneath them. Their internal dialogues must have been confused, angry, frightened, despairing. To be subject to another's will leaves us to contend with our own character, to rely on it entirely. In that part of the world, people must be coming to know themselves more completely than they ever wished.

In the public schools that have produced so many British politicians, it used to be held that character could be beaten into children. As we know, the truth is that it can only be beaten out of them. Whilst flogging and caning are no longer acceptable practices, the shadow of that thinking still falls across our culture. The lie that hard experience, rather than love, produces useful personalities propels damaged individuals to the top of organisations of every sort. We know better but we still allow it.

On the plane, skirting Iran on the rejigged flight path, it struck me that we have, in the UK, been extraordinarily lucky to avoid the sort of disaster that is ruining people's lives in the Middle East. Over the last few years, we have allowed palpably weak people to run our affairs and to escape censure for their misdeeds. Their malfeasance, particularly during the pandemic, has brought misery to millions of us but they haven't, thankfully, been exposed by an active, determined enemy.

In Israel, before October 7th, Benjamin Netanyahu was facing the end of his political career and a probable prison sentence for corruption. Thousands had taken to the streets enraged that he was attempting to change the constitution so that he could avoid that outcome. So, when Hamas attacked, its leaders knew that they were dealing with a man who was compromised to the point of desperation. He had *shown* them that his instinct for self-preservation would always supersede whatever sense of duty he had. He could be relied upon to do the wrong thing, to outrage the world with his lies and cruelty. Inherent to this thesis, of course, is that they knew he would kill many thousands of their people. Just as he was willing to spend Israel's standing on saving his skin, they were willing to sacrifice as many Palestinians as necessary to let him do it.

Back at home, I heard a Conservative spokesman say that their priority was that at least one plane full of asylum seekers leave for Rwanda before the general election. It would, he said, demonstrate that the policy had been feasible. It no longer matters, it seems, whether the plan has any positive effects at all. The futures of the people on this yearned-for flight are to be mortgaged on an election that the party knows it can't win. They are to be shifted to another continent for the rest of their lives to make a point, or perhaps save a marginal seat or two.

Dull people never tire of telling us that idealism is childish. In the *real world*, they scoff, moral compromise is the currency of mature statecraft. Well, that has brought us to Trump, Johnson, and Netanyahu. It has the putative leader of the free world on trial for bribing a porn actress whilst hot metal falls on children every day. It has our Foreign Secretary so snookered that he calls for a ceasefire whilst defending the sale of weapons to one side of the conflict. It has made us ludicrous and, like Israel, vulnerable.

Most of the world faces elections this year. We should look deeply into the eyes of those we elect because people who wish us harm surely will, and we won't escape consequence forever.

193

No Measure of Health

21 April 2024

We don't tend to think of Rishi Sunak as being intimidating. If he was in the Rheola in Porth on a Saturday night and started effing and blinding in front of the ladies, I'd have no hesitation in stepping up to him and issuing a reprimand.

'I don't know how you carry on in the nose-to-tail gastropubs of Richmond, North Yorkshire, butt,' I would tell him, 'But round here we mind our language. Now, sit down and finish your Babycham.'

I wouldn't anticipate any further trouble from Sunak. If anybody spent breaktimes at school with his head down the toilet looking for the blue goldfish, it's him.

Intimidation takes many forms, however, and the Prime Minister comes into his own when he's using his 'caring' voice. We're not often treated to this. More commonly, he's flanked by union flags comically trying to put the frighteners on people-smuggling gangs or attempting to troll Keir Starmer at PMQs… 'Yeah, but you were mates with Jeremy Corbyn!'

It's only when he's trying to project kindness that his black heart is properly revealed. At the outset of this week's speech on illness and economic inactivity, the PM sought to reassure us that *of course* he would never make life more difficult for people who faced *genuine* health challenges. The tone of voice he employed for this section of the speech was legitimately terrifying. His caveats were slathered with an unctuous insincerity that set off every fight or flight alarm I possess. Part Bitcoin grifter, part Stepford wife, one can imagine him being employed to tell people that an AI programme has selected them to be euthanised. He is a walking Happy Meal, the ostensibly human equivalent of an online mortgage application. *We are sorry, you have been unsuccessful…*

All of which, of course, is of a piece with the substance of what Sunak had to say. The casual assumption that there are millions of workshy parasites gaming the system for an easy life is a go-to trope for failing regimes everywhere. It's not *you* of course, it's those *other,* the lead-swinging malingerers who are to blame for our ills. I can't remember a time when politicians hadn't suddenly realised that the latest cohort of working-age people was letting the side down. It's so familiar in its desperation that much of the speech could have been written at any time during the last 200 years. Sunak is, of course, relying on an increasingly elderly segment of the electorate to turn out and vote so wheeling out condemnations of feckless youngsters will be a feature of the next few months.

So far, so depressingly predictable. What *was* new and far more alarming, is Sunak's suggestion that GPs be stripped of the power to issue sick notes, or 'fit notes' as they are known in the newspeak of our times. The responsibility for this is to be handed to unspecified 'professionals' who won't feel the 'pressure' to issue them experienced by family doctors. These 'professionals' will undoubtedly be employees of private companies whose government contract will specify that they return as many people to work as possible. So, if you need time off, the conversation you have will not be with a clinician who is trained to ensure your wellbeing, but with someone financially incentivised to persuade you into work. Will such an employee be interested in the chronic shortage of medication that is a feature of post-Brexit Britain?

Sunak specifically highlighted mental health issues such as depression and anxiety as targets for 'help' in returning to work. Ignoring the 1.9 million people on waiting lists for mental health treatment, he implied that many if not most sufferers should be dragging their conditions to the workplace where the 'dignity' of work will do them the power of good.

Labour rightly pointed out that much of this problem stems from underfunding of the NHS. It didn't, however, attack the moral premise of the speech and that is a concern. Is it now a given that people who feel unwell are to be mistrusted at the institutional level? In the absence of an explicit pledge *not* to pursue this line of thinking, the comforting reality that Sunak is in no position to enact anything might soon be replaced by the realisation that Labour has accepted his position as the status quo.

Tony Benn once remarked that the treatment of refugees was instructive as to how governments would treat the rest of us if they could get away with it. As the monstrous Rwanda plan meanders towards legislation, we are seeing its dehumanising language directed towards the population at large. The glassy-eyed, casual cruelty of governance in the UK is bearing down on more of us by the day.

'It is no measure of health to be well-adjusted to a profoundly sick society.' – Jiddu Krishnamurti

Blood-Soaked Rodeo

25 April 2024

There is nothing quite so unsettling as hearing the current generation of politicians projecting moral certainty as the rationale for their actions. After everything we've been through over the last few decades it's challenging to accept on face value their earnest pronouncements about protecting 'our' values and serving the cause of liberty. It's not our first rodeo; in fact, we have been trampled by the bucking bronco of their murderous dishonesty so frequently that we can barely sit upright on our horses.

So, when London and Washington announced eye-watering increases in defence spending this week, it was to populations who have every right to question the morality behind those decisions. The UK, you will recall, has recently abandoned HS2, its only recent investment in large-scale infrastructure. We in Wales, having contributed to it for no obvious return, watched the government write off our cash as the project was deemed unaffordable. Our councils are teetering on the verge of bankruptcy and slashing services. Our taxes are the highest they have been in modern times.

We have pledged, none the less, to fund Ukraine to 'do what it takes' in its war with Russia. Given the near impossibility of Ukraine winning a war with Russia, there are only two potential outcomes to this. Our money will be spent *prolonging* the war, at incalculable human cost to the Ukrainian people, or else NATO joins the war and the world as we know it passes into history. The bean-counting utilitarian arguments upon which our government so blithely relies when it is denying essential services to its own people do not, seemingly, apply to its foreign policy. At home, there is no magic money tree, everything must be 'costed' and if that means your granny has the heating turned down in her care home then wise-up, bucko, because we live in the real world. When it comes to unwinnable conflicts, though, limitless resources can be found and justified on moral grounds alone. We are 'standing with' the Ukrainian people, right behind them until there are so few left that a grubby compromise is brokered, and our arms companies pay out their dividends.

Sunak is the fourth consecutive Prime Minister to refuse an inquiry into Russian interference in the Brexit referendum. The extent and purpose of Russian donations to Conservative MPs in recent years remains a matter of intrigue.

Our proudly virtuous country is, of course, also supplying weaponry to Israel. As Rishi Sunak was explaining the inviolability of Britain's commitment to international law, mass graves were being uncovered in the ruins of Palestinian hospitals, the bodies within having their hands tied behind their backs and bullets through the backs of their skulls.

This week, the same Rishi Sunak claimed victory for his bill to deport refugees to Rwanda, a bill that deems that country to be safe in contravention of legal findings and despite proof that it shot refugees dead only five years ago for the crime of asking for better food.

Still, Sunak stood and spoke, his voice a caricature of dignity, his record an inventory of disgrace. Without a mandate, he presumed to speak for us, to impoverish us further in the pursuit of conflicts over which we refuse to negotiate. Are we to believe that the traumatised residents of Gaza will somehow become more moderate as a result of what is being visited upon them, that the thousands of orphaned and homeless children there will grow up to reject the philosophy of Hamas and embrace Israel as their friend? Is Russia going to respond to temporarily sterner Ukrainian defence by seeing the error of its ways and resolving to become a nice, cuddly social democracy? Is the youth of Europe happy to be conscripted into an extinction-event war without our governments even *exploring* the possibility of a negotiated settlement?

As blood-soaked warhorses ran amok through London on Wednesday morning, the myth of British decency ran with them. The day before, St. George's Day, the union flag was once again waved by Tommy Robinson's drunken fools as they spat

198

the last gobs of nationalist bile at their own police force. Wales has never been part of that flag, and I have never been so glad of it.

The Last Days of Frome

28 April 2024

Dan Poulter's defection from the Conservatives to Labour marks a new stage in the party's descent towards oblivion. He won't be the last rat to flee the ship, leaving Rishi Sunak perched on the stern like Leonardo DiCaprio in sliders.

In retrospect, it was always on the cards that Boris Johnson would bring about the death of the Conservative Party. He has lived his life as a human wrecking ball, destroying all around him as bystanders felt compelled to watch in rapt horror. He's cheap entertainment, though, a YouTube compilation of car crashes with a comedy voiceover. The party's decision to let him bluster through the endless difficulties of Brexit, brushing them off with flippant jingoism was short-sighted but when the pandemic blew in on his watch, the party's innate superficiality was laid bare for all to see.

Serious conservatism was always paternalistic. The Harold Macmillan style of patrician governance recognised the responsibility implied by privilege. Whilst the lower orders were to be kept well away from the family silver, they should be allowed their comforts and recognised for the work they had done. That all ended with Margaret Thatcher's middle-class insistence on 'aspiration' as the prime national virtue. After 1979, the poor man at his gate was assumed willing to put in 20-hour days to dislodge the rich man in his castle and encouraged so to do. Aristocratic disdain for effort and professionalism seemed to have disappeared forever beneath a tidal wave of mercantile vulgarity. Grouse moors acquired gift shops and Alan Sugar raced up the ranks of nobility like a bulldog with a dab of Colman's mustard on its arse.

The return of governance by toff, in 2010, came as a profound shock to me. Whilst Blair's government contained plenty of privilege, with John Prescott retained as a sort of mascot for the proletariat, it was *desperate* to play down

200

embarrassingly comfortable origins. Yes, Blair had been to Fettes but his schtick was determinedly of the people. John Major, meanwhile, actually *was* of the people. He liked frozen peas, apparently. Imagine!

So, how was it that David Cameron and George Osborne managed, at a stroke, to turn us back into a feudal society? Not only did they sweep into power with unashamed received pronunciation and famously grand family histories, but their policies also overtly penalised anybody unfortunate enough to be asset-poor. It wasn't even sugar-coated. Austerity was imposed on the nation from a great social height, and in England, they put up with it and voted for more.

Watching in the wings, meanwhile, Boris Johnson could see his path clearing. If the English electorate would put up with the faux-paternalist, take-your-medicine arrogance of Cameron and Osborne then surely the full end-of-the-pier poshboy act he'd spent his life perfecting, complete with scattergun Latin and comedy hairdo, was bound to succeed.

The road from John Major to Johnson travels through the English psyche and reveals a nation that never grew up. Major is a recognisable character from any walk of life. Essentially decent, he tried hard, didn't sell himself very effectively, and left high office quietly. There are people like him in every workplace. He represents an authentic version of southern English masculinity.

What he *didn't* represent was the wild fantasies of imaginary England. Whilst a walk through Reading or Basingstoke might see you encounter a hundred John Majors bimbling round Marks & Sparks in their Saturday slacks, you would need a psychotherapist to show you the forces that unleashed Boris Johnson on to the world stage. Much has been made of his supposed imitation of Churchill. That, however, is to underestimate the depth of the delusion to which he was playing. The cultural touchstone he was really invoking was, I can reveal, Henry VIII. All English insanity springs from the idea of this gluttonous, vicious despot around whom an industry of dishonest exceptionalism has revolved for centuries.

A class system which devolves all drudgery downwards produces a peculiar sort of longing. Your personal potential might be limited to becoming Assistant Manager in charge of haberdashery in the Bournemouth branch of Dunelm, but the wildness in you, the bit that might look smokily at Edwina Currie, dreams of medieval rampage. Johnson – amoral, sexually incontinent, rich, lucky, and ultimately accountable to nobody – can live that for you.

Now that the rampage is over and Rishi Sunak is picking through the wreckage looking for anything still intact that he can offer to the electorate, I wonder where that impulse will find its next conduit. There will be a few years of Starmerite dreariness during which some repairs will be undertaken, but soon enough the fantasists will be bored and looking for a new psychopathic overlord to brighten up their serfdom.

There's some debate over whether Cymru was or is a colony. My belief is that it certainly was. Nowadays, it is more accurately the collateral victim of a nation destroying itself. The death throes of the Conservative Party will reveal a wider malaise in England. Its sense of self is as fragile as it is preposterous.

Under the Spotlight
2 May 2024

Donald Trump famously observed that he could shoot someone on 5th Avenue and his poll ratings would only go up.

In Wales we have a rather different situation; our politicians could rampage through Roald Dahl Plass, laying waste to the citizenry and it wouldn't make the UK press unless the Duchess of Sussex happened to be visiting at the time.

So, it is ominous for the First Minister that disquiet around his campaign donations has, eventually, found its way into *The Guardian*[1].

A 'senior Labour figure' – anyone up for a sweepstake? – has disclosed that Keir Starmer's office is 'very concerned'. Gosh, that's flattering, isn't it? Imagine someone in Sir Keir Starmer's office knowing what goes on round here!

It's probably the bloke in charge of ironing union flags but still, this is unprecedented attention for us. Well done, Vaughan!

If an uncomfortable conversation with Starmer is on the cards, it would be interesting to observe Mr Gething's attitude. His Senedd exchanges of late have been redolent of Charles I, tetchily outraged that the great unwashed might question their natural superior.

The affably collegiate atmosphere of Cardiff Bay is, however, a world away from Westminster. If the First Minister is perceived as a negative in the upcoming general election, he can expect the *Goodfellas* treatment.

It's all so lowering, isn't it? Questionable behaviour is nothing new in politics, and neither is it confined to cartoon Tory villains. We are usually, however, entitled to expect a few months of best behaviour from our masters when they assume

---

[1] https://www.theguardian.com/politics/article/2024/may/02/labour-concern-donations-vaughan-gething-campaign-wales

office.

For a while, they should at least look as if they *want* us to believe they are honest. Gething's 'politics is expensive' remark was dismissive in the tradition of Marie Antoinette. So is food, and gas, and council tax, Vaughan. You do remember who is paying for all this, right?

In the scheme of things, a couple of hundred grand is peanuts, especially when weighed against the fortunes diverted by Westminster during the pandemic, and more generally to government-friendly companies over the last few years.

A rotten prawn stinks out the house as badly as a haddock, though, and for this odour to be clinging to the First Minister from day one is bad for a democracy that commands little enough respect as it is.

The tuppeny-halfpenny nature of this controversy is no mitigation of its severity. Rather, it is a warning of how vulnerable Welsh politics would be to bad actors who know what they are doing. When Adam Price floated codifying political honesty this week, he warned that Wales was not immune from 'post-truth' politicians.

We have seen Andrew RT Davies' creative narratives sweep across social media in recent years.

You are never far from someone who is convinced that the Welsh Government is paying all asylum seekers a king's ransom every week, for instance.

His bluster is containable, though, and voiced from a position of electoral irrelevance.

The problem will come if an incoming Labour government in Westminster is unpopular in Wales.

Given the economic and social conditions it will inherit, this seems like a near certainty to me.

In those circumstances, voters will be vulnerable to organised liars with simplistic solutions. We are yet to contend with an accomplished, homegrown Farage or Trump, and nativism is at the heart of any grifter's appeal.

Welsh politics generally, and Labour in particular, should

204

not assume that the cosiness of its position is any protection against the tumult of years to come.

Only through rigorous and unsparing insistence on honesty and transparency can we defend our democracy against those who would subvert it. The wider world is watching now, what will it see?

Turned Out Nice Again

5 May 2024

Whenever Boris Johnson appears to be 'bumbling' it's wise to be suspicious. His mendacity is such that there's always a better than evens chance he's play acting for some personal outcome we'll find out later. You'll remember his bizarre claim of spending leisure time making models of London buses. It's been suggested that this was a ploy to game Google results so that his most famous lie, £350 million per week to the NHS from Brexit, which was plastered across a bus, became obscured.

Why he contrived on Thursday to arrive at a voting station without the photo ID he'd mandated by law isn't clear, but it got him noticed again and he rarely does anything at all without purpose. We'll see.

This week's elections for police commissioners, mayors, and English councillors were the first to require voter identification and the discussion around this reveals the threadbare nature of democracy in the UK. Turnout, we've been assured, was only slightly down and supporters of the change have been keen to list the many forms of ID that are acceptable. This line of thinking ignores the glaring reality that turnout in UK elections *without* ID was so low as to render their results undemocratic in any meaningful sense.

It is a mantra of conservatives that the state is too powerful. This idea is supposed to be the bedrock of their ideology. The introduction of voter ID by a Tory government exposes this for the sham it is. The state *is* terrifyingly powerful. It can lock you up, take away your resources, decide whether to treat your illnesses, dictate what your children are taught, and send you to war. The only scant response we have to its activities is the rare opportunity to vote, and even that is rendered meaningless for most of us in Westminster elections that are decided by the first-past-the-post system.

You would expect the Tories, self-proclaimed defenders of personal liberty, to be outraged by any move to place barriers between the individual and his or her access to democracy. The truth, of course, is that they adhere to no such ideology. They are perfectly happy for the state to march over your liberty to protest, vote, or receive an education that might enlighten your political outlook. Their 'light-touch government' applies only to touching their wealth. Any notion that this belief forms part of an overarching libertarian philosophy is for the birds.

The problem this policy purported to address, voter fraud, is virtually non-existent. Organising hundreds of imposters to vote in place of people who must be relied on not to turn up is impossible. On the other hand, you can be confident that the majority of people who can't put their hands on passports or driving licences come election day will be from the poorer section of society. That such a law can be passed without violent resistance, speaks itself to the hopeless disengagement that most of the country feels from the mechanism of government.

The results of this week's elections underscore the inevitability of an incoming Labour administration. The triumphalism displayed by the party in Wales over police commissioner victories achieved with minute turnouts is dispiriting. If Labour mistakes widespread disgust at Tory misrule for enthusiasm as regards its own uncertain offering it will be making a grave error. The UK requires fundamental constitutional reform. It must devolve power properly across the nations as well as the regions of England. Proportional representation should be immediate Labour policy if it poses as a progressive force. Voter participation should be prioritised as an urgent concern. Why, for instance, is election day not a Bank Holiday? If politics continues to be something that is done to people, rather than a process over which we feel ownership, then the drift towards corporate governance will become irreversible. Whether your priority is independence, the environment, equality, personal liberty, or economic change, your chances of achieving it via the ballot box are few and shrinking. Politicians should quake in fear of a responsive electorate; their every decision should carry personal consequence.

The first question we should ask of Sir Keir Starmer when he assumes office is,

'How do we get rid of you?'

Gift-Wrapped Power
9 May 2024

Less than a week after the English electorate made it clear that the Conservative Party was about as welcome as a fart in a spacesuit, Sir Keir Starmer responded by adding a little more Tory to his Labour offering. This time the newcomer is Natalie Elphicke, the MP for Dover. There is a tradition of Tory MPs jumping ship when it starts to list, but these have generally been from the One Nation end of the party, the 'wets' as Margaret Thatcher dubbed them. Nowadays, of course, there is no One Nation end of the party so all that remains are different flavours of Brexity. Even in that context, however, Elphicke, who succeeded her ex-husband as candidate for Dover following his conviction for sexual assault, is considered a right-winger by 'Brexit hardman' Steve Baker, the Minister of State for Northern Ireland.

'I have been searching in vain for a Conservative MP who thinks themself to the right of Natalie Elphicke,' he tweeted after her defection.

She previously made the headlines for receiving a suspension from the Commons for attempting to influence the judge during her husband's trial.

None of this, however, is considered any bar to her joining the Labour Party as it is today. Her decision was announced moments before PMQs and allowed Sir Keir an unmissable opportunity to skewer wretched Rishi. His point, that the country needs an election because the Government cannot rely on the support even of its own MPs is indisputable. The price he is willing to pay for these moments of triumph, however, may prove to be higher in the long term than he appreciates.

You will have noticed, thanks to the work of this vigorous organ, that our own Labour supremo has not got off to the best of starts. As Vaughan Gething begins to slide down the greasy

209

pole he has so tenaciously, and recently, clambered up, it is telling how few voices are being lent to his support. The allegations against him are serious, for sure, but not of the Jeremy Thorpe dog-shooting order usually required to shake the political class from self-serving loyalty. Gething's problem, as much as the accusations surrounding him, is his political emptiness. When scandals arise, a politician needs to be able to point to his principles and ask those around him,

'Are you willing to throw away all this good stuff we believe in over this temporary embarrassment?'

What, of that sort, can Gething stand on? For which crucial reforms is he the driving force? What of substance will Labour, as a whole, be losing if he goes?

Now, think a few months past the honeymoon of a Starmer victory and apply the same test to him. His current strategy is to position Labour so that it wipes the Tories off the map. To do that he has reversed not only the commitments he made to Labour members, but even subsequent pledges to the wider electorate. Only this week, union leaders are warning that his flagship workers' rights charter is poised to be watered down.

All governments become embroiled in scandal. Their work is messy, compromised, and done in a rush. From the moment they assume office they need to be able to rely on the benefit of the doubt and, ultimately, the forgiveness of those who share their fundamental principles. Labour, at the moment, seems to have one fundamental principle, which is to achieve power. When that is achieved, most likely without any external threat for many years, around what will its leadership inspire loyalty?

By glad-handing right-wing Tories, diluting policies, and prevaricating on issues of international morality, Starmer is weakening his own position as he piles up votes. We know a thing or two about Labour hegemony here in Wales and it can be an ugly business. As the First Minister discovers the limits of gift-wrapped power, the putative Prime Minister should take note.

People Speak Up

Rhian Elizabeth, clare e. potter, Bella Collins

12 May 2024

As the sun streamed down on Llanelli Thursday evening, there seemed to be an easy wellbeing about the place. People were enjoying an al fresco drink and assembling for the People Speak Up[1] show at Ffwrnes Fach. It's a beautiful venue housed in the old Zion Chapel, and the ethos of the place is an organic fusion of rooted culture and modern sensibilities.

The communal atmosphere reflects the building's history. It's a place people have gathered for a very long time, and, under the pipe organ, it seems natural to chat to whomever is at the next table. Equally, though, these events are created to meet the needs of today's audience. Warm and welcoming, they are planned to be as inclusive as possible with refreshments available for an optional donation and break-out spaces for anyone who needs to step away for a while.

As the name suggests, People Speak Up is all about showcasing and nurturing voices. Tonight's bill features three very different takes on the world.

Bella Collins[2] is a beloved talent on the Welsh music scene. In demand as a singer/guitarist and bassist, she possesses one of those voices that's seems to wrap you up in rich tonality, only to sting a little when she pushes it or elevate when she leans back and lets it float. It allows for a wide range of emotions to find its way to the audience, whether through the jazz and blues standards she interprets or her fine, original songs. Accompanying herself on acoustic guitar, her playing is led by strong basslines and jazzy chordal inflections. Her own 'Part

---

[1] https://peoplespeakup.co.uk/index.html

[2] https://www.instagram.com/bellacollinsmusic/

Time Lover' carries a jaunty playfulness reminiscent of Nina Simone in cheerful mode, whilst a spontaneous 'Wade In The Water', played by audience request, showed the emotional heft that her formidable musicality can wield. Effortlessly spellbinding, Collins' cool-as stage savvy and easy wit are the launch-pad from which she soars.

The poet clare e. potter is many elements all at once, fizzing and overflowing as she corrals them into a compelling stage presence. Her collection, *Healing The Pack* (Verve Press), was launched last week and is an affair of the heart, 18 years in the writing. Potter's poems deal in memory, family, and trauma. They are hymns to the people and places she grew up around in Cefn Fforest, adult appreciations of childhood impressions that made her. Their language is the rainbow virtuosity of Valleys English, shot through with snatches of Cymraeg. (Her next collection, she tells us, will be in the language). There is rhythmic storytelling, filmic in its clarity and set beside poetic observations of majesty in tiny moments. The poems find beauty in hardship and caveats to joy. Potter's performance inhabits that dichotomy as she ascends into certainty before cutting herself down to vulnerability and clambering back up, clinging to her beautiful words as a guide to redemption. An emotional high-wire act, she is as fierce as she is fragile, Mam and daughter at once. She is extraordinary, a Valleys Piaf.

Rhian Elizabeth is a study in understatement. Acclaimed for her 2018 collection, *the last polar bear on earth* (Parthian), her poems in her new book *girls etc.* (Broken Sleep Books, 2024) are finely chiselled and unsparing. Having flashed us a knowing smile and announcing, 'some poems about lesbians and Taylor Swift', she stands still and works on the lonely spaces inside us all. Space is important in Elizabeth's work. Things are left unsaid, wrenching all the more in their absence. Unspoken events whisper through delicate descriptions of their aftermath. Listening to this work is to stand on the rumbling of a distant earthquake, far enough away to be safe but close enough to tremble. That smile is there for a reason, though, and after the poems have unsettled you, they often curl away into wise humour. Calmly, they take you where you are afraid to go, before leading you back home and setting you down to think.

The breadth of perspective on show thrilled a capacity audience in Llanelli. Each one of these performers can reach people with rare artistry.

The Cosmos According to Facebook

12 May 2024

Well, I see the sky has gone woke[1]. In my day, the night was a pitiless void upon which your existential dread could be projected as you shivered under a thin, nylon sheet. We didn't expect frivolous light shows and flat screen TVs.

If my old dad had seen Friday night's vulgar display of Technicolor luminescence, he'd have assumed the Nazis were bombing Swansea docks and gone to hide in the toilet.

Not that we got to see it up our way. Oh no.

Whilst Facebook was full of gloating Treorchy residents posting photos of Blaencwm looking like the Las Vegas strip, Rhondda Fach passed Friday evening in its customary sombre tones, disturbed only by the occasional tinkling of broken glass, or rustling of chip paper.

You can blame Rhondda Cynon Taf council for that. We don't even have a railway line up here, let alone a Fancy-Dan, award-winning High Street so what hope did we have of them staging the aurora borealis in the Fach?

All those corrupt, good-for-nothing councillors, fat on free chips from A Fish Called Rhondda, can't find a few quid to fix the potholes in Pontygwaith but can somehow fund an extreme G5 electromagnetic storm on the other side of Penrhys.

Shame on you if you enjoyed the northern lights, anyway. I boycotted the event for political reasons. How you hypocrites can enjoy the spectacle of solar flares turning the sky into entertainment when there is so much suffering in this world sickens me.

This is the *same* sky through which innocent birds fly into wind turbines, did you even consider that? Why, it seemeth nothing to me than a foul and pestilent congregation of vapours.

---

[1] The Northern Lights were visible across Wales. Well, most of Wales.

All you sheeple, staring up at the pretty colours just like the WEF wants you to. Baaaa, Baaaa, Baaaa!

While you were busy being mesmerised by the 'once-in-a-lifetime' event, The Elite were quietly installing spyware on your devices that interacts with the Covid vaccine to track subversive thoughts.

The mainstream media won't tell you that!

There's a cost-of-living crisis on, though, and we all know how tough it can be to find treats for the family nowadays. So, (admin please delete this if not allowed), I've created a range of bespoke 'Haribo bouquets' to commemorate the phenomenon for the children.

Available in small, medium, and type 2 diabetes sizes, these cellophane-wrapped gifts are a fun way to celebrate the vulnerability of mankind to random, cosmic happenstances through brightly coloured sugar.

DM me to reserve your child's bouquet, they'll be ready for collection on Wednesday and include a *FREE* printout of a photo I took outside Morrisons on the night itself. Cash only.

I like to think that within all of us, a small voice yearned for the polarity of the earth to be reversed on Friday night, for a hushing of the endless chatter as global misery is beamed into our daily experience at a rate that outpaces our capacity to understand.

It was a reminder that there is, always, something outside of the godawful mess we seem to have made of our world.

Like and share, like and share.

It's Not Going Awfully Well

16 May 2024

Transitions of power are often jolting, as a management style to which people have become accustomed is replaced by something else. In a functioning democracy, they would usually be in response to the people's will. An example of that would be the cautious, torpid air of John Major's administration giving way to the energy and ruthlessness of Tony Blair. It was the mood of the UK at the time, so it found political expression. In a de facto one-party state like Wales, however, the preferences of voters are of little import. Leadership of the Labour Party guarantees power here and the wider UK positioning of the party is a major factor in determining its character in Wales.

Mark Drakeford, in his gentle, if occasionally tetchy, way was a headache for the party in London. His leadership was policy-led and informed by his commitment to devolution as the form of governance that suited Wales. The pungency of objections to those policies, and to his opposition to independence serves to underline the doggedness with which he pursued them. 'Welsh Labour' is not a thing outside of campaigning leaflets and the platitudes of politicians. The party here has no independence from UK Labour and doesn't even run its own bank accounts. Party officials here are hired from London and the leadership in the Senedd has no authority over Labour MPs in Westminster. Drakeford's success in putting a little tangible distance between UK policy and that in Wales belied the constitutional weakness of the party in Wales. He benefited from two phenomena: a UK party that was preoccupied with tearing itself apart during Jeremy Corbyn's leadership, and a Conservative government in Westminster that dominated the news cycle by virtue of unprecedented incompetence. In effect, the Drakeford government went under the radar.

UK Labour in 2024, however, is a very different beast. On

216

the cusp of power and tacking rapidly to the right in the belief it can capture Tory England forever, it is no longer in the mood to indulge radical experiments in Cardiff Bay. Before the Welsh leadership election was even announced, Vaughan Gething was benefiting from *Guardian* puff pieces announcing him as the coming man in the Senedd. Upon assuming office, he was immediately invited to attend a shadow cabinet meeting, an honour that was never bestowed upon Drakeford. Policy-free, and not given to public statements of principle, Gething's rise seemed to be pre-ordained. Despite unpopularity amongst the party in the Senedd, it appeared powerless, and largely voiceless, as he emerged the victor. The implication that he is Starmer's man in Wales seems beyond dispute. He is there to keep Wales on message and prevent us from becoming an embarrassment to the UK party in election year.

It's not going awfully well. Whilst he has mastered the Starmerite technique of firing anybody who threatens the leadership's line, he has failed to see the distinction between doing this for perceived party advantage and resorting to it to quell urgent concerns about his own fitness for office.

In the short time Gething has been in post his dismissal of legitimate questions about his professional behaviour has been a defining characteristic. 'Politics is expensive', he told us when we learned of the enormous funds he received from a questionable donor. Questions about his deletion of messages related to the Covid enquiry were met with blank denial and apparent contempt for those asking them. Now, as the voices grow louder, he has dismissed a colleague for disloyalty without troubling the record with any proof to counter her denials.

The sparseness of Gething's defence is underlined by the ease with which Andrew RT Davies is making mincemeat of him on social media. The First Minister has, in a few weeks, contrived to make Davies seem sensible. Let. That. Sink. In.

Gething's antics today again made the UK press and just as the London Labour party can impose leaders on us so they can remove them when they become an embarrassment. It is telling, don't you think, that the much-vaunted professional operation

217

behind Sir Keir Starmer was unable to see through the pliable acquiescence of Vaughan Gething to the questionable nature of his success. Personal ambition has defined Gething's political career since his days on Cardiff Council. As long ago as 2013 he was facing allegations of electoral misconduct when he narrowly defeated Betty Campbell in Butetown. A simple Google search could have told the 'forensic' leader of the opposition that.

As things stand, the prospects of a bronze Vaughan Gething statue gazing out across Cardiff are very slim indeed.

From the Senedd to the Roofs

19 May 2024

I went to see the National Theatre's production of *Nye* on Friday evening.

We could have seen Michael Sheen's magnificent performance in person, there's a few tickets available at the Millennium Centre, but the filmed version at Hopkinstown Community Hall seemed more appropriate somehow.

Watching the play in a small, Valleys venue with a village feel and a table of retired NHS nurses passing round a box of Cadburys Roses underscored one of the play's themes, that the values of Wales birthed the UK's greatest social institution.

Bevan inspires a religious devotion in many of us. Flawed as he was, our perception is of a man whose motivation was principled and heartfelt.

As the solidity of 20th-century industrial life has given way to a technological quicksand that seems to give way beneath our feet, he is a touchstone of humanity in politics.

Religiosity, however, is a dangerous tendency when it comes to politics. For many of us with roots in industrial communities, putting a cross next to the Labour candidate is as reflexive as the one Catholics make when they see a funeral procession.

We're brought up on a whole testament of stories that see the Attlee government delivering us from evil forever and ever, amen.

If religions point towards the divine, it is persistent human error to start worshipping the finger and round here it can feel that way with Labour.

From Neil Kinnock onwards, a red rosette has frequently been employed not to celebrate the blood and guts of communities demanding change, but to conceal the timidity of those without the minerals or inclination to insist upon it.

Labour politicians in South Wales are amongst the most comfortable mammals on the planet.

Whilst I was watching socialism happen in the theatre, the Senedd Labour group was meeting to discuss something to which they are wholly unaccustomed: sustained scrutiny of their behaviour from within Wales.

Nation.Cymru's Martin Shipton and Emily Price have, over the last few months, brought to Welsh politics the journalistic rigour that a mature democracy demands.

Their questions of the First Minister have been necessary and would be considered standard practice in Westminster, Washington, or Paris.

Vaughan Gething's refusal to engage seriously with the concerns that surround his election as Labour leader, and his conduct during the pandemic would provoke a political crisis in any free society.

Consider, for a moment, what it is like to be a Labour supporter or activist at the moment.

Your work colleagues never shut up about 20mph speed limits and are convinced that the Senedd is stuffed full of gravy-train riders who don't understand the lives of ordinary people.

You're terrified yourself that you might pick up points on your commute to work; how will you afford the insurance?

Still, you tell yourself, personal sacrifice is the noblest aspect of community service. You've read the statistics on road traffic deaths, and this is just something we all need to live with.

It's the same as when you must remember to decelerate to 50mph on the M4. Doing so reduces air pollution which can damage the developing lungs of children and make life hard for older people too.

It's a pain in the arse when you just want to get home and there's next to no traffic, but that's how we roll. Those are our values. The blokes at work might take the piss but you're holding the line because it matters.

Now, imagine being that person when it emerged that the new leader of your party had taken two hundred grand in campaign donations from a convicted polluter.

How do you think the tea-break convo at work goes then?

Given the enormity of the death toll, you can assume that at least one colleague there lost a person dear to them during the worst stages of the pandemic.

What do you say to them when they ask why Vaughan Gething can't explain the deletion of crucial messages demanded by the Covid inquiry?

Apparently, you should accuse them of being racists.

Reports from the Labour group meeting describe the First Minister characterising the questions asked of him by the press as 'racially driven'.

On Saturday the Welsh Labour (sic) BAME Committee issued this statement:

We should be rightly proud that the appointment of Europe's first Black leader happened here in Wales.

As First Minister, Vaughan Gething represents all the people of Wales, whatever their background or political identity, and the fact that he is Black demonstrates that Wales is proud of all its children in all their diversity.

However, as Welsh Labour's BAME Committee we feel that we must also state that this achievement brings with it the danger of surfacing racist attitudes in the media and elsewhere. We would like to call on all in Welsh Labour to stand together to resist this path.

For so many BAME people in Wales the last few weeks have been disturbing, unsettling and yet very familiar. In the Welsh media the treatment of Vaughan Gething has gone well beyond what one can reasonably call fair scrutiny.

This led to, and was compounded by, a despicable article about the First Minister in the Daily Mail over the weekend, which used racially charged language of the sort we may have thought was a thing of the past.

We fully endorse thorough political scrutiny from a free press and from an active political community. However, we feel that this scrutiny in recent weeks has crossed a line between fair examination and racially influenced attitudes and judgements, with a Black person being held to a higher standard.

The issue also has consequences which reach far beyond the current political debate. We have always believed that Wales needs more people from the BAME community coming forward into our political institutions. The treatment of the First Minister over recent weeks will mean more BAME people thinking Welsh politics, and public life in general, is not for them.

Not only that, it remains the case that statistics show that if you are born Black in Wales you are more likely to have poorer education outcomes, as well as poorer representation. The struggle to achieve equality, not only in public view, but in the hearts and minds of all people, is ongoing. This project is something that is currently being set back at a time when we might all have hoped that it would take a step forward.

There have been many moments of reflection over the last few years in which people and institutions have accepted how subconscious racial prejudice can creep into the things they do and say. We believe we are seeing this play out before us, and we must act to stop it.

This is why we are speaking out, standing firmly behind Vaughan Gething, and calling on all in our movement to be allies, not bystanders.

Ruba Sivagnanam   *Mahaboob Basha*
Vice Chair   *Chair*

Now, the over-scrutiny of BAME politicians, along with that of females is most assuredly a real problem in UK politics. It takes many forms.

We have seen the absurd over-reporting of Diane Abbott drinking a mojito on the London underground and the inflation of her misstep in calculating the cost of police recruitment into a campaign of sustained national bullying.

Currently, the penny-halfpenny details of Angela Rayner's

historic house sale have generated exponentially more column inches than the many questions surrounding billions spent by Conservative ministers during the pandemic.

On the other side of the coin, left-wing journalists often suggest that politicians like Kemi Badenoch and Suella Braverman are to be condemned more vehemently than others for their views because their ethnicity implies a kind of betrayal.

All this journalistic practice is overtly prejudicial and common in UK publications.

By citing the *Daily Mail*, the Welsh Labour (sic) Committee seeks to draw equivalence between the dogwhistle filth of billionaire-owned tabloids and the scrutiny that Vaughan Gething is facing from the Welsh media.

The questions Mr Gething faces are not inflated 'gotchas' to further a separate agenda, they speak to fundamentals in our political landscape.

Mr Gething was previously Minister of Health during the most harrowing period of national life since the war. Subsequently, he has been elevated to the position of First Minister, the greatest entrustment that Wales can bestow.

To question the validity of examining his conduct during the pandemic and how he assumed his current office is outrageous.

If the press is to be constrained from doing the basic work the electorate demands of it, then why are we here?

It wasn't long ago that Andrew RT Davies was on the floor of the Senedd demanding the closure of *Nation.Cymru* because it was a government mouthpiece.

He still hasn't invited me for a pint, mind.

The meeting was held in response to Plaid Cymru ending their cooperation agreement with the government.

Here is where this incident becomes more urgent.

If we are racist for asking questions of the First Minister, then is Plaid also racist for withdrawing formal support for his government?

Racism has rightly become the most serious accusation in

public life. My own position is that antiracism is the only non-racist position a person or organisation can adopt.

To fall short of active opposition to bigotry is to tolerate it.

With that accusation on the table, the responsibility now lies with Labour members of the Senedd to state their position.

Do they believe the Welsh media, and specific journalists, to be racist or not? Do they believe Plaid Cymru's decision to be based on acceptance of a racist premise?

As Nye fades away at the end of Tim Price's play, held safe until his final moment by the NHS he created, that legacy is still stewarded by his party in Wales, and soon in the wider UK.

If there's a prejudice at play in the coverage of Vaughan Gething it is rooted in a distrust of his commitment to the historical values of his party in Wales.

His patrician contempt for those challenging him is at odds with the communities he seeks to lead, regardless of their ethnicity.

His problem is not that he represents the BAME people of Wales, but that he seems only to represent himself.

Confident as Labour candidates may be of Welsh crosses next to their names, they should remember Luke 12:3:

'What you have said in the dark will be heard in the daylight, and what you have whispered in the ear in the inner rooms will be proclaimed from the roofs.'

Crying in the Rain
22 May 2024

As Rishi Sunak stood outside Downing Street in the pouring rain to announce an election on July 4th, the optics matched his prospects. Over 14 years, the Conservative Party has lost its reputation, its credibility, its sanity, and its dignity. By the time Sunak assumed the helm, it was already listing in the water and beyond repair. It is a measure only of his vanity that this government has carried on so long.

Today's announcement was an admission that where we are now, with 0.6% growth shading us out of recession, and inflation somewhere within reason at last, is as good as it was going to get. This, it seems, is Sunak's electoral happy place. Bad weather in the channel is stemming the arrival of wretched souls on the beaches of Kent for a while and that will have to do. In an inversion of Tony Blair's theme song, things can only get worse. It's time to cut and run.

The first-past-the-post system means that UK elections are only ever about a handful of constituencies and polls suggest that this time the Conservatives will retreat into the innermost ventricles of its heartlands. Their campaign will be nothing to do with you. Money, grins, and slander will be expended on areas of England they have hitherto taken for granted as Central Office fights a rearguard action on behalf of MPs who believed their tenure to be for life. The cumulative horrors of Brexit, the Covid response, Boris Johnson's disgrace, and Liz Truss's disastrous farce, along with the financial pain they caused have left nearly every household in the country with a personal reason to vote the Tories out. Many find their obsession with immigration to be immoral and cruel, but even those who share their sentiments are furious that they have failed to enact any of the measures they proposed. This is less an election than an expulsion.

Which is not to suggest any widespread enthusiasm for Keir

Starmer's Labour Party. They may yet surprise us with a manifesto choc full of innovative solutions to the social ills blighting every village, town, and city in the country but, if so, they've done an unprecedented job in concealing them. More likely, we will be offered a programme of tinkering that leaves Brexit untouched and accepts austerity as principle of public finances.

There will be flags, oh my there will be more flags than you have ever seen. Neither Sunak nor Starmer will leave the house without a Union Flag to hand, and possibly draped around them to ward off the SNP.

The only variable at play is the size of Labour's victory. With Reform UK's Alf Garnett-fluffing shysters siphoning off some of the more distasteful Tory vote, it could be a majority that ends the Conservative Party as an electoral force. Has it ever gone into an election that it *couldn't* win? Not to my recollection, and such things tend to be habit-forming as the Liberals discovered after WW1.

With a Labour victory assured, it's possible that some areas of the country feel emboldened to vote more creatively than usual. Here in Wales, many people are not currently very enthusiastic about Labour and this time, can't rely on the coercive power of threatening us with a Tory government if we don't vote for it. There is a clear opportunity for an election in Wales that is defined entirely differently from the one going on over the border. Plaid Cymru, the Green Party, and even Reform UK could harness local grievance here much more effectively than they might in a tighter national race. It will be interesting to see which of these rises to the challenge. With Labour poised to control the Senedd and Westminster, many voters might see a clear advantage in sending a message that, for once, we aren't to be taken for granted. It is allowed, you know.

Taking a Dive

26 May 2024

We're wasting our time here, folks. Our gerrymandered, media-commanded charade of a democracy is essentially meaningless at the best of times but this year we are going through motions without any sense of jeopardy or need for debate at all.

Seventy-eight Conservative MPs have, at press time, announced that they are standing down to spend more time with their non-executive directorships. It had previously been assumed that Michael Gove could only be removed from national life by a trained professional with a tick hook, so news of his voluntary exit has a particular Robert-Maxwell-on-the-boat vibe about it.

So, very few 'Portillo moments' to look forward to on election night for those of us who have howled outrage at the outgoing delinquents throughout their wretched period in office.

Elections are never for people like us, though. If you're this far into *Nation.Cymru*'s opinion section, down here in the murky wallows of ill-natured speculation and spiteful gossip, then you share my unhealthy obsession with the doings of our elected representatives. We may differ in our conclusions, but we have more in common than we do with the people who decide elections.

Election time for us is to be a regular in the pub at Christmas. Your carefully ordered environment is briefly invaded by hordes of arrivistes shouting and unable to handle their drink. Your usual table in the corner, where you read the paper over a restorative lunchtime pint, is swarming with tinselled office workers who don't know how to order at the bar.

'A Crème de menthe and ginger, please. It's Christmas!'

That's who elections are for. Unfortunately, the world is crammed full of people who have a wide range of interests, a functioning family life, and insufficient time to drill down exhaustively into the blackened heart of the body politic. The best we can hope for is to peel them off, one at a time, when they are at their lowest ebb, and reveal to them the full horror of what we know. Get to them after a relationship breakup is my advice.

The only people who seem genuinely surprised by the timing of this election are out-of-the-loop Tory backbenchers who had been banking on another six months to set up post-parliamentary gigs to support their lifestyles. Labour, and Tories close to power, seem to have eased into the campaign without any sense of urgency or excitement. Even the participants are behaving like spectators to an inevitable process.

The only point of intrigue in all of this is whether the Conservatives are deliberately taking a dive. From announcing the election in the pouring rain to appearing in the Titanic district of Belfast and enquiring about football in Barry, Rishi Sunak seems to be going out of his way to ensure there is no possibility of victory. This weekend's offering is a promise to bring back National Service, complete with graphics that look suspiciously like a National Express advert.

We have now moved beyond the performative politics of the Rwanda plan, in which an unfeasible policy was suggested in the knowledge that it would never happen. In that scenario, the policy had support amongst a percentage of the electorate who could then be gaslit into believing it had been obstructed by sinister forces in the 'woke' establishment. It was grubby but had its own twisted logic.

Here we are presented with a parody of Conservative philosophy. It exists in the same cultural space as Lenin T-shirts as a signal that a previously powerful ideology has been defanged. The idea of herding unwilling teenagers into the modern armed forces or, God help us, NHS hospitals is so absurd that its message is clear. You are to vote Labour. The media have told you to, defecting Tory MPs have told you to, and the visuals of the Conservative campaign are telling you to. If you do *not* vote Labour, you are either immature, immoral, or insane. Just as in 2017 and 2019 it was socially unacceptable to vote *for* Labour, now it is taboo to vote against them.

After the election, when the tinsel has been swept up and we're able to get to the bar, we'll see what all this is about. My feeling is, if Michael Gove is fleeing the scene, it's about to get very ugly indeed.

Is he up to it?
30 May 2024

When Rishi Sunak took office as Prime Minister, there were a couple of hours after his opening speech, in which he promised to restore accountability to politics, when it seemed possible that we had seen the end of the Johnson/Truss circus of absurdity. Then he reappointed Suella Braverman at the Home Office and that hope was over. Dysfunctional organisations produce disordered outcomes, and the Conservative Party is, at best, nearing the end of a cycle of existence if not permanent extinction. So, in retrospect, it's simple to draw a line from Sunak's ill-conceived 'Eat Out to Help Out' catastrophe to the continuing performance of the government under his leadership. For a moment, though, something about his affect and presentation suggested to many that he represented a return to the 'grown-up' politics we had lacked since the beginning of the Brexit campaign. He seemed managerial and self-effacing when viewed in relief to the egotistical bombast of Johnson and ideological recklessness of Truss. His policies may have been anathema to those of us on the left, or extreme right, but nothing about him during his leadership campaign suggested that he was an agent of chaos.

I wonder if the nation is experiencing the same blind spot when it comes to Sir Keir Starmer. Objections to Starmer have tended to be ideological. The right distrusts his commitment to Brexit, whilst the left decry a perceived unwillingness to redress inequality alongside a foreign policy that appears to shadow the government. Neither of these groups have mounted a case that Starmer's government might prove to be incompetent.[1] If anything, his detractors are worried that it will be *too* effective in implementing a programme they dislike. Both sides warn of an immovable centrist force in government; a bland machine

---

[1] I hate to say I told you so…

imposing its will so insidiously that by the time voters wake up to the changes it has made, they will be irrevocable.

Starmer's record as a politician, however, suggests otherwise. As shadow Brexit Secretary, he wielded a lot of power in the Labour Party. Such support as it retained during the Corbyn years was heavily reliant on opposing the various government Brexit strategies. There was a point during Theresa May's premiership when party politics became almost irrelevant. Both parties were split and if either had advanced a coherent plan to get us through the post-referendum confusion, it would have been placed to shape the next decade. In pushing for a second referendum, Starmer lost the opportunity to secure a soft Brexit that would have respected the vote whilst preventing its most pernicious effects. Swathes of traditional Labour voters were lost in the process. Jeremy Corbyn's shortcomings as a leader are never far from the lips of UK politicians and commentators. Starmer's misreading of the nation at this crucial time seems not to have made it into the accepted narrative.

More recently, Starmer allowed himself to be boxed into endorsing Israel's threat to cut off water and power in Gaza. This happened during an interview with Nick Ferrari, LBC's veteran presenter, and it illuminates some dynamics in Labour's current performance. Ferrari is a grizzled and wily operator on the right of British politics, and he clearly smelt weakness during this encounter. Under pressure, Starmer appeared to explicitly endorse war crimes and has had to spend the last six months finessing himself out of that corner. I'm more forgiving than some on this particular incident. I don't believe that Starmer is ideologically rabid enough to believe in the outcome he appeared to suggest. One of his trumpeted attributes is that he is not a career politician; he's a lawyer who has come into politics because of a sense of duty. He is, though, about to plunge into a world where Nick Ferrari is the least of his problems. Everybody from Putin and Xi Xinping to unfriendly figures in the Civil Service will be lined up against him and they know he can be wrongfooted. Centrist politicians lack the

231

comfortable certainty of those with ideological ballast. Margaret Thatcher's appeal lay in the simplicity of her arguments, much the same could be said for Tony Benn. It is much trickier to sell the centre position, laden as it is with compromise, contradiction, and nuance. To pull it off requires the political instincts and singlemindedness of a Tony Blair or Bill Clinton.

Many close to Blair were surprised at his refusal to expel Jeremy Corbyn when the electric gardener was openly calling for a leadership election. Blair's position was that his strength derived from the structural integrity of the Labour Party as a recognisably progressive force and that to offload Corbyn would threaten that. This week's floundering over Diane Abbott suggests that Starmer, with Peter Mandelson in his ear, has mistaken political expedience for strategy. The appeal of not being the Tories will evaporate upon contact with power and the ex-Tory voters to whom Abbott has seemingly been sacrificed will be the first to reject Starmer when immediate solutions to endemic problems are not forthcoming. To whom will he turn then?

B&M or Home Bargains?
2 June 2024

Thank God for democracy! In return for not lopping off the heads of the Windsor family we get to send *whomever we like* to parliament on our behalf. It is, in theory, the only agency a person can exercise that isn't determined by wealth. Just as in our free market economy, where you are at liberty to express your very dignity by deciding whether to buy pan scourers from Home Bargains or B&M, you can choose between red and blue at the ballot box. It's slightly different this time, after the management at B&M nicked most of the stock and set fire to the store but you're still in control, sovereign citizen. Tremble before the majesty of your decision.

The homogenisation of life in the 21st century gives me the ick. Wherever I go in the world, people are selling the same tat, all sourced from central warehouses and circling the globe in shipping containers before being passed off as local handicrafts to saps like me. My spirit rages against it even as my card details are being captured by a bloke in traditional dress and sent to Visa or Mastercard.

The revulsion of everything being a simulacrum of life as it used to be is clinging to me during this election. I'm fine with politicians lying to me. It's what they do. We price in a healthy percentage of bullshit promises at election time just as we know that souk-purchased Rolexes are unlikely to have been crafted within earshot of a cuckoo clock. The base line, after all the flannel, was that taxes were supposed to go down under the Tories and public services were supposed to improve under Labour. In practice, the difference was far less than promised but those were the ambitions. The rich want lower taxes, the poor want better services and those in between decide the election depending on how far the pendulum has swung. Your only obligation is to vote for your own interests.

Not this time, apparently. We have heard much about

Labour's 'Ming vase' strategy in this election. The party has been disciplined not to promise anything that might spook the electorate out of trusting it with power. 20% ahead in the polls and rising, the strategy seems to have been a success. The only public figure who still believes that Keir Starmer can be derailed on his way to Downing Street is Peter Hitchins, in his role as the mad old aunt of British commentary.

But, despite the Ming vase being swaddled in three yards of bubble wrap and under 24-hour guard by Special Branch, Labour is adamant that it could shatter at any moment. Only by chasing down every last Conservative voter, deep into the leafy lanes of Surrey, can victory be assured. Sir Keir's 'changed' party must become the natural party of government, as appealing to business as it is to workers.

The problem here is that the interests of hardcore Conservative voters are diametrically at odds with those of traditional Labour voters. Put baldly, them 'uns have all the stuff and us 'uns want some of it. They have no incentive to see our services improve, and we have no interest in seeing their share dividends flourish further. That presents Labour with a choice. They *could* choose to square that circle by putting the case for a more equal UK to those who have benefited from Conservative rule. Poverty breeds crime and indolence, whilst a prosperous general population will, over time, spend their money on goods and services that provide a return to investors. It's a simple argument but one that requires an appeal to long-term thinking. Boris Johnson made this case with his levelling-up agenda, only to abandon it when the going got tough.

That case is not being made by Labour. Instead, it is appealing to Conservative voters with explicit promises not to disrupt their privilege. Instead of selling the benefits of equality, it is quelling fears of it coming about. Meanwhile, those of us in deprived areas are receiving moral instructions that we are committing heresy if we so much as grumble about the party's offering. Not only are we to vote for policies crafted to appeal to people who share none of our concerns, we are to do it with a smile on our faces or be lumped in with the Tories.

The sole benefit of the first-past-the-post system is its reflection of local character. To mitigate the absence of direct influence on government, we are permitted to send our brightest and best to advocate for us. If that check is removed from the process, it becomes a tyranny, regardless of which party is in power. As Labour candidates are imposed on Welsh constituencies, and a closed-list system looms for Senedd elections, we are becoming wholly divorced from our governance. What possible incentive will a UK Labour government have to act in our interests if the only jeopardy it faces comes from voters in the traditionally Conservative constituencies of England? What resistance will it encounter from Labour members of the Senedd whose candidature is gifted by the UK party?

As the parties lay out their wares at this election, we need to be inspecting them carefully. Democracy in the UK has always been a compromised and flimsy concession of influence. To enjoy even that, we had to threaten disorder on a regular basis. What we're being offered now looks like a Chinese knock-off to me.

The Toxic Entitlement of Labour
6 June 2024

How times change. The last I remember, *Nation.Cymru* was being condemned in the Senedd as a Pravda-style mouthpiece for the Labour government, whilst Plaid Cymru's Senedd cohort were the toothless handmaids of its agenda. Martin Shipton, Adam Price, and Mark Drakeford were equal partners in a bicycle repair business that was set to cash in on a 20mph tyranny over Welsh motorists. Chinking glasses of Chablis as they smiled contentedly over Cardiff Bay, the triumvirate conspired to deny plucky Andrew 'Real Ting' Davies his seat at the table. Muwahahaaaaa!

So, what's going on by here now in a minute?

First off, let's raise a cap to Hannah Blythyn and Lee Waters. Objecting to your boss by pulling a sickie is the most authentically working-class action conceivable. I'd be disappointed if they didn't treat themselves to a pub lunch after croaking their apologies down the phone.

There's nothing quite as enervating as a suddenly understaffed workplace. Everybody must rush around picking up unfamiliar tasks and speaking to people they know don't know. In Labour's case yesterday, that meant the people of Wales.

'Hello, I'm concerned that the First Minister is only in place because of questionable donations from a convicted criminal whose wealth derives in part from loans the First Minister facilitated.'

'I'm terribly sorry, we're understaffed at the moment, but it says here that you're a racist.'

'Good morning, is it right that the First Minister lied to the Covid Inquiry about deleting messages it had asked for?'

'I haven't read the notes so I'm going to assume that you are a Tory who wants eight-year-old children to be forced down

236

the mines. Thank you.'

'Hello, I've never called in before but I'm worried that the dignity of Welsh democracy is under threat and...'

'Will you shut up, it's D-Day for God's sake!'

Labour has never come under this sort of media pressure before in Wales and its fragility was on full display yesterday.

Hefin David MS has spent the week flouncing around like a grounded teenager, issuing preachy tweets with the replies disabled, and insinuating that any dissent must be grounded in prejudice. Mike Hedges MS appeared so broadsided by events that he relinquished syntax in favour of an incoherent soundtrack to his mimed outrage. When no Labour members of the Senedd agreed to appear on BBC Wales, Stephen Kinnock MP stepped in to instruct the nation that Vaughan Gething was a man of integrity and honour.

The cumulative impression given by Labour figures is that commonplace scrutiny is an impertinence. By yesterday evening, the wider Labour family was joining in.[1]

> Todays vote was a desperate gimmick to distract from the Tories & Plaid Cymru's faltering election campaigns
>
> With two Senedd members on the sick, this was always a cheap political trick [...]
>
> – @GMBWSW, the GMB Wales & Southwest X account
> (June 5, 2024)

Tweets like that attracted dozens of outraged responses which went ignored. The institutional pillars of Labour: the MSs, MPs, union officials and party workers were content to pronounce and then leave their statements to stand alone.

Well, they would, wouldn't they? The entire civic structure of Wales has been moulded by Labour over the last century. Anybody who works for the government, most councils, the charitable sector, the media, and, increasingly, private business, knows their position exists in relation to its monolithic presence

---

[1] https://x.com/GMBWSW/status/1798399626636382567

237

in national life. *I'm on the committee, Butt...* The Labour establishment in Wales seems as entrenched and interdependent as the public-school mafia in England.

So, when Adam Price reflected the ghost of Aneurin Bevan back at the Labour benches during yesterday's debate, it was received as heresy.

'Shame on you!' called the Gething loyalists.

On telly, Kinnock denounced Plaid Cymru as being 'in bed with the Tories' in this 'gimmick', this 'stunt'. Specific objections, it seems, can only be part of a juvenile and partisan hostility to the governing party.

An overwhelming Labour majority seems inevitable in Westminster and the party in Wales needs to buckle up. With no Tory overlords to blame for hospital waiting lists, exam results, potholes, or endemic regional poverty, the automatic moral superiority implied by a red rosette will be revoked.

The Senedd has no confidence in its leader. That is a hard fact, not something that can be politicked away. The people telling us to ignore it are also insisting that clever men from London are required to represent our parliamentary constituencies. The toxic entitlement of the Labour Party in Wales is creating a vacuum in representation last seen by Scotland during the Blair years. If it refuses to listen, then it must be made to hear.

The Wages of Sin
9 June 2024

If you feel guilty about the impulse to laugh at those in discomfort, you should give yourself a break.

It's a necessary psychological process to cope with the knowledge of your own mortality and there's nothing you can do about it.

Especially when the butt of the joke is the Tories.

Observing the Conservative death-spiral is to experience the Platonic ideal of *Schadenfreude*.

It is to be present at the comically botched execution of a heinous criminal who refuses to relinquish his favoured role as executioner, even as the noose is slipped around his neck.

Better yet, no hood is being employed so you can watch his facial expressions. So far, we've seen derision, contempt, and disbelief.

Over the next few weeks, we have anger, terror and resignation to look forward to as the murderous architects of austerity finally realise that the vultures circling overhead are for them at last.

Well, them's the breaks. Be sure to add your own guffaw to their final moments.

In the meantime, though, I urge all decent people to enjoy the spectacle. The incoming mauve administration offers even less in terms of comedy than it does as regards social reform, so now is the time to revel in this era-defining event.

Because they're not just going to lose, it's going to be an extinction event.

One of the circling vultures is N. Farage esq. and he has already stated his intention of 'taking over' whatever is left of the 'natural party of government' providing that he wins a seat.

'All Eyes on Clacton' might sound like a racy 1970s

239

comedy starring Robin Asquith but is, in fact, far tawdrier than that.

The Conservative & Unionist Party, previously stewarded by Disraeli, Churchill, and, er, Iain Duncan-Smith is now facing the sort of cultural makeover that Sports Direct recently inflicted on House of Fraser.

Hook it to my veins!

They are currently still in the bargaining stage of grieving their relevance in British life.

During last week's Sunak v Starmer yawnsville debate, the PM was understandably keen to avoid discussion of his party's record in office.

His tactic was to roll his eyes and admonish Starmer for being 'obsessed with the past' whilst he, Sunak, was looking to the future. It was desperate stuff but at least rooted in an acknowledgement of reality.

Unfortunately, the immediate future held Sunak's ill-advised disappearing act from the commemoration of D-Day in Normandy.

The following day, Tory MPs were trying to close down questions about this on the basis that 'we've all moved on' and 'need to look to the future.'

In the panic of imminent annihilation, the Tories now require us to wipe clean the slate every morning and be reborn into a blameless idyll where consequence is forgotten.

It is the fantasy of the condemned. And condemn them we must.

Finally, after all these years, the despicable tone of their governance has finally been turned on them.

Forever fetishising the past, and consistently colluding in the racist dog whistles of its defenders in the press, the Tories are caught in the slurry pit of their own immorality.

Much of the criticism of Sunak this week hinted at an innate deficit of patriotism in the UK's first Asian Prime Minister.

He attended most of the commemorations then left the international segment to his Foreign Secretary whilst he went home to try to salvage whatever he could for the party that elevated him.

He was crucified for it because the xenophobic, shallow jingoism of his party's corrupted soul was destined to get him in the end.

He's getting what he deserves, and so are they.

For Welsh Labour, See UK Labour

13 June 2024

The manifesto published by Labour today mentions Wales 20 times in its 135 pages. The majority of these are 'England & Wales', or 'Scotland, Northern Ireland & Wales' general references with the rest confined to the Wales-specific section reproduced below.

Welsh devolution and the Wales Office Wales has been failed by a chaotic and divisive Conservative Government that does not understand the ambitions of the Welsh people and refuses to work with the Welsh Government to achieve them.

Labour will serve Wales with a plan that matches those ambitions. We will strengthen the relationship between the governments in Westminster and Cardiff Bay. The two governments will work collaboratively to deliver Labour's national missions. Labour recognises that the Welsh Fiscal Framework is out of date.

We are committed to working in partnership with the Welsh Government to ensure the framework delivers value for money with two Labour governments committed to fiscal responsibility. Labour recognises the value of integrated public services, which are more efficient and create better outcomes.

As part of the strategic review into probation, we will explore the devolution of services to enable them to be more locally responsive. We will work with the Welsh Labour Government to consider devolution of youth justice.

In line with our commitment to devolve employment support in England, Labour will devolve employment support funding to the Welsh Government.

Welsh culture, products and services are renowned around the world – from the thriving tourism sector and highest-quality steel to Welsh Lamb and semi-conductors. Labour will harness

242

the UK's diplomatic and trade networks, working with the Welsh Government to champion Wales across the world.

With Labour, the Wales Office will once again become an advocate for Wales at home and abroad and facilitate closer collaboration between our governments. The Wales Office will ensure on issues under the competence of the UK Government the voice of Wales is properly heard.

In fairness to Labour, this vague offering is of a piece with the rest of its manifesto which, above all, seems crafted to reassure rather than inspire. There is recognition that the Welsh Fiscal Framework is 'out of date' but this is swiftly followed by a commitment to 'value for money' and 'fiscal responsibility'. If Labour had intentions of redesignating Welsh investment in HS2, or devolving administration of the Crown Estates you can be sure it would be in included here, so forget about that.

There are minor devolutionary ambitions for probation and youth justice. These two areas are wholly contingent on non-devolved economic and social policy, so a cynic might conclude that what's being devolved here is blame.

The wider picture is hinted at by the statement that, 'The two governments will work collaboratively to deliver Labour's national missions.' These 'national missions' are also mentioned in the section devoted to Scotland, so we can assume that the nation in question is the UK, rather than Wales.

This suggests a substantive change in the workings of devolution, as might be expected when the same party oversees both institutions. With the Conservatives in power at Westminster, the UK Labour Party benefited politically from Welsh Government policy diverging from UK norms. If policies worked well, it was proof that progressive Labour government delivered, if they failed, the Tory government could safely be blamed on grounds of national underfunding.

After July 4th, the Welsh Government is to be harnessed in service of a UK-wide programme which has been mandated by many traditionally Conservative areas of England. How that can

243

be married to the socio-economic concerns of Wales is unclear.

When Rhodri Morgan stood up to the Blair government at the turn of the Millennium, it defined Welsh democracy as a distinct, radical force that aspires to self-determination and meaningful influence on UK policy.

There is no Labour figure in Wales today who carries the authority or goodwill that was enjoyed by Morgan. Nothing emanating from its leadership in the Senedd suggests that it has any appetite for challenging the UK party one iota.

Plaid Cymru's own manifesto, which was also launched today, casts a canny eye over the landscape that will emerge after the election. If Labour in Westminster discounts the singularity of Welsh concerns whilst, at home, its leadership continues to lose the trust of the people, then the conditions that saw the SNP usurp Labour in Scotland for a generation may emerge here.[1]

---

[1] This is what youngsters call 'cope'.

The Centre Cannot Hold

16 June 2024

How long to go, another two weeks? We're into the uphill portion of the election now. Anything remotely interesting that the parties might have had to reveal has been said so all that's left is for politicians to run around the country bellowing slogans in the hope that the UK's densest citizens wake up to their appeal.

'Keir, we need you in Cwmcarn, there's a man here who says he doesn't know your dad was a toolmaker, we're sending the chopper.'

Now that the fickle masses have cottoned on that it's socially acceptable to bully Rishi Sunak, he'll face a lifetime's hardship quota in 18 days, likely emerging with the embittered worldview and ciggy habit of late-period Bet Lynch in *Coronation Street*.

'I'll tell ya, kid, you can't trust them. My trouble was I loved too much...'

This election has a dreamlike quality to it. The substantive outcome is guaranteed, so our attention is captured by anything that might provide a more nuanced insight into the 'Tories bad, Labour good' fanfare of the result.

In our peripheral vision, strange apparitions vie for attention. David Cameron is everywhere, pronouncing in that reassuring, polished voice he has as if the last nine years didn't happen at all.

2015 has entered the chat...

Ed Miliband, another tonal reminder of life before the flood, adds his jolly, self-deprecating input, as if his electoral failure didn't usher in a catastrophe of governance that is etched on the graves of Covid victims and austerity martyrs.

It is comforting, I suppose, to hear the voices of politicians who are associated with simpler times. Democracy was a lot

245

more navigable before we were all forced to get our heads around WTO rules, spike proteins, and Lee Anderson. The electorate is coming down from a particularly heavy trip and it craves familiarity.

We're not going to get it, though.

Watching the 7-way debate on telly the other evening, I was struck by how strangely unbalanced it was. The ruling party was represented by Penny Mordaunt, an ersatz Boudica who, I am willing to risk a libel action, withdrew from the Tory leadership contest in return for carrying a sword at the Coronation. If the Conservatives were to win this election, it would inconvenience her plans for the future.

Ranged against her, Angela Rayner looked like Kurt Cobain on a record company-mandated appearance on The Muppet Show. You could imagine the chuckling at Labour HQ as Rayner squirmed while selling the most watered-down Labour offering in history. Boasting an origin story that is everything Keir Starmer pretends to be, Rayner didn't join Labour for this. You could see it in her eyes. After the election, she'll be a problem.[1]

So, the main event was contested by actors who didn't believe in their roles. The central space where the UK's issues are traditionally decided has become one of those rip-off Winter Wonderlands that are a mainstay of Christmas headlines. 'I took my child to his first election and all he saw was Wes Streeting in an elf costume. Michael Gove didn't even turn up.'

Around them, however, an actual debate was happening. Nigel Farage's position is far more bracing than expected. Whilst everyone who has followed his career knows that he is all about the money, he seems emboldened to say the quiet bits out loud now. With toxic rhetoric on immigration now an established feature of UK politics, Farage has pushed the envelope to overtly support the dismantling of the NHS.

In the red corner, Rhun ap Iorweth of Plaid Cymru and Stephen Flynn of the SNP mounted explicit defences of

---

[1] More cope.

immigration and investment in public services. There, between Farage and the progressive edge of Wales and Scotland, exists the real, meaningful battle for the UK's future.

Labour's line that investment can happen without extra taxation is dependent on economic growth that is not predicted for the UK economy. For all the performative caution of their presentation, the Labour offering is pure Mr Micawber: 'Something will turn up.'

If something *doesn't* turn up, then the election after this will see Labour where the Conservatives are now. This is the Last Chance Saloon for a traditional party to deliver for the traumatised people of the UK. If Labour fails to effect meaningful change, its victory will be Pyrrhic.

The Way and the Light
19 June 2024

What is it with Labour in Wales and answering questions?

The First Minister treats enquiries about his various irregularities as an impertinence or, latterly, evidence of prejudice on the part of those asking.

This week, the Shadow Secretary of State for Wales, Jo Stevens, seemed to regard Catrin Haf Jones's impeccably crafted interview questions as irrelevant to her role.

Clearly irritated with the line being taken, Stevens gave the impression that the issues at hand were a distraction from the big picture of UK politics.

Right off the bat, Stevens disclosed her caste of mind. Asked how a Labour victory would lead to change in Wales, she explained that,

'The UK government controls a lot of what goes on in Wales.'

As the interview unfolded, it became evident that this state of affairs is not merely acceptable to the incoming Secretary of State, but desirable. In her own words, 'Devolution is an agreement, not a demand.'

Well, good to get that learnt.

Conservative plans to electrify the North Wales Main Line may not, it seems, be affordable. The money invested by Wales into HS2 is apparently 'not there' anymore.

Repeatedly promising to 'work hand in hand' with the Welsh government, Ms Stevens seemed not to recognise its legitimacy as regards longstanding demands for the devolution of criminal justice.

We discovered that recommendations to devolve probation and youth justice are not to be implemented but, rather, explored. Pressed on whether this represented a betrayal of devolution, Stevens invoked the desires of 'the people of

Wales'.

These 'people of Wales' aren't interested in 'fiddling around with structures and systems.'

Vaughan Gething, she claimed, is also listening to the 'people of Wales'. Dismissing the recent vote of no confidence as a stunt mounted by the Conservatives in connivance with Plaid Cymru, Stevens effectively erased the democratic legitimacy of the Senedd.

The 'people of Wales' can have a parliament, but the Secretary of State is the way and the light. Only through her can the 'people of Wales' reach the ears of power.

A clear picture of how Wales is to be governed after the election is beginning to emerge. Earlier this week, *Nation.Cymru* revealed that Labour's Westminster whips' office had attempted to bring pressure on members of the Senedd before the First Minister's confidence motion.

Last week, Ms Stevens told us that money to replace EU funding would be distributed not by the Welsh Government, but by 'representatives of Wales'. A cynic might infer that both the 'people of Wales' and the 'representatives of Wales' are, in fact, the incoming Secretary of State herself.

Progressive reforms in Wales have, until now, been politically useful to the national party.

As the UK has suffered under Conservative austerity, Labour have been able to point to the Welsh government as an example of social justice.

Now that the party has accepted the current government's fiscal rules, that situation is reversed. Unless the economy grows far more quickly than most experts predict, Labour will need to find £17 billion in cuts to public services over its term in office.

Welsh measures, like free prescriptions, which were once a matter of pride for the UK party are set to become a stick with which it can be beaten. If the rest of the UK is not to be levelled-up in terms of social justice, then the pressure will be on to level-down the spendthrifts in Cardiff Bay.

Wales' loyalty to Labour is, perversely, its weakness once

the party is in power. Juicy, safe seats have been handed out as rotten boroughs to potential fast-tracked ministers, whilst funding is removed from Welsh democratic control.

Devolution has indeed been an agreement rather than a demand in Wales. Belief that Labour UK governments will eventually do right by us has fostered an affable 'jam tomorrow' atmosphere in our relationship with Westminster.

Political positions, however, can change, as Ms Stevens well knows. As recently as 2015, she was calling for unilateral nuclear disarmament. In 2013, she was mourning the socialist leader of Venezuela, Hugo Chavez, whom she described as her 'political hero'.

What happened to all that?

Jo Stevens' remarks this week sought to diminish self-determination as a factor in every question she faced. She reduced Welsh nationhood to cultural window dressing, and our Senedd to the talking shop the Conservatives always accused it of being.

In an election that seems unnaturally predetermined, it is Wales that has the most at stake.

Our rugby team are playing a home match at Twickenham this weekend. Watch the boys and remember how it feels.

Landed on Mayfair

23 June 2024

Does anybody even know the rules to Monopoly? If we ever did, they are lost to time when the set is brought out to distract everyone from ancient, family resentments.

Never trust anyone who wants to be the top hat, I'm always the little dog myself: unthreatening and unassuming, yet stolid and determined.

At the end of the game, when a ghastly brother-in-law has accumulated unsurpassable tracts of prime London real estate, and you're left with the deeds to the gasworks and Old Kent Road because you 'don't live in the real world', it ceases to be a pleasant pastime and takes on the soul-crushing inevitability of life in general.

Marcus – let's call him that, because I want you to hate him, and everybody hates a Marcus – is desperate for the game to continue.

As you dream of a walk in nature, away from this grotesque charade, he wants to lend you £2000 in fake money, so that he can take it off you on your next go round the board and whoop to the thrill of his ape dominance over your childhood home at Christmas.

That stage of the game was reached in 2008, when the world's capital was sucked up, like a line of coke, by the world's ultimate shitty brother-in-law, the banks.

Hindsight is 20:20, but its abundantly clear that the board should have been turned over then, the table pushed back, the family guillotine wheeled in from the shed, and the coal bucket emptied as a receptacle for the head of your sister's unfortunate marital error.

Instead, we've allowed Marcus to pay us off with PIP, furlough, cost-of-living payments, and mortgage deferments as if the rotten, autumnal droppings from his tree were compensation for a life lived on the forest floor.

Sixteen years of economic stagnation has settled on the people of the UK like a degenerative disease. All we can rely on is that next year will be worse than this.

One wrong move at work and the little security you have will be taken from you and your credit score obliterated.

Like medieval serfs, our wellbeing is dictated by whims we can never comprehend.

'Why has my mortgage doubled?'

'Because Liz Truss questioned transubstantiation.'

Are you surprised, then, that wild ideas are taking hold? When you are walking round the post-apocalyptic high streets of post-industrial Wales, where the only viable businesses pander to vices or peddle Chinese tat, can you tolerate it?

Labour's stately procession towards stewardship of our decline doesn't reflect the seriousness of the situation. Even here, where making the best of things is a matter of pride, nobody is happy, are they?

Look at your local Facebook group and observe decent people channelling their rage into complaints about overflowing bins and dog shit.

'It's the council! They are all in hospitality suites at the Taylor Swift show whilst XL bullys drop empty Prime bottles where the playground used to be!'

Not to worry, though, Sir Keir Starmer, Sir Rachel Reeves, and Sir Wes Streeting MFC[1] are here to euthanise our dreams politely and with dignity. Your call is important to them.

It's not important to Nigel Farage, either. He has, though, at least taken the time to record an entertaining answer machine message.

As you hang on to communicate your frustration to Nigeco Ltd, he tells you of a 20% income tax threshold, 50%

---

[1] This is an acronym of my own devising that sailed through the *Nation.Cymru* editorial process without challenge. Fans of Enid Blyton's *Magic Faraway Tree* series will be best placed to decipher it.

nationalisation of utilities, and that your kids being conscripted into a Russian war is preventable.

Human beings can't live without hope.

Every story we devise leads to our redemption and, crucially, centres us personally as the authors of it.

I see no hero's journey for any of us in Labour's offering, no route out into the sunlight, just another go around the board with humiliation at the end.

If they don't ginger things up when they get into office, the siren call of populist hucksters will amplify.

Something must be done, this is something, therefore it must be done.

The Dignity of Toil
27 June 2024

You have to hand it to the Conservatives. Having besmirched the body politic with indulgence in seemingly every conceivable human frailty and vice over the last 14 years, they've managed to squeeze in gambling as the fat lady's final note is decaying into silence. Their sheer commitment to grubbiness is unmatched outside of ecclesiastic circles.

Which made it all the more risible during last night's debate when Rishi Sunak wheeled out the belief most beloved of all politicians: that we, the swinish multitude, derive 'dignity' from work.

I would dearly love to meet whoever first advanced this idea, so that I could look him in the eye and shake him warmly by the neck. Dignity, indeed! Uniquely amongst the dishonest, manipulative tropes that politicians lob at us, they undoubtedly believe this one. As you are scrabbling around in the dark at 6am, in search of a sock without a hole in it so that you can get on the road before it bottlenecks into a car park, Johnny Politico likes to imagine your eagerness to contribute to the national cause. When you arrive, sweating and apologising for the traffic making you late, he pictures you wrapped in a flag, frustrated that your productivity has been constrained. At lunchtime, as you dive into Greggs to cram down a steak bake whilst your boss barks further instructions down the phone, your elected representative sees you sat on a Constable waggon wheel, taking a moment to survey the bucolic perfection of the morning's ploughing. As direct debits hurtle out of your account on pay day, pushing you into the red if you escaped it in the first place, he takes comfort that you have earned the respect of your peers. Finally, when you're carted up the local crem years before your time, with cemented arteries and a spine like a coat hanger, you have his ultimate respect.

If you were a miner, he might have once suggested that you

were 'the enemy within'. Perhaps, as a junior doctor, he called you a 'doctor in training'. Never mind, 'lefty lawyers', 'lazy council workers', 'ideological teachers', 'overpaid train drivers' and the rest of us are all forgiven once we've been worked into the grave. A six-foot hole full of dignity awaits us all if we are fortunate enough to avoid the hell of a life lived off investments.

At some point next Thursday morning, a victorious politician will tell us how he is looking forward to 'rolling up his sleeves' because there is so much work to be done. Both main candidates know all about this, after all their parents had jobs, apparently.

Like you, though, they aren't in it for the money. Inspired by the dignity that dripped off their fathers into the tin bath by the fire, they are fuelled only by 'service'. Ever so 'umble they are, and unable to conceive of a selfish thought. So, forgive them if they romanticise your relationship with work a little. These vessels of honest duty just see themselves in you. Silhouetted against the fire of a blast furnace, you gaze skywards in their mind's eye, soundtracked by the Morriston Orpheus Choir and smeared in soot, you carry their dreams in your snap tin.

But remember, if you have to be replaced by AI, it's your own fault.

Voting With My Heart

30 June 2024

When the crack troops of nondescript centrism descend on my timeline to chide me for failing to leap aboard the Starmer train, their charges are always some combination of the following:

Enabling the Tories[1]

To be honest, anyone capable of enabling the Tories at this stage should be founding a religion based on their powers of revivification. They have, as John Cleese had it, turned up their toes and gone to join the bleedin' choir invisible. It is testament to the trauma they have inflicted upon us all that even now, as the hearse idles on Smith Square, their waxen rictus can still inspire fear. But no, refusal to vote Labour is not going to invoke the ghost of Margaret Thatcher to rise in the Rhondda and privatise Ponty lido. The Labour vote around here will be weighed on industrial scales as usual, with Chris Bryant MP experiencing fewer election night jitters than typically endured by Kim Jong Un. Using fear to motivate a Rhondda resident to vote Labour is like expecting an otter to apply moisturiser.

It's easy to be a cynic

It is, isn't it? You could, for instance, win the leadership of a political party by making a series of principled, written pledges on policy, only to abandon them all and tell the people who voted for you to sling their hook if they don't like it. Alternatively, you could spend years demanding billions in reparations for a failed high-speed rail project, only to revalue it

---

[1] Actual people that I know and have encountered in three dimensions accused me of this. Their names have been added to a list.

to fourpence when it looks like your party's government might have to cough up. Perhaps you are tanking in the polls after accidentally endorsing war crimes in the Middle East, time to be 'absolutely clear' that you've always called for an immediate ceasefire *terms and conditions apply*.

So, yes, I'm cynical. Anybody paying attention to all this would need a head that buttons up the back not to be. Experience has taught us that shining-eyed optimism is rarely wise when it comes to politics, but we do usually have to wait until they are elected before being gutted. Starmer's Labour, after peeing down our legs and telling us its raining, can't really object if our trousers whiff a bit.

Immature idealism

As well as being the embittered spite of cynical losers, objections to Labour are simultaneously founded upon a childlike belief in a better world that only belongs at the top of magic, faraway trees. Fans of Enid Blyton's wonderful forest trilogy[2] might enjoy imagining Wes Streeting as Moonface, and Jo Stevens as the washerwoman, but we discuss serious politics here, so do it in your own time.

I can't speak for you, but my grand hopes for change are rather more timid than they used to be. Nobody's nationalising the banks, I get that. *Love Island* will not, in my lifetime, be replaced on ITV by proletarian dramas produced by workers' creative units as part of their 25-hour/week employment contracts. Neither will Alan Sugar be forcibly re-educated and taken on tours of the nation's schools to repudiate his filthy, exploitative past and promote a spirit of egalitarianism amongst the nation's children. By the same token, though, I don't accept that enforcing £18 billion[3] of cuts on public services that have already been picked bare by Tory vultures is somehow a grown-

---

[2] The only 'literature' I have ever needed.
[3] How did I know this *before* Rachel Reeves 'opened the books' and discovered her blackhole? It's one for Scooby Doo and the gang.

up thing to do.

The Tories have destroyed trust in politics so you must vote Labour

Vaughan Gething has entered the chat. *Parachuted candidates have entered the chat*. *Westminster whips threatening Members of the Senedd have entered the chat*.

So, here's where I'm at, for what it's worth. A Labour government is inevitable. They know it, the Tories know it, Farage knows it, and the media knows it.

What remains at stake in this election is how this government behaves. The Senedd election in 2026 is timed to act as a mid-term gauge of Labour's popularity in the wider UK. With the threat of Tory governance gone, Wales is in a position *now* to send a message to UK Labour that it is in peril here and needs to fear Welsh voters in a way it never has. Huge majorities here in Wales will render us an irrelevance as Starmer governs to keep newly won constituencies in England and Scotland.

If the party sees signs on Thursday that it could face embarrassment in 2026, it will think twice about how its decisions affect us here. Impressive progressive cases have been made in this campaign, but not by Labour. I'll be voting with my heart, it's not quite broken yet.

Cleansing rain falls on
a Tory-free Wales

5 July 2024

Out, damned spot! Cleansing rain fell on a Tory-free Wales this morning after the UK acted in concert to evict the party not only from power, but from the national conversation. After five years that saw us enduring hardship and upheaval that has changed us forever, the driving emotion of this election result was revulsion.

For people bereaved during the pandemic, homeowners whose mortgages have soared, people suffering from cuts to a range of public services, and those whose pensions have been devalued, governance since 2019 has seemed like abuse. At the very time when wise and gentle leadership was needed, the Conservatives offered irresponsible, callous politicians whose personal behaviour often reflected the public decline they oversaw. Many chose not to face the electorate at all, standing down before the public could issue its verdict. Those who remained, including the inconsequential Rishi Sunak, didn't so much campaign as cower through the last six weeks, bracing themselves for their just desserts. The result is less a political decision than it is a trauma reaction from voters whose decency has been outraged and who needed to be seen.

Refreshing as rain can be, though, it doesn't provide a backdrop for a new day in the nation's mood. A disciplined Labour campaign saw the party achieve an unprecedented majority without significantly increasing its share of the vote. Many of its gains were the result of the Tories haemorrhaging votes to Nigel Farage's Reform UK. You Gov published a poll[1] this week of people's reasons for voting Labour. 48% responded that their motivation was to remove the Tories, a further 13%

---

[1] https://yougov.co.uk/politics/articles/49947-why-are-britons-voting-labour

because the country needed a change. Only 5% of respondents cited approval of the party's policies as their reason.

It's far from clear what the party intends to do in office for many people, me included. A vague manifesto and a front bench that lacks many recognisable figures leaves the party with a huge mandate but no defined mission. While the public is clear that it demands sensible behaviour, the result offers little insight into *how* voters want the country to change.

Labour's support in this election is so broadly drawn that some of it is likely to evaporate as soon as policies are announced. It's not possible to govern for the equal benefit of traditional voters in the Valleys, for instance, and those in English constituencies that previously voted Conservative as a matter of religion. Something will have to give, and which way Starmer's government leans will have far-reaching consequences.

In France, Emmanuel Macron moved into the centre ground from the left and tried to cohere the nation around traditional economics and cautious social reform. Labour will be eyeing the results on Sunday's French election to see if managerial polish is, in fact, enough to stabilise a nation that is unified in dissatisfaction with the status quo.

With anti-Tory sentiment the overwhelming factor in today's result, it may transpire that second places and shifts in vote share reveal more about the nation's feelings than the headline figures. Reform's 13% is significant enough to demand attention but also evidence that Farageiste populism doesn't cut the mustard for mainstream right-of-centre voters. Subtract Farage himself from the equation and, for now at least, there is not a base for radical conservatism in the UK. Nature abhors a vacuum, however, so if Starmer's Labour steps into the huge Tory-shaped hole on the right of UK politics, the Lib Dems, Greens, and Plaid Cymru have the momentum to grow exponentially on the left. The SNP, paradoxically, have squandered that position by underperforming in office. Labour should be taking notice of that, too.

Decency drove last night's result. Voters lashed out at its

scarcity in the Conservatives and signalled their approval for it in the Lib Dems, Greens, and Plaid Cymru. The recent machinations of internal Labour politics suggest they may be disappointed in that regard when it comes to Labour but, for now, Keir Starmer has a clean slate and a mandate to draw up a new UK. We'll all thrash out the implications of that when he gets started. Today, let the rain wash away the stench of 14 years of disgrace. On that, for once, we can all agree.

4D Chess
7 July 2024

Amongst those sucking deeply on the post-electoral copium pipe, are people who ascribe Reform UK's 17% share of the vote in Wales to English immigrants. Here's a tweet[1] from this morning:

> Llanelli has remained Labour since 1922. A proud socialist community. The figures below are alarming! I was in Llanelli recently. I heard some local accents and 2 or 3 couples speaking Welsh. But I might well have been in Solihull or Croydon. Electoral demographic shift. [...]
>
> — @leighcanham (5 July 2024)

Leaving aside the rich irony of this position — *to defeat Farage, you must become Farage* – a less alarming rationale is available. The Tories have spent fourteen years making themselves unelectable, and right-wing voters still exist. There you go, cleared that one up.

The outright unpleasantness of politics on the right recently has led many to view it as something to be excised from the culture. I joined in with the 'Tory-free Wales' jubilation on Friday morning myself. The banishment of Conservative MPs in Wales and much of the UK, however, doesn't indicate a shift leftwards in the electorate, so Labour's vast majority has left a huge contingent of people unrepresented in parliament and that could lead us to some dark political scenarios.

The case against first-past-the-post is conclusive after this election. Try to fit the following facts about UK elections into your head simultaneously without reaching for the ibuprofen.

Labour's 2024 majority is the largest since 1997 and the

---

[1] https://x.com/leighcanham/status/1809360405216567633

third largest since universal suffrage.

In 2019 Labour recorded its worst result since 1935.

More people voted Labour in 2019 than in 2024.

There is no doubt that Labour has played the game as it is constituted with consummate skill. On a positive note, it suggests that there are people in the party who absolutely know how to deliver an objective. The strategy required to achieve such a result, however, is removing governance yet further from voters.

When Keir Starmer admitted the right-wing Conservative MP Natalie Elphicke to the Labour Party in May, there was outrage amongst traditional supporters who saw it as a betrayal. Soon, however, the narrative emerged that this move was evidence of Starmer's political genius. He was 'playing 4D chess' we were told. Welcoming Elphicke gave traditionally Conservative voters 'permission' to switch allegiance to his 'changed party'. By astutely targeting seats in which this process could occur, Labour could become the natural party of government for a generation.

Press narratives have a tendency to override reality as their authors' reputations rest on their validity. The idea that Starmer has steered Labour towards an electoral sweet spot in the centre of UK politics, convincing Tory voters of a progressive course, has persisted beyond an election that painted a very different picture. Labour's share of the vote remained static, whilst opposing voters reorganised themselves to the detriment of incumbent Conservatives. The turnout of under 60%, driven by stay-at-home Tory voters, further skewed the result in Labour's favour.

The defence of this is that the electorate is sophisticated enough to participate in the first-past-the-post system intelligently and tactical voting is the reason for Labour's disappointing share of the vote as contrasted with its parliamentary majority. Well, maybe, but in itself that is problematic.

You may have noticed that nobody has the slightest idea

what Labour is going to do. It managed to arrive in office without disclosing detailed policy on anything. We are yet even to find out if Labour will close the spending deficit by raising tax or cutting services. That is a fundamental binary choice that the government will face immediately, about which it has stated no position.

Theresa May's 'nothing has changed' policy reversal on social care during the 2017 election has written a new rule into the 4D chess playbook. When voters are studying their tactical voting maps, you don't want them distracted by policy. Their motivation must be that your candidate is 'decent', so to vote against his/her interests is a moral failure. The nature of his/her decency need only be revealed after victory.

This removes the final defence for the system. First-past-the-post is traditionally criticized for producing elected dictatorships. In response, supporters point to the governments of 1945, 1983, and 1997 to demonstrate their transformative vigour. The point here is that the intentions of those governments were obvious when they were voted in. This election has delivered a thumping mandate for an unknown agenda. Whilst proportional representation produces compromise governments, voters can indicate their priorities in the election that precedes the negotiations, mandating single-issue candidates if necessary.

Governments are understandably fond of thumping majorities, so a change in the Westminster voting system isn't on the agenda. Here in Wales, though, we have proportional representation and that is going to be a very big story in 2026 when we see if Reform UK's support and an uptick for Plaid Cymru translates into votes in the Senedd. In that election, we will see a far clearer illustration of where opinion sits than we have now. Consequently, the next couple of years in Welsh politics will take on a UK-wide significance. The introduction of Adam Price and Lee Waters' legislation on political integrity is groundbreaking on a global scale and could, potentially, put Wales at the forefront of democratic process. I am not a supporter of the closed-list system. Personal accountability is important, and the system will obstruct voters' connection to their candidates. It could, however, produce an emphasis on content over personality, provided the media doesn't over-emphasise party leaders.

Last Friday, on the BBC, David Blunkett looked horrified at the suggestion of PR for Westminster. His objection was that it would allow for the representation of the far-right. UK-wide, the Reform UK vote was 14%. You can be sure that grievance over lack of representation will be key to Farage's appeal in trying to increase that figure. Blunkett fails to see the danger in unrepresented views being left unchallenged in the echo chambers of the internet. A few more underprepared Reform MPs being exposed in parliament for all to see is less dangerous than millions of voters becoming convinced that they are being silenced. Labour's success in gaming the voting system may not represent the return to stability that so many crave. In his post-election speech, Nigel Farage vowed to 'professionalise' and 'democratise' his party over the next five years. The danger is that he learns to play 4D chess too. After the 2026 Senedd election, Reform Members of the Senedd will be elected in proportion to their actual popularity and their ideas tested in a debating chamber. The delusional, online confidence of its supporters will flourish in England but meet reality on the floor of the Senedd. Wales must show the UK electorate what a functioning democracy looks like.

Cymrectitude*

11 July 2024

When Chancellor Rachel Reeves was pretending to have had first sight of the government finances on Monday, her speech was an object lesson in performative indignation. Pitched between Emile Zola and someone on a local Facebook group whose bins haven't been collected, Reeves bristled at the irresponsibility of her predecessors.

The public ledger is in the worst state since World War II, I mean FFS, what have these people been doing?!?!?!

The data is, of course, available to anyone online and always has been, so the big reveal wasn't quite the shock it was billed as, but well done to Rachel for carrying off the performance like the tipped-off recipient of a surprise party. *OMG!!!! I had NO idea...*

The UK's public finances aren't, in fact, in their worst state since the war but that isn't the point. We, the hardworking people, are outraged by mismanagement of the country and our new government is inhabiting that fury on our behalf. The vibe is of parents returning from a weekend at Center Parcs to find the fallout from a teenage party in their suburban home. *We hoped you were better than this...*

Sir Keir himself is, of course, possessed of a potentially lethal sense of integrity. When he ties his shoelaces, he feels a greater burden of responsibility than you did upon becoming a parent. He burps ethically. During one of the leaders' debates, Starmer was asked whether he, a millionaire, would consider paying for private healthcare if a close family member was gravely ill. How very dare you?! The putative PM looked as if he'd been stung by a wasp at the very suggestion. Stuttering a

---

* With apologies to Peter Finch.

little, he explained that 'in his house', where he is the sole moral arbiter, nobody had even heard of BUPA. His expression suggested a religious aunt who had been offered a line of cocaine at a wedding.

All of which is wretchedly inconvenient for Vaughan Gething. Timing is everything in politics and his emergence on to the national scene as it embraces puritanical rectitude must be a proper ball-ache for him. A few months ago, when Westminster was all popping champagne corks and Covid contracts, Gething's ask-me-no-questions-I'll-tell-you-no-lies style would have been of a piece with the wider scene. One can picture Boris Johnson knowingly joshing him, *you old roister doister, you...*

Now, though, with the earnest, bequiffed Starmer wrapped in a Union Jack and turning national life into an interminable Morrissey concert, the shenanigans down the Bay look jarringly at odds with the zeitgeist. Today, the Senedd Labour Group were off for an 'away day' designed to cohere them around the First Minister. One can only imagine the scenes in the minibus when *Nation.Cymru* confirmed[1] that Hannah Blythyn was not the source of Vaughan Gething's woes. Reports that Mike Hedges attempted to lighten proceedings with a chorus of 'Ging Gang Goolie' are unreliable and possibly a result of incoherence.

Whatever transpired at today's David Brent meets Richard Nixon corporate beano, we're left with the impression that Labour in the Senedd is the ugly stepchild of the national party. In Westminster, for now, everything is shiny-new and untainted by the sludge of realpolitik. Here in Wales, we are decades into entrenched Labour governance and the inevitable stench of complacency is about to waft over the border. How the party deals with the multiple scandals enveloping the First Minister could have far-reaching consequences for devolution. Nothing that Keir Starmer or, more worryingly, Jo Stevens has said indicates any enthusiasm for Wales as a political entity. On

---

[1] https://nation.cymru/news/hannah-blythyn-was-not-our-source/

267

returning from their outward-bound course this evening, Labour Senedd members need to construct a case for their usefulness to the political process. For all that Labour's predicament might delight opposition parties; by embarrassing their Westminster bosses, they could disenfranchise the nation.

The Conditions for Tyranny

14 July 2024

I was planning to write about America today. President Biden's descent into puzzlement is a Shakespearian narrative that will touch us all in some way. We're experiencing it as a human tragedy, familiar to many of us who have struggled as family members sank into cognitive decline, but also as a public catastrophe, with stewardship of a military superpower teetering on the brink of incompetence. There's more than enough to chew on there, I thought, before opening Twitter/X this morning to find that 'Civil War' was the top trending topic.

The language of history lessons is increasingly being applied to current affairs. It is jarring to read news stories that speak of insurrections, and fascism, and pogroms. For decades these words spoke either of the past or to the frothing discontent of people on the far fringes of the political conversation. Now, in a global situation too complex to comprehend, old and ugly solutions are being repackaged as if trying to fix your laptop with a hammer will turn it into a steam engine. Awash in a deluge of contradictory, often fabricated, information we have been herded into camps that hold up totems of the past to project authenticity and inspire loyalty. Here, Labour will sell you a Nye Bevan tea towel whilst deciding how much of the NHS to privatise whilst Boris Johnson invoked Churchill despite palling around with a KGB officer.

In America, much was made of Donald Trump having a portrait of Andrew Jackson in the Oval Office. Jackson is the pin-up of the 'peasants' revolt' strand of US politics. In this fairytale, the people are sovereign over entrenched elites, whose governance is condemned as self-serving and derived from European corruption. It is fiercely nativist but paradoxically hostile to aboriginal people. Jackson's rhetoric against First Americans led to the Trail of Tears and is echoed in Trump's remarks about Mexican immigrants. In style, it's folksy, simplistic and bombastic as the situation demands. It's appeal to Americans is such that half the nation is willing to believe that a man born into privilege, who lives in a gold tower on Fifth Avenue is somehow a conduit for their grievances.

'Make America Great Again', along with 'Take Back Control', and 'Stop the Boats' are pegs upon which people can hang their feelings. People feel got-at, controlled, and diminished by societies that are changing at a rate that leaves no time for reflection or to consider what's being lost along the way. A more honest slogan would be 'Make It Stop'.

As wealth continues to be hoovered up from communities into the offshore accounts of billionaires, blame becomes valuable political currency. Trump, Farage, Le Pen, Orban and the rest have a simple job which is to direct our eyes away from the flow of money outwards and towards the flow of people in.

At the time of writing, there's no authoritative word on why Donald Trump was shot last night. It doesn't matter. Within minutes of the incident, you could follow strands of opinion that led to a Deep State assassination attempt on one hand, or staged fakery on the other. The all-pervasive confusion of the internet era will offer you a personalised truth dependent on what you're inclined to click on.

What *does* matter is the imagery. As a blood-stained Trump got to his feet and raised his fist in defiance, he was backed by the US flag and huddled by a group of servicemen. It recalled the iconic, and staged[1], image from Iwo Jima that has stood as a totem of American resolve for 80 years.

If you interrogate patriotism of any sort, you'll find manipulation and, frequently, outright lies. We already feel something for our nations, if someone is telling us to then they have an agenda.

At Mar-a-Lago, Trump has a team of people planning the agenda for his second term. They are reportedly considering mass deportations, using federal troops to go after migrants, prosecuting Biden, pardoning participants in the January 6th

---

[1] https://edition.cnn.com/2015/02/22/world/cnnphotos-iwo-jima/index.html

Capitol insurrection, and wholescale replacement of the civil service with political supporters.

Last night's event will dominate the mythology of Trump's campaign and potential second term. Trump will be elevated from his position as an avatar of his supporters' concerns, having been sanctified in blood. With a partisan Civil Service and immunity from prosecution already granted by the Supreme Court, removing him in 2028 may take more than an election, presuming there is one.

Why Thomas Matthew Crooks caused a trickle of blood to run from Trump's ear last night will be contested forever. Whether it's allowed to swell the Potomac rests with the uncertain capabilities of his frail successor on Pennsylvania Avenue. The world watches.

Labour in the Dock

16 Jul 2024

Keir Starmer expended 17 lines marking the departure of Gareth Southgate from the England kickball job today, and only 11 on Vaughan Gething's resignation. Having backed the First Minister during the recent election, characterising his loss in a vote of confidence as 'a stunt', the Prime Minister could find no defining achievement around which to frame his tribute, other than Gething's success in achieving office.

The lack of original policies attached to Gething's name has worked against him in two ways. Firstly, it left him nothing substantive to point to when his position came under scrutiny. Secondly, there was no compelling reason for his colleagues to stand by him when the pressure came on. Politicians can survive scandals if their agenda is worth fighting for. Starmer's lukewarm statement unwittingly captured the suspicion that Gething's election as First Minister had been his primary, and perhaps sole, objective in politics.

We were, of course, facing a situation in which the government was unable to pass a budget. This would have marked a subtle transition from doing virtually nothing to absolutely nothing. If I were writing about its substantive work, then yesterday's stand-out announcement would have been consideration of banning pop refills at Harvester.

This sort of social tinkering has been a hallmark of recent Welsh governance. We are offered a Christmas dinner with elaborate trimmings but no turkey, as innovative projects on the fringes of life crowd out the urgent concerns of the electorate. I can put up with driving at 20mph to A&E but find my goodwill tested if I must then wait 18 hours to be seen. I'll never understand why I hear more about the former than the latter.

In some areas of Wales, Labour is so embedded into the national consciousness that it is difficult to see where its interests end and the nation's begin. The party's perception of itself as the inheritors of Nye, and the wider social struggles of the 20th century, belies the 21st-century reality of a party that is an agreeable career move for the professional and managerial classes.

It is against this backdrop of top-down, unchallenged complacency that Mr Gething rose to prominence. Having dropped £170,000 on his side of the scales in the leadership election, he assumed a position so remote from the lives of voters as to be unquestionable. The inner workings of the Labour Party in Cardiff seem to proceed on an ethereal plane, only to be revealed in the form of appointments and occasional legislation.

So, it's unsurprising that this quasi-religious organisation reacted so ineptly to the novelty of press scrutiny. Ironically, only Gething himself was genuinely revealing. His refusal to engage with any of the questions put to him, beyond impugning the motives of those asking, showed him in a clear, unforgiving light. What about the rest of them, though? Do all those anonymous briefings and questionable sick notes put as much ethical distance between them and their boss as they'll soon be claiming?

I doubt that Keir Starmer's Westminster party, Jo Stevens included, could care less whether devolution continues in a meaningful fashion. As soon as the election was over, Gething went under the bus, and it was on with their day. So, it's time for the Labour Group in the Senedd to engage with some existential contemplation. Devolution can only thrive with the enthusiasm of the population. If that is seen to wane, then it will be chiselled away to puppetry by the UK government. If their careers mean more to them than an agreeable lifestyle, Labour representatives need to put forward leadership candidates with robust and meaningful policy objectives that acknowledge the urgency of problems in people's lives. They should be shaking the Westminster tree for funding and doing so publicly; they should be engaging all over Wales to determine voters' priorities. The noise they make should be audible across the border, and inescapable here.

Wales is not a laboratory for insipid, progressive notions.[1] Nor is it a rotten borough over which privilege can be projected without accountability. Its governance is a mighty privilege, and, in its current embarrassment, Labour must find a purpose worthy of that.

---

[1] Well, it is. What I was trying to say is that it shouldn't be.

God Save the Labour Party

21 July 2024

With Baroness Morgan of Ely seemingly set to join Sir Keir Starmer at the top table of the Labour party, it would seem a fitting moment for the sans-culottes to respectfully enquire as to their intentions for our nation.

Certainly, today's coordinated statements of support from the Senedd Labour group suggest a preference for the abstract over anything as vulgar as a slate of policies.

Jeremy Miles, having relinquished his putative role as Labour's Robespierre, set the tone for the upcoming coronation.[1]

'The values she champions – of fairness, prosperity for all, a greener future and a strong devolution settlement – are ones which I passionately share. Welsh Labour under Eluned would reach out and represent all parts of our nation.'

That would be nice, wouldn't it? It would make a welcome change from Welsh Labour reaching out and trying to throttle each other or reaching out for several hundred thousand pounds in questionable readies, for that matter.

Prosperity for all! Huzzah! It's time to break out the travel brochures and get on down to the Tesla dealership as the team that made our NHS the envy of the world bring their Midas touch to our bank balances

Who knew it was this simple? The Labour Party should have been run by knights and baronesses all along.

Dr Hefin David, who is 'proud to call Jeremy Miles a friend', welcomed[2] the proposed appointment of the 'brilliant' Baroness:

---

[1]   https://nation.cymru/news/eluned-morgan-in-line-to-be-first-minister-as-jeremy-miles-says-he-will-not-run/

[2] https://x.com/hef4caerphilly/status/1815031815662395790

> We move forward together to serve the people of Wales. I'm proud to call @Jeremy_Miles a friend and he has shown courage and vision today. I too will be nominating the brilliant @Eluned_Morgan for leader of @WelshLabour

Some voters responded to this splendid news by making tawdry demands for evidence[3] of the Baroness's policy successes in her previous roles:

> Please name one success you can attribute to Eluned Morgan in any Ministerial position she has held?

If Welsh democracy has a flaw, it is tolerance for this sort of lowering discourse. Jack Sargeant[4] reminded us all of the higher calling that resounds for our ruling class:

> I'm proud to support @Eluned_Morgan for leader of @WelshLabour and Prif Weinidog. Her skills and experience at the head of a Welsh Labour team can unite our Party and ensure we continue to deliver for Cymru.

Echoing the Baroness's own statement, 'There'll be one of us and one of their mob, so it'll be fine,' Sargeant emphasised the need for unity.

Because, aside from effecting a green future and universal prosperity, the Baroness's primary purpose is to stop her Senedd colleagues from fighting like stoats in a sack and prevent Labour from sliding further into public derision.

---

[3] https://x.com/NickTFish3/status/1815038017381228652
[4] https://x.com/JackSargeantAM/status/1815050147031613606

Implicit in this is the notion that a healthy Labour Party means a healthy Wales. It needn't stand for anything in particular so long as it looks credible and keeps its internecine treachery out of sight. It is less a political movement than a royal court, within which legislation occasionally emerges having been 'championed' by one of the participating aristocrats.

Amongst responses to today's news were reminders of the remoteness that many in Wales feel from their government.[5]

> We were told by her top officials it 'would not be appropriate' for Eluned to meet public about her NHS. This is her culture in her department. Treating the patients she is responsible for with contempt.

If it follows the UK Conservative Party in appointing a leader in office without so much as an internal contest, that remoteness will be felt all the keener. In the imagination of its politicians, the electorate is anxiously waiting for good news about the health of the party. Certainly, any sustained criticism of it is treated as treasonous and grounds for accusations ranging from dishonesty to racism. If the gleam of the Senedd building reflects the mood of Labour within its walls as this is stitched up to save its embarrassment, the rest of us can look to the crumbling, derelict edifices a few yards away on Bute Street for our architectural metaphor. 'The Internationale' is seldom sung at party events these days, still less 'The Red Flag'. 'God Save The King' seems more in tune.

---

[5] https://x.com/ChannonRobert/status/1815063300327318009

Flogging a Live Horse
25 July 2024

I only watched a few seconds of the video showing Olympian dressage star Charlotte Dujardin whipping a horse 24 times. I'm weak, I suppose, such things upset me for so long after viewing them that I just can't cope with it. She's ruined, of course. Bracketed forever with that woman who threw a cat in a bin, Dujardin is on the national shit-list: someone over whom we can all feel morally superior.

Morality, though, is quicksand in our Godless, atomised world. There is no authoritative clergy to govern our behaviour now, and praise-be for that. Instead, we make our own rules, within the law, until the arc beam of social media illuminates our doings for judgement before the mob.

Last night in the Commons, an amendment to the King's Speech, which would have lifted the two-child cap on benefits, was defeated by 363 votes to 103. Only seven Labour MPs voted for the measure, and all were immediately suspended from the party. None of the seven represents a Welsh constituency. The measure currently affects 1.6 million children.

So, those are the plain facts.

Here's Swansea West's new MP, Torsten Bell, writing 12 weeks ago, about the urgency of scrapping the cap.

'The limit has to go. The costs are real (£2.5bn a year), but small compared to the damage. Abolition would lift half a million children out of poverty.'[1]

His article in April was titled, 'It's immoral to push children into poverty, but that's what the benefits cap does…'

Now, I didn't come down the Taff on a bubble and neither did you. Compromise is a necessary part of politics, and nobody

---

[1] https://www.theguardian.com/commentisfree/2024/apr/27/abolish-two-child-ban-child-poverty-torsten-bell

wants a legislature where intransigence prevents reasoned progress. Here, though, at the outset of this government's term, we seem to be in a place where an MP considered so integral to Labour's mission that he was imposed on a constituency about which he knew next to nothing, is required to vote against an explicitly moral position that he expressed less than 12 weeks ago. Having escaped a 14-year abusive relationship with the Tories, what have we ended up with on the rebound?

Nobody expected any wild redistribution of wealth under this government. Its adoption of the existing fiscal rules signalled that bold measures were never on the cards. As Bell makes clear, though, the misery-to-cost ratio of this issue is stark. For context, the UK is sending £2.5 billion to Ukraine next year.

People *do* have a right to expect a change in priorities from an incoming government, alongside a change of tone. The refusal to fund this measure is all about the latter. Sir Keir 'isn't afraid of the big decisions', 'the sums must add up', etc. etc. All well and good, but not of a piece with refusing to reform Capital Gains Tax, is it?

I'm forgetting, of course, that Sir Keir is playing 4D chess, as is his habit. What a fool I will appear when, having done 'the sums', Rachel Reeves announces the repeal of the cap in her first budget. Sensibilists across the UK will triumphantly crow at the lesser minds who were so naïve as to object to the government's initial caution. Analysts will marvel at Sir Keir's efficiency in ejecting dissenting voices from his swollen parliamentary ranks when he was going to scrap the measure all along.

Between now and then, though, little bellies will rumble across the UK for a few months more. Not as loudly as the crack of a whip on a horse's thigh, but just as plaintively for some of us.

All Hail Baphomet!

28 July 2024

Like many of you, I have a Cornish wife. I should be clear, though, that I acquired mine before they became fashionable during the pandemic and Mrs W. is bedecked with a dizzying array of attributes and accomplishments beyond her Cadbury's Caramel rabbit cadence and tin mining expertise. She's a trained boxer, for one thing, so this may prove to be my final column.

We're in Cornwall this week, and its similarities to Wales have been comforting as the UK has erupted into a fresh spasm of identity-based confusion. We stopped en-route in Shepton Mallett to have a look at some revolutionary artwork.[1] I rarely go to England nowadays, so it was salutary to be reminded that it hasn't been entirely subsumed into Farageiste xenophobia or Starmeroid union jackery. There might be hope for it yet.

Kernow has always been its own thing and, despite lacking a devolution settlement, the cultural shift is palpable when you cross from Devon. The Cornish flag is widely flown and, increasingly, bilingual signage is cropping up.

This was evident at the supermarket we stopped at on the way to Boscastle. Asda, sniffing some of that sweet, sweet national identity cash, has put the opening hours up in Cornish, in the same spirit that sees any product that has so much as travelled on the M4 labelled 'Welsh' to loosen our purse strings.

In Boscastle, after downloading a parking app that evaporated our cash into the swollen cloud of transnational finance, we dodged the showers with a visit to the Witchcraft and Magic Museum. This was a kindly indulgence on the part of Mrs Wildsmith, whose uncompromising rationalism is often at odds with her husband's lazy attachment to unfounded superstitions and speculative notions.

---

[1] https://www.the3foundation.co.uk/

I wasn't alone, though, as the museum is clearly a gold mine. In its cramped environs, we shuffled past pop-culture representations of the occult in uncomfortable proximity to a disagreeable grandmother who kept bellowing,

'I don't know why I'm here; I can't read any of it!' as her granddaughter patiently read out the explanatory cards next to the exhibits. We scooted past her at the dunking stool and hoped for the best.

Next up was a display of 'family items' used in defiance of the clergy. These included a 'cock rock' and a 'fanny stone' that had been in use until the 1920s to encourage fertility.

'Of course, Meghan Markle is into all this!'

I turned to find I was being addressed in Brummagem tones by a tall woman who later emphasised her Egyptian descent.

'Is she?' I asked, warily.

'Oh God, yes. Why do you think our Royal family are all ill?'

'Good luck to her,' I offered, hoping this might conclude matters. Nope. In the next room, having been caught up by Mrs W. who, clearly, had been lingering over the 'family items', our new friend continued:

'My brother is in the police; he's forever investigating West Africans who have sacrificed children!'

'Gosh,' I replied weakly. Absolutely adrift I was, readers, and she hadn't finished yet.

'Did you see the Olympics opening ceremony last night?' she demanded.

'Erm… I caught the end it seemed really beautiful with the flame rising into the sky in the rain and Celine…'

'It was a disgrace! They were mocking the Last Supper with all these woke weirdos and a *child* present. Is that what you want, is it?'

I find myself being harangued about The Woke on a tediously frequent basis nowadays. At work, online, in the pub there are people who need to know whether you share their sentiments on the supposed erosion of traditional values as an entrance qualification to their company. I'm used to failing this examination under all circumstances and here, in a cramped, windowless room, with my interrogator backed by a nine-foot effigy of Baphomet, I felt even less inclined to fall into line.

So, escaping into the Cornish sunshine, I idled through Twitter whilst waiting for Mrs W. to emerge. Tommy Yaxley-Robinson-Lenin was apparently leading a march of people who 'want their country back'. Children were slipping around on the rocks in Boscastle harbour and Cornish pasties, Cornish cream teas, and Cornish crabs vied for tourist cash. Back on my phone, I learned that the Romans banned the Olympic Games for being anti-Christian remnants of Pagan culture. How woke is that?

Post-Truth Blues

1 August 2024

When Andrew 'Real Ting' Davies gets his gilet in a twist about true facts reported in the press, sometimes on this website, he is occasionally misguided enough to seek redress through the authorities that exist to ensure our output is truthful. When, however, he is seeking to mislead the nation about payments to care-leavers, he makes sure to do it on Twitter/X. The reason for this, of course, is that no commensurate bodies exist to regulate output on social media platforms and, thus far, their billionaire owners have succeeded in convincing the UK government that they are not publishers.

The consequences of this state of affairs have been all too evident this week as the UK has struggled to make sense of the awful events in Southport. When the broadcast media remained silent about the identity of the person arrested for the atrocity I, like many others, was tempted to see what might have leaked out on social media. Reports that the perpetrator was a Syrian Muslim who had recently arrived in the UK as an asylum seeker were widespread on X within an hour of the attacks becoming known. The supposed source for the information looked like a cropped photograph of a print news story. That detail bears some analysis, I think, as it points towards the enormity of a crisis in credibility that is threatening the coherence of society. Why, with no byline or named newspaper in the picture, would a supposed *print* source have so much persuasive power that the originator of the lie would go to the trouble of fabricating one?

Part of the answer is, as described, the remaining regulatory framework around legitimate news outlets. With no author or brand visible, however, I suggest that the semiotics of old-fashioned print offer a more worrying attraction to those who seek to mislead. Print newspapers are a relic of the past, a time when people imagine that they could access reliable information. If the olden days say it's true, then it must be.

If the olden days also happen to be confirming prejudices we already hold, then a heady mixture of nostalgia and confirmation bias can override critical thinking altogether.

Nostalgia, as we know, ain't what it used to be. Facebook pages and groups have attracted huge audiences by encouraging it amongst their consumers. 'Who remembers when you'd go out a six in the morning, play all day and your mother wouldn't expect you back until it got dark?' seems a trite question. Ask it on Facebook and see the huge response it provokes. As quasi-communities grow around thin remembrances of the past, they become saleable commodities, and with the addition of AI-generated pictures, the reality of the past can be manipulated into something sinister. All year I've been puzzling over bizarre collages of thatched-cottage Britain, complete with overhead spitfires and suspiciously cheerful white people. These images have darkened over the months to feature frightened looking white children shadowed by cartoons of surly, dark adults with beards. This week, I've seen multiple variations on this theme featuring knives being shared by acquaintances I would have assumed to know better. When challenged, the people sharing this filth indignantly deny any suggestion of racism. I *know* them, they say. I *know* they aren't racist. It's me who is deluded, I haven't woken up to the new reality. The process has all the hallmarks of cult membership, and, for me, it's been highly distressing to see people I've known for decades be caught in its jaws.

The official response to the violence we've seen around the UK this week is decidedly 20th century. Downplaying the 'tiny minority' of thugs who actually show up to riot ignores the wider problem at play. Huge swathes[1] of the population are being deluded into false, hateful beliefs and, in a democracy, even one as rigged as ours, that holds the seeds of our destruction. A common call this week has been to proscribe the English Defence League as a terrorist organisation. The problem here is that the EDL no longer exists. Organisations like that

---

[1] HUGE, I tell you.

used to need membership lists to disseminate information. Now, 'Tommy Robinson' can tweet from anywhere in the world and anybody remotely interested in his ideas will get the message immediately.

We need to be passing laws fit for the century we live in, and we need to do it immediately. Social media sites should be legally accountable for the veracity of their content and politicians who amplify falsehoods must be sanctioned without fear or favour. A society that cannot set the parameters of debate will lose sight all sense of itself. Those who the gods would destroy, they first make mad.

The Chaos is the Point

4 August 2024

Deciding how seriously to take things is becoming a real challenge. We are in permanent crisis and have been since the 2008 financial crash. Austerity flowed into the division and political violence of the Brexit referendum. Then the pandemic shut down life as we know it and its aftermath coincided with the return of war in Europe to usher in the cost-of-living crisis that we're enduring now.

It's psychologically impossible to afford all those events the gravity they deserve. It's been so relentlessly harrowing, for so long that we have to ration our emotional engagement with current affairs as a survival strategy. How we feel about life in the UK is further complicated by the sheer, batshit *weirdness* of much that is unfolding in front of us. Whether I'm watching an occasional guest host from Have I Got News For You sit in front of a flag and tell us all to remain in our homes on pain of arrest, or I'm staring at a bottle of olive oil in Lidl muttering, 'Eight quid, *seriously?*' everyday life seems to veer out of known parameters so frequently that my conception of reality is threatened. I can't be alone, can I?

This week has been another in which a year's worth of processing energy has been expended. Monday's news from Southport was so horrifying that, in the past, we'd have allocated some time to digest it properly, to feel the unfathomable sadness in the air and breathe it as an act of empathy. Those days are gone, though. In six days since the tragedy, we've seen it bent through a demonic prism of bigotry and personal ambition. When we should have been lighting candles, we've been giggling as a rioting imbecile was smacked in the knackers with a stray brick or cheering on a police dog who knows a fascist backside when he sees one. *Not* to laugh at the high farce of much that is going on would be to surrender to its insane logic. We laugh when we can because if that's taken

286

from us, what is left?

Mid-chortle, though, the true degeneracy of it all ushers us back into despair. Just when it seems possible to understand the riots as the latest opportunity for a perennial minority of coked-up beer boys to disgrace themselves, the picture shifts to reveal people of colour being tactically isolated so they can more easily be attacked. Today, a Rotherham hotel housing migrants has been set on fire. People in this country who were living in peace last week are now in fear.

Of all the absurdity we've witnessed, I was struck by the burning of a Citizens Advice Bureau. These little beacons of humanity have long been the last resort for people who couldn't fathom the unknowable cruelties of the system. Years ago, when I was lost, I turned up at one in debt and at the end of my tether. They gave me a cup of tea and began calling my creditors, explaining my situation and negotiating payment plans when I was way past being capable of those conversations. I don't care what perceived grievance the mob harboured when it burned down the CAB in Sunderland but, for absolute certain, I know it wasn't done on behalf of the 'ordinary people' the rioters pretend to represent.

The 'ordinary people' I know are caught between laughing, crying, and numbed stoicism. We're walking along derelict high streets, driving over potholes, trying to find a dentist, being sent round a call centre maze if we ever need anything. We're poorer, sicker, and less confident than we used to be because we've been living through permanent decline and instability for decades.

These riots are a vile performance, orchestrated by sinister forces and acted out by clowns. Early indications are that the foot soldiers will face harsh justice and the rest of us will lose a chunk of civil liberties in the process. If the government is serious about addressing these events, it needs to go further than that. Sitting in front of flags and threatening the populace with Chinese-style facial recognition technology may look robust but it's remedial at best. A *Labour* government, of all things, should be pursuing the financial interests behind toxic disinformation loudly and as a matter of principle. More broadly, it should be pinning the blame for our diminished circumstances where it belongs, around the necks of corporations that have so ruthlessly drained the vitality from national life.

After a landslide election, we should be seeing radical action from the government to redress years of underfunding and widening inequality. Put simply, after the unfettered profiteering of 14 years under the Tories, 'ordinary people' need to feel change. George Osborne, this week, referred to Rachel Reeves as 'mini-me'[1] and observed that her economics were similar to his own efforts. George's efforts brought chaos into the lives of us all. Every interaction we have with the state is marred by unsustainable workloads, understaffing, and a lack of facilities. Some of us have died as a result. For Labour to persist with the economics that caused all this is recklessness posing as caution.

The UK's chaotic civic life now has a correlation in scenes on its streets. If Labour does not do the job it was founded for and restore a quality to public services that dignifies the populace, it will further normalise dysfunction. Be sure that Musk, Farage, 'Robinson', and the rest want them to carry on as they are. For them, the chaos is the point.

---

[1] https://www.thenational.scot/news/24495275.george-osborne-rachel-reeves-mini-me/

Make Him Go Away

8 August 2024

Sipping from a can of Monster, 'Andy' (not his real name) struggles to articulate what caused him to become embroiled in this week's far-right controversy.

'I dunno, it wasn't really me,' he shrugs, puffing furiously on his Poundland vape. 'People was coming up to me, right, 'cause they know I've got an X account.'

I ask Andy what they wanted, and he looks around furtively.

'I've got to be careful,' he explains. 'G's round here will cut you if you're a snitch.'

Round here is Cowbridge, a tough Vale of Glamorgan sink estate where Andy grew up.

'There's bad mans round here,' he warns. 'Almost everyone's in the NFU.'

'Are you a member?' I ask.

'Couldn't say,' Andy sniggers. 'Let's just say I know my chine from my sirloin and leave it at that.'

I press him on why his X account is so controversial and he darkens.

'Look, people wanted to know about the meat, see? You're not from these ends, you wouldn't get it. It's alright for you, traditionally slaughtered livestock are all we've got round here.' To emphasise his point, Andy reaches into his North Face jacket and waves a packet of pork scratchings in front of me.

'It's our culture!'

Lacking a mandate, Andy relies wholly on the Welsh Government for his income and save for a brief spell as a farm labourer, has been neither use nor ornament his entire life.

'What are you for, Andy?' I ask him.

'I'm out here keeping it real,' he says, scratching at a

congealed Bovril stain on his trousers.

'Speaking truth to the elites.'

'About what?' I ask.

'Well, me and the boys used to drive from here to Pentre Meyrick in Gerald's Land Rover and we'd smoke everything we passed, some of them going 30, or 35mph. It was sick.'

'Sorry, what's your point, Andy?'

'Well, it's shit now, isn't it? We have to go at 20mph because of The Drake.'

'Sorry, what is The Drake?'

'Don't mention The Drake,' Andy hisses, 'not in an NFU pub.'

'The A48 there has an exemption from the 20mph regulations though, Andy.'

'That's what they *want* you to think,' Andy laughs. 'Honestly, wake up, Bruv, haven't you got GB News?'

I was puzzled as to why Andy had exhorted his followers on social media to 'Burn the Senedd'.

'Andy, you and your friends are all paid by the Welsh Government, why on earth would you want to destroy it?'

'I'm an edgy rebel who plays by his own rules,' Andy asserts.

'That's a line from *The Simpsons*, isn't it Andy?'

'Whatever. Suck your mum.'

Sensing that Andy was becoming agitated, I ask about his plans for the future.

'Gonna be a YouTuber,' he announces, brightening.

'I'll be on a like-and-subscribe tip, you feel me? I'll be out there spitting bars and making coin. Gold Landie with a ragtop, wagyu for breakfast, and custom Hunters on my feet, Bro. Might move to Berkshire but I'll always have love for my peeps in the 'bridge.'

We reached out to the NFU for comment and a spokesman said, 'Not him again! For the last time, we have no idea who he is. Make him go away.'

290

The Triumph of the Will
11 August 2024

We've seen this week what an elected government in the UK is capable of if it is motivated to act. Far-right rioters have appeared in court quickly and been sentenced without recourse to probation reports or consideration of overcrowding issues in prisons. In a moment of seeming national crisis, the system jolted into action in a way that we haven't seen since the pandemic and, before that, the last riots in 2011.

Observers of British life over the last thousand years will be aware that the supposedly ironclad separation of the executive from the judiciary is more of an ideal than a reality. The nebulous nature of our constitution allows for all manner of cross-pollination between the two spheres, and, in an emergency, that can facilitate urgent action. Keir Starmer is, of course, uniquely well placed to locate the correct levers when it comes to criminal justice, and it has been widely reported[1] that he 'leaned' on the justice system to act as it has.

So, in the first instance, let's applaud that. It was a situation that could easily have spiralled out of control, and, for now, that's been prevented by governmental decisiveness backed up by the system. The UK was on fire and now it's not, only a fool wouldn't welcome that outcome.

Interestingly, there has been little objection to the process outside of complaints from those – Musk, 'Robinson', Farage, Tice etc. – whose views reflect differing shades of those held by the rioters themselves. Amongst the rest of the population, there seems to be general agreement that the urgency of the situation justified suspending conventional practices.

There is a lesson for elected representatives here. We put them into power with the expectation that they will wield it on

---

[1] https://inews.co.uk/news/politics/how-judges-saved-starmer-from-losing-control-as-rioters-violence-spread-3219091

our behalf. That power is considerably more potent than politicians of all stripes would have us believe. In 2008, it was used to bail out the banking sector to the tune of £137 billion. The pandemic furlough scheme cost £70 billion. These spending decisions were made quickly and without a mandate as circumstances demanded. In both cases, they were made against a backdrop of neglect, in banking regulation and pandemic preparedness respectively.

So, we have seen that government is adequately empowered to enact legislation quickly, compel agencies to implement it, and to raise finance as necessary. The system, it seems, works, but is only made to under threat of impending disaster.

The question for Starmer going forward is how to keep the systems of government running like this so that points of crisis are averted in the first place. My own view is that the perceived problems around immigration are more of a symptom than a cause of the widespread dissatisfaction amongst the British public. It is now so embedded in the national consciousness as a set of serious issues that it needs to be addressed specifically. In recent years, it has been government policy simultaneously to inflate the seriousness of the problem and then feign powerlessness in the face of judicial restraint. That game needs to be brought to a very public end. Labour was circumspect about its plans for immigration measures during the election campaign, presumably feeling that whatever it proposed could be misrepresented. It now has a decisive majority and no credible opposition in parliament. However, it seeks to address the issues, whether by negotiation with the EU or via domestic legislation, the government needs to be clear, decisive, and resolute.

The same attitude should, of course, be taken towards the crisis in public services. We have seen with our own eyes how much can be achieved quickly if there is the political will to act. The rhetoric of this government tends to conflate inaction with caution, as if it were a safe option. A Conservative government is elected with a mandate for that line of thinking, as it is charged with maintaining the status quo as regards the distribution of wealth. It has led to a tearing of the social fabric which is becoming more expensive with every botched repair.

Here in Wales, no such remedial power exists. Our government cannot print money nor borrow it in quantities to address the fundamentals of our economy. It is, however, in possession of a pulpit from which it can preach the urgency of the situation. It was, then, excruciating to hear Baroness Morgan use her *first* speech as FM to instruct us that more austerity is on the way. If you ask any Labour politician whether George Osborne's economics were ruinous for the UK, they will agree that they were. They were ruinous in poorer areas, many in Wales, to a disproportionate degree. To persist with underinvestment when the electorate has rejected it is perverse.

The 'our hands are tied' defence for neglecting serious issues in this country is dependent on discredited economics that were a trojan horse for further enriching the investment class. This government, as we have seen, is capable of acting when it needs to. It has a thumping majority and minimal internal dissent. The question we should be asking of Starmer and Morgan is, what do you *want* to do? We've heard enough of what you *can't* do to fill a courtroom.

Conquering the Post-Eisteddfod Blues

18 August 2024

With Baroness Morgan embarking on her 'listening exercise' around the nation this month, wouldn't it be enlightening if she undertook the journey on public transport? I feel certain that she'd encounter some fellow passengers who would be happy to share one or two concerns with the First Minister.

The rail line from the Rhondda to Cardiff was recently closed for *eight months* whilst Transport for Wales worked on electrifying the line. Local people were placated with half-price travel and the promise of a futuristic new system, including an integrated hub for buses at Porth and a monorail over the Rhigos to link up with the zipwire at Hirwaun. I'm unsure of the details. Rhondda residents, we were assured, would only have to think about Cardiff and we'd be tucking into a Clark's pie before we'd had time to put our big coats on.

Thus far, the hub in Porth remains a mirage, with 'finishing touches' being applied. All requests for a finish date, from residents and councillors alike are met with your-call-is-important-to-us obfuscation.

The electric trains did happen, though. As you know, Pontypridd briefly became the centre of the Cymric universe last week, doing a superb job of hosting the National Eisteddfod. The town looked fantastic, with a breathtaking new mural and visitors remarking online about its welcoming and vibrant atmosphere.

Those arriving by rail were carried on the new electric trains for which we suffered so long. Those eight months of commuting hell were swept away by the dawn of the new era, as the cultural and technological achievements of the nation flowed joyously into Ponty.

50,000 people had been successfully transported crowed

Transport for Wales in its press release.

But, as the bunting came down in the post-Eisteddfod drizzle, there was another announcement. The new electric trains that had made their debut in the sunshine and public glare of last week's festivities were to be 'redeployed' and replaced by the ones we had before.

Now, there is nothing as wearisome as the tendency of right-wingers to characterise anything to the left of Genghis Khan as 'Communism', especially when applied to the wishy-washy liberal tinkering of the body politic here in Wales. You must concede, though, that this has all the hallmarks of the North Korean tourist experience, in which Western visitors are taken to see happy villagers enjoying lavish meals which are confiscated as soon as the tourists leave. Rumours that public discussion of the bus hub would require offenders to attend struggle meetings at Bronwydd Park are unconfirmed at press time.

Post-pandemic life can often seem like one long rail-replacement bus journey. Our politics is preoccupied with grand, strategic ideas whilst the nuts and bolts of our lived experience seem never to work as they should. This has a real effect on the viability of long-term planning, as support from a continually disappointed populace is difficult to generate.

Good ideas, like expanding 20mph zones and having a national airport become mired in cynicism because the public contrasts their cost and profile with the invisible misery of their own battles just to get home from work at night.

Grand, transformative visions are what float the egos of politicians. It's the part of the job that motivates them to put up with criticism and abuse. They are also, though, the fun bit of what they do. Making what we already have function properly is the grunt work: the solid scrum that allows your backline to create magic.

As we head towards the Senedd election, we need to hear from politicians who are motivated to fix our everyday interactions with public services as their driving priority. Every minute spent waiting for a bus, on hold to a GP's surgery, or trying to find an NHS dentist, drips into a swelling reservoir of common disillusionment with governance in general.

An Honest Day's Work

18 August 2024

A friend of mine, who works for an English local authority in the parks department, was hauled up before a disciplinary meeting this week accused of making a political post on his personal Facebook page during an election campaign. I can only imagine the whitening of his knuckles, gnarled as they are by decades of remorseless labour, when an HR operative, who wouldn't know a cultivator from a pogo stick, explained that political silence was stipulated by his terms of employment.

For we human resources, the PAYE chumps so hopelessly stuck in a 20th-century mindset that we still believe in working for a living, that's the way it is. If we are lucky enough to have a proper contract of employment, it is opaquely laden with potential reasons for our dismissal. Employers are empowered to stalk our utterances and monitor our behaviour in and out of the workplace. If they want rid of us, they will find a way.

Not so for the beneficiaries of Ripoff UK, which long ago codified rewards for spivvery at the expense of working people. As surveillance culture has intruded into the home life of anyone with a job, deregulation and the normalisation of Johnsonian amorality have made the UK ever more fertile for a parasitical class of unproductive liars.

This week, we learned that Nigel Farage, Arthur Daley's coat on Oswald Mosley's back, is trousering £97,000 *a month* for his show on GB News, plus another four grand for his newspaper column. This would be a profoundly depressing statistic if all it denoted was the public appetite for his millimetre-short-of-the-line divisiveness. The truth, however, is far worse than that. Neither his show nor his column has enough drawing power to justify that level of remuneration. He is the beneficiary of old-school patronage, whereby the wealthy tip the scales of national discussion in their favour by purchasing visibility for those who will do their bidding. It is, ironically, antithetical to the 'free market' principles that Farage poses to hold sacred. The historical roots of his place in British life lie not in Friedman and Hayek but in the feudal practices of the Medieval aristocracy. Compare the grand families of Europe with American corporations and you'll find the precedents for Farage in the arts and the church.

Alarming as Farage's media ubiquity is, it has become far more dangerous with his election to parliament. I doubt even he would expend much effort persuading us that the driving ambition behind his candidature was to become the public voice of Clacton-on-Sea. His constituents know that and those who voted for him were content to be of use. The implications of Farage's elevation to representative politics lie not in his potential to influence policy, Labour's majority is too wide for that. Rather, he is in a position to *make* the news he discusses on his show. Every outrageous speech he gives in the House will become fodder for his GB News appearances. In turn, remarks by him and guests on the show will create enough unrest as to require parliamentary discussion. In subverting the roles of journalist and legislator he can create a perfect loop of outrage that will generate ever more money for him, and political heft for those who pay for it.

The courts have continued this week to send a powerful message about rioting and online incitement. Keir Starmer, by facilitating this, has succeeded in showing a muscular attitude towards the boundaries of acceptable debate in the UK. Locking up the dregs of society, however, is low hanging fruit. If we can be prosecuted, or lose our jobs over social media posts, then a way can be found to purge British public life of Farage's dangerous pantomime. If the HR team at the House of Commons is struggling to find a rule upon which to string him up, perhaps they should ask the Westminster parks department for advice.

It may well be that what passes for democracy in the UK is already doomed, but if the government has ambitions of reviving it then it needs to pass legislation regarding outside media roles for MPs, and it needs to do so quickly.

A Blue Moon for Red Tories

23 August 2024

Were you all out for the blue supermoon on Monday night? If you enjoyed it then, truly, I'm happy for you. Personally, I'm done with supermoons. Every month or so a new variant seems to come along, heralded in the papers as if it were the portent of the Age of Aquarius, promising delivery from the riot-beleaguered, Ed Sheeran-soundtracked, have-you-forgotten-your-password hellscape in which we somehow persist. There's only so many times, however, that you can work up a spark of celestial optimism only to yourself standing on the patio in wet socks peering up at the clouds and asking,

'Is that it?' before trooping back inside to resume recreational doomscrolling. It's not the despair that gets you; it's the hope.

The prospect of change is the currency of elections. *It's all going to be different,* we're told. *Our best days are ahead of us! If only we'll belieeeeeeeeeeeve enough to put a cross in a box next to the right name, happiness and contentment will return to the realm. The chaos will stop, no return to boom or bust* etc. etc. etc.

After our first electoral victimisation, we naturally become more sceptical about political promises. Having been led up the garden path once, we realise that we're not going to be unwrapping a new bike on Christmas morning. It is reasonable, however, to expect *something* when we elect a new government; some token measures to acknowledge that we weren't happy with the previous lot.

So far, Labour seems to be sending the message that voting is for suckers. Feigning shock at an £18 billion hole in the public finances that was widely reported[1] during the election campaign, the government has resisted measures, like lifting the

---

[1] See earlier in this book…

two-child cap, that would signal a change in moral priorities in the nation's governance. Indeed, by cancelling the winter fuel payment for all except the poorest pensioners, it seems to be ramping up performative impoverishment as if it accepts the fundamental ethics of Tory politics.

Money has been found, however, to settle the pay claims of junior doctors and train drivers. Justified as these demands were, the government's stated rationale for meeting them – that prolonged strikes are disruptive – is neither moral nor sensible. As well as setting a clear precedent for other unions to follow, it rewards two groups of workers that enjoy sufficient financial security to sustain indefinite strike action. Those in jobs that pay less are unlikely to secure the majorities required to follow suit simply because they can't afford to lose regular days' pay.

We also learn that Labour plans to fund the building of social housing by increasing rents above inflation for ten successive years. If you can find a Labour voter who expected that when they left the polling booth, I'd be very surprised. Housing is a devolved matter, so if you encounter Baroness Morgan on her 'listening exercise' around Wales this month, please ask if she can rule out taking this approach here. The viability of devolution rests upon decisions like this, and the glib assumption that a Westminster government will act in the interests of people who voted for Labour in the Senedd will be tested as soon as the summer recess ends.

Nobody doubts the economic challenges facing the country. It's clearly going to be a tough job to reverse the decline we have suffered during 14 years of incompetent government, and the financial crash that preceded it. Politics is increasingly, however, being done online and, recently, on the streets. If people are to believe in democracy, an incoming government should demonstrably reflect the values of its voters. A failure to do so in the name of caution is recklessly complacent in troubled times.

'I personally can't tell the difference between a supermoon and a regular moon,' Fred Espernak, scientist emeritus for NASA's Goddard Space Flight Center told *Morning Edition* this

300

week. 'And I've been looking at the moon all my life.'

Letter from Goa
30 March 2024

At the phone shop in Chaudi our taxi driver, Vincent, is making sure we get a SIM card. It's the second one he's taken us to and the refusal of the first has chafed at him.

Half-serious, he smiles at the guy in his 'Jio Mobile' T-shirt.

'They get these good jobs with Jio,' he teases, 'and they are up here. Meanwhile us poor people are ringing them up with problems and they are not answering the phone.'

The Jio guy grins and enters his own Indian ID number on the computer, thus fooling the system and allowing us our SIM.

Outside at the main crossroads, scooters converge on the junction in a cacophony of tooting. Approaching a bend? Toot your horn to warn oncoming traffic. Passing a cow? Toot at it.

Displeased with the road positioning of a vehicle? You'd better know that's getting a toot. See someone you know? Repeated toots. Toot, toot, toot until there is nothing but toot.

Tooting is life.

On the beach at Patnem, we potter about in reverie. Between the bath-warm water and the coconut palms, I feel uncomfortable at first, an unsightly speck on paradise.

I lumber about, consciously avoiding ectomorphic Western yoga students and cleaving towards happy, splish-splashing Indian families who, like me, prefer parathas for breakfast.

If you enjoy detox smoothies and superfood salads, you'll find plenty of places for them, but the old charge that Goa isn't the 'real India' is out of date.

Real India is doing better economically nowadays and at weekends the beaches throng with people from all over the country, flying into the new Manohar airport and expecting food and customs to suit them.

Your beach hut might be run by someone from Punjab, your chef might be Nepali.

Away from the beaches, though, on the back roads where spices grow, water buffalo bellow, and monkeys chatter, it's still Goa.

In the roadside taverns you can have your fish reachardo fried with kismoor (dried prawns), sukkah clams and a bowl of digestive solkhadi to wash it down.

At night, this time of year, you need air conditioning, or at least a fan. The temperature only drops by a couple of degrees from its midday height of 33 to 35 degrees and humidity makes it feel hotter still.

Alstid, who owns the little group of huts we are staying at, warns us that we'll be without electricity for four hours this evening between 10pm and 2am.

'The government of Canacona is shutting it off so that everyone stays indoors tonight.'

A god, which appears as a ball of light, is making its way down the Canacona highway towards Agonda this evening and it is imperative that everybody be off the roads whilst the police escort it on its biannual journey.

'Have you seen it, Alstid?'

'No, I'm not sure it exists, but friends of mine say they have. Apparently, it travels at knee height. If the police catch you out, they will knock you off the road.'

At distant Talpona beach, the next day, we watch as two Italian women are ordered out of the water by lifeguards.

They have been pulled towards the rocks by a riptide.

We walk up the beach to the jetty where a gentleman makes his living taking people across the river to Rajbagh beach, from where you can walk back to Patnem.

The sun begins to set as he poles his boat towards the shore, and everything sinks into the caramel luminescence that marks the end of every day in this blessed place.

I'm lost in gratitude for what I'm experiencing.

God knows what awaits at home. My work phone will be clocking up messages concerning this disaster, that catastrophe, or the other tragedy.

It sits there in the Rhondda, on my desk like a reproach, pinging away belligerently.

Walking up Rajbagh, I watch the fragile sandpipers rushing forwards as a wave recedes, hoping to snatch up bugs.

They run on thread-thin legs, poking at the sand urgently until forced back by the returning wave.[2]

Sometimes the tide brings them something, mostly it doesn't.

---

[2] You can see my ~~holiday snaps~~ excellent professional photographs with this piece on *Nation.Cymru*. (https://nation.cymru/feature/letter-from-goa/).

Acknowledgements

Thanks to Mark Mansfield at *Nation.Cymru* for publishing the articles and allowing me free rein. To Sarah Morgan Jones for all her help and to Jon Gower for kind encouragement and wise guidance. To Chris Jones at Cambria for realising my work in book form. To Susie Wildsmith for her frequent inspiration and impeccable proofreading.